ATLAS OF JEWISH HISTORY

by the same author

ATLAS of JEWISH HISTORY

DAN COHN-SHERBOK

London and New York

First published 1994
by Routledge
11 New Fetter Lane, London EC4P 4EE

Simultaneously published in the USA and Canada
by Routledge
29 West 35th Street, New York, NY 10001

© 1994 Dan Cohn-Sherbok

Typeset in 10/12 point Baskerville by
Solidus (Bristol) Ltd, Bristol
Printed in Great Britain by
Clays Ltd, St Ives plc

British Library Cataloguing in Publication Data

A catalogue record for this book is available from the British Library

Library of Congress Cataloging in Publication Data
Cohn-Sherbok, Dan.
        Atlas of Jewish history / Dan Cohn-Sherbok.
            p.   cm.
        Includes bibliographical references.
        1. Jews–History–Maps.   2. Jews–History.   I. Title.
    G1030.C559   1994 ‹G&M›
    909.′04924′00223–dc20   93-15018 CIP

ISBN 0–415–08684–1

For Lavinia

CONTENTS

PLATES

MAPS

ACKNOWLEDGEMENTS

In writing this book I have used the following books as sources for maps: Martin Gilbert, *Jewish History Atlas*, Weidenfeld & Nicolson, London, 1985; Herbert G. May (ed.), *Oxford Bible Atlas*, Oxford University Press, London, 1962; *New Bible Atlas*, Inter-Varsity Press, Leicester, 1985; Evyatar Friesel, *Atlas of Modern Jewish History*, Oxford University Press, Oxford, 1990; *The Illustrated Atlas of Jewish Civilization*, André Deutsch, London, 1990; Nicholas de Lange, *Atlas of Jewish History*, Thames & Hudson, 1982; Robert Seltzer, *Jewish People, Jewish Thought*, Macmillan, New York, 1980; *Encyclopaedia Judaica*, Keter, Jerusalem, 1972– .

We are also grateful for permission to reproduce the plates. Sources are given in the respective caption.

1 THE ANCIENT NEAR EAST AND THE ISRAELITES

Ancient Mesopotamian and Canaanite civilization

The rise of ancient Mesopotamian civilization occurred at the end of the fourth millennium in southern Mesopotamia alongside the Tigris and Euphrates rivers, where the Sumerians created city states, each with its local god. In Uruk there were two main temples: one was for Anu, the god of heaven; the other was for Inanna, the mother goddess of fertility, love and war. In addition, other deities were worshipped at other places – Enlil, lord of the atmosphere at Nippur; Utu, the sun god, at Larsa; Nanna, the moon god, at Ur. Each of these gods had a family and servants who were also worshipped at various shrines. The temple itself was located on a high platform and housed in a holy room in which a statue of the god was washed, dressed and fed each day. Through the centuries, Sumerian priests recounted stories about these gods, whose actions were restricted to various spheres of influence. In addition, the Sumerian myths contain legends about creation: Enlil, for example, separated heaven from earth, and Enki created man to grow food for himself and the gods.

During the next millennium, waves of Semitic people (known as the Akkadians) settled amongst the Sumerians, adopting their writing and culture. From 2300 BC, when Sargon of Akkad established the first Semitic empire, they dominated Mesopotamia. At this time Sumerian stories were recorded in the Semitic language, Akkadian. These Semites reshaped Sumerian culture, equating some of their gods with the Sumerian ones. Anu, for example, was identified with El; Inanna with Ishtar; Enki with Ea. In Akkadian schools epics of the gods were chronicled. The Gilgamesh epic, for example, depicts King Gilgamesh, who ruled Uruk in about 2700 BC.

For the Sumerians and the Akkadians, life was controlled by the gods. To obtain happiness, it was mandatory to keep the gods in a good humour through worship and sacrifice. None the less the gods were unpredictable, and this gave rise to the reading of omens. In the birth of monstrosities, the movements of animals, the shapes of cracks in the wall and the oil poured into water these peoples perceived the fingers of the gods pointing to the future. Thus if a person wished to marry, or a king chose to wage war, they would consult omens. Another frequent practice was to examine the liver of a sacrificed animal – a special class of priests was trained to interpret such signs.

At its height Sargon's and his descendants' empire stretched from the Persian coast to the Syrian shores of the Mediterranean. However, this kingdom collapsed in about 2200 BC through invasion and internal conflict. Among the new arrivals in Mesopotamia were the Amorites, who dwelt in Mesopotamian cities such as Mari and Babylon, where they assimilated Sumero-Akkadian culture. Other Amorites penetrated into ancient Canaan, where they retained their separate tribal structure. The collapse of the

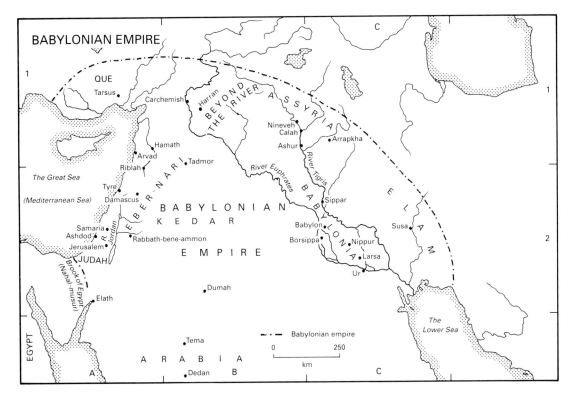

BABYLONIAN EMPIRE

QUE

Tarsus

Carchemish

Harran

BEYOND THE RIVER

ASSYRIA

Nineveh
Calah

Ashur

Arrapkha

Hamath

Arvad

Riblah

Tadmor

River Euphrates

River Tigris

The Great Sea

(Mediterranean Sea)

Tyre

Damascus

EBER-NARI

BABYLONIAN

KEDAR

Sippar

BABYLONIA

Samaria

Ashdod

Jerusalem

R. Jordan

Rabbath-bene-ammon

EMPIRE

Babylon

Borsippa

Nippur

Larsa

Susa

ELAM

JUDAH

Brook of Egypt
(Nahal-musur)

Ur

Elath

Dumah

The
Lower Sea

EGYPT

Tema

ARABIA

Dedan

A

B

C

–·–·– Babylonian empire

0   250
km

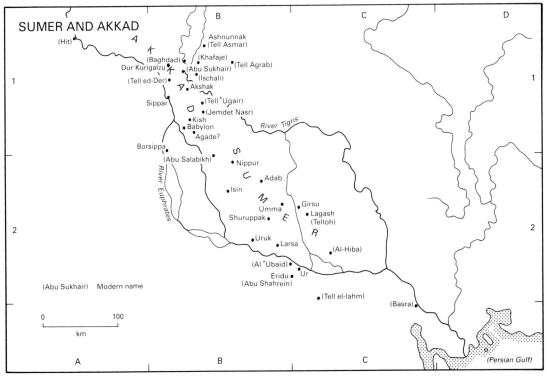

SUMER AND AKKAD

(Hit)

A
K
K
A
D

Ashnunnak
(Tell Asmar)

(Baghdad)

(Khafaje)

(Tell Agrab)

Dur Kurigalzu

(Abu Sukhair)

(Tell ed-Der)

(Ischali)

Akshak

(Tell 'Uqair)

Sippar

(Jemdet Nasr)

River Tigris

Kish

Babylon

Agade?

Borsippa

(Abu Salabikh)

S
U
M
E
R

Nippur

River Euphrates

Adab

Isin

Umma

Girsu

Shuruppak

Lagash
(Telloh)

Uruk

Larsa

(Al-Hiba)

(Al 'Ubaid)

Eridu
(Abu Shahrein)

Ur

(Tell el-lahm)

(Basra)

(Abu Sukhair)   Modern name

0   100
km

A   B   C   D

(Persian Gulf)

2

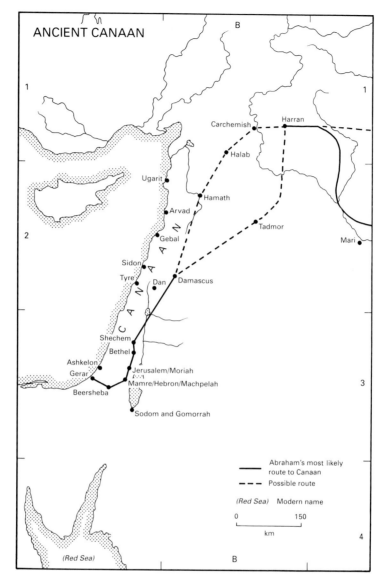

ANCIENT CANAAN

Abraham's most likely route to Canaan
- - - Possible route

(Red Sea)   Modern name

0   150
      km

Akkadian empire was followed by a Sumerian revival in the Third Dynasty of Ur (2060–1950 BC). During this period Hammurabi of Babylon reigned from 1792 to 1750 BC; as a tribute the Babylonian creation story ('Enuma Elish') was composed in his honour. In c. 1400 BC the state of Assyria grew strong in northern Mesopotamia and later became the dominant power in the Near East. The Assyrian kings imitated the Babylonians; they worshipped the same gods, but their chief god (identified with Enlil) was Ashur.

In the second millennium, the inhabitants of Canaan were composed of a mixture of races largely of Semitic origin. Excavations have unearthed the remains of small temples in Canaanite towns; these housed cultic statutes in niches opposite doorways. When temples had courtyards, worshippers remained outside while priests entered the sanctuary. A large altar was placed in the courtyard and a smaller one inside the temple. The animal remains from these places of worship suggest that offerings consisted mainly of lambs and kids. Liquid offerings of wine and oil were also contributed, and incense was burned. In some temples, stone pillars were erected as memorials to the dead; other pillars served as symbols of gods. Statues of gods and goddesses were carved in stone or moulded in metal overlaid with gold, dressed in expensive clothes, and decorated with jewellery. To the north of Canaan, excavations of the city of Ugarit have provided additional information about religious practices. The texts of Ugarit emphasize that the gods of Canaan were like many others of the ancient Near East: they were powers of the natural world. El was the father of gods and men;

his wife was Asherah, the mother goddess. El had a daughter Anat who personified war and love and is portrayed in some accounts as the lover of her brother, Baal (the god of weather). The texts of Ugarit depict Baal's victory over Yam (the sea) and against Mot (the god of death). Additional gods include Shapash, the sun goddess; Yarikh, the moon god; Eshmun, the healer. This Canaanite religious structure as well as the earlier Sumerian and Akkadian civilizations provide the backdrop for the emergence of the religion of the Jewish people.

The patriarchs and Joseph

The biblical account in Genesis depicts Abraham as the father of the Jewish nation. Initially known as Abram, he came from Ur of the Chaldeans – a Sumerian city of Mesopotamia. Together with his father Terah, his wife Sarai and his nephew Lot, he went to Harran, a trading centre in northern Syria. There his father died, and God told him to go to Canaan: 'Go from your country and your kindred and your father's house to the land I will show you. And I will make of you a great nation' (Genesis 12:1–2). During a famine in Canaan he went first to Egypt and then to the Negeb. Finally he settled in the plain near Hebron, where he experienced a revelation confirming that his deliverance from Ur was an act of providence: 'I am the Lord who brought you from Ur of the Chaldeans to give you this land to possess' (Genesis 15:7).

Because Sarai was barren Abram had relations with her servant girl, Hagar, who bore Ishmael. However, when Abram was ninety-nine and Sarai ninety, God gave them a son, Isaac. It was at this time that Abram received his new name Abraham ('the father of a multitude'), and Sarai was renamed Sarah ('princess'). When Isaac was born, Abraham sent Hagar and Ishmael away at Sarah's insistence. During this period God made a covenant with Abraham symbolized by an act of circumcision: 'You shall be circumcised in the flesh of your foreskins, and it shall be a sign of the

covenant between me and you' (Genesis 17:11). Subsequently God tested Abraham's dedication by ordering him to sacrifice his son Isaac, only telling him at the last moment to desist. When Isaac grew older, Abraham sent a servant to his kinsfolk in Hebron to find him a wife. The messenger returned with Rebecca. Later God answered Isaac's prayers for a son, and twins (Esau and Jacob) were born. Jacob bought his brother's birthright for food, and with his mother's help secured Isaac's blessing, thereby inflaming Esau's wrath. Fleeing from his brother, Jacob travelled northward toward Harran; en route he had a vision of a ladder rising to heaven. There he heard God speak to him, promising him that his offspring would inherit the land and fill the earth (Genesis 28:12–14). After arriving in Harran Jacob laboured for his uncle Laban for twenty years as a shepherd. There he married Laban's daughters, Rachel and Leah; they and their maids (Bilhah and Zilpah) bore him twelve sons and a daughter. Eventually Jacob returned to Canaan. On this journey he wrestled with a mysterious stranger in the gorge of the Jabbok river, a tributary of the Jordan, where God bestowed upon him the new name, 'Israel'.

When the man saw that he did not prevail against Jacob, he touched the hollow of his thigh; and Jacob's thigh was put out of joint as

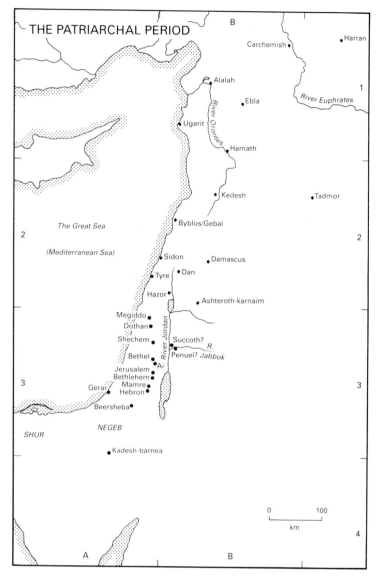

THE PATRIARCHAL PERIOD

he wrestled with him. Then he said, 'Let me go, for the day is breaking.' But Jacob said, 'I will not let you go, unless you bless me.' And he said to him, 'What is your name?' And he said, 'Jacob'. Then he said, 'Your name shall no more be called Jacob, but Israel, for you have striven with God and with men and have prevailed.

(Genesis 32: 25–8)

Eventually Jacob was welcomed by Esau, but then the brothers parted. Jacob lived in Canaan until one of his own sons, Joseph, requested that he and his family settle in Egypt, where he died at the age of 147.

The history of the three patriarchs is followed by the narrative of Jacob's son, Joseph. As a young boy, Joseph was given a special long-sleeved robe as a sign that he was his father's favourite. With his brothers he tended his family flocks in Shechem, but he infuriated them by recounting dreams in which they bowed down to him. Furious at this presumption, they plotted his death. However, Reuben, one of the brothers,

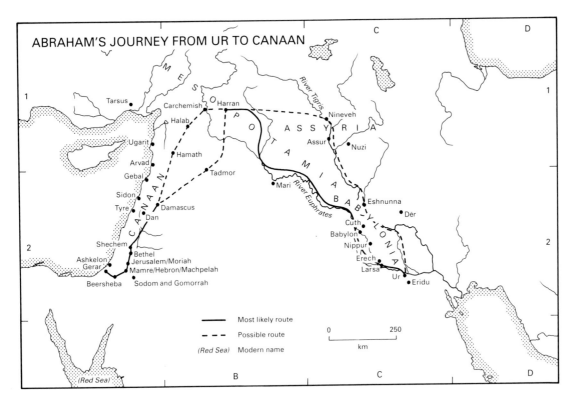

ABRAHAM'S JOURNEY FROM UR TO CANAAN

Tarsus

Carchemish Harran Nineveh

Halab ASSYRIA

Ugarit Assur Nuzi

Hamath

Arvad Tadmor

Gebal Mari

Sidon Eshnunna

Tyre Damascus Der

Dan Cuth

Shechem Babylon

Bethel Nippur

Ashkelon Jerusalem/Moriah Erech

Gerar Mamre/Hebron/Machpelah Larsa

Beersheba Sodom and Gomorrah Ur Eridu

MESOPOTAMIA

CANAAN

BABYLONIA

River Tigris

River Euphrates

——— Most likely route

- - - - Possible route

(Red Sea) Modern name

0 250
km

(Red Sea)

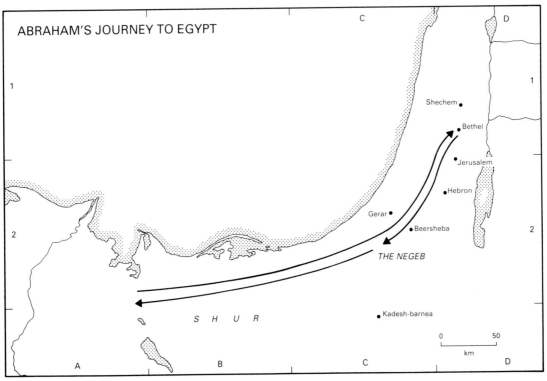

ABRAHAM'S JOURNEY TO EGYPT

Shechem

Bethel

Jerusalem

Hebron

Gerar

Beersheba

THE NEGEB

S H U R

Kadesh-barnea

0 50
km

Figure 1   Jacob wrestling with the angel, Rembrandt (Gemaldegalerie, Staatliche Museen Preussischer Kulturbesitz, Berlin)

persuaded them to wait, and another, Judah, suggested that Joseph should be sold as a slave rather than be killed. Eventually Joseph was taken as a slave to Egypt; his brothers dipped his coat in a kid's blood, declaring to Jacob that he had been mauled by a wild animal. In Egypt Joseph first served in the house of Potiphar, but was falsely accused by Potiphar's wife of rape. As a result he was cast into prison. In time he was released by the reigning pharaoh in order to interpret his dreams; subsequently he became chief minister of the land. After the outbreak of famine, he enabled the country to become rich. When his brothers came before him to buy grain, he revealed to them his identity, assuring them that all was guided by God's providential care:

I am your brother Joseph whom you sold in Egypt. And now do not be distressed because you sold me here; for God sent me before you to preserve life.

(Genesis 45: 4–5)

At the age of 110 Joseph died, and his family remained in Egypt, where they prospered. Yet with the arrival of a pharaoh 'who did not know Joseph' (Exodus 1:8), the Jewish people were forced to labour as slaves on the construction of the royal cities of Pithom and Raamses. According to Scripture, this pharaoh declared that all male offspring should be killed at birth: 'Every son that is born to the Hebrews – you shall cast into the Nile, but you shall let every daughter live' (Exodus 1:22).

Ancient Egypt

Paralleling the rise of Mesopotamian civilization, Egyptian culture reached great heights in the third millennium. In c. 3000 BC an Upper Egyptian king, Narmer, conquered Lower Egypt, unifying both portions of the land. With the collapse of the Old Kingdom in c. 2200 BC Egypt suffered political anarchy and civil war which lasted over two centuries. However, with the accession of Amenehmet I of the Twelfth Dynasty (c. 1990 BC), the Middle Kingdom enjoyed considerable prosperity – this period coincided with the patriarchal period in Palestine, and it appears that interrelations existed between the two regions.

In c. 1780 BC the Middle Kingdom collapsed. As a result, chaos ensued. About fifty years later the Delta was ruled over by the Hyksos of Asian descent; their rule lasted until c. 1570 BC. Around 1550 BC the Egyptian rulers of Thebes began a war of liberation against the Hyksos – this resulted in the capture of the Hyksos capital at Avaris, and the Hyksos were expelled from Egypt. To prevent the reccurrence of such foreign domination, the rulers of the Eighteenth Dynasty extended their domination east and north into west Asia. Under Thutmose (c. 1490–1436 BC), the foundations of Egypt's Asiatic empire were

laid. His two successors continued his policies until the reign of Amunhotep III (c. 1405–1367 BC). During this period the national god, Amun of Thebes, was regarded as having given victory to Egypt.

Under Amunhotep's son Akhenaton (c. 1367–1350 BC), a social revolution occurred. Akhenaton attempted to revolutionize religious life by suppressing the cult of Amun and other major gods and replacing them with worship of the sun-disk Aton. Such reforms resembled monotheism, yet Akhenaton's revolution did not survive his death. At the death of Akhenaton's successor Tutankhamun, Egypt was defeated in Asia in a war against the Hittites and a civil war in Egypt led to the independence of Canaan. From c. 1304–1200 BC the Ramesside kings of the Nineteenth Dynasty re-established Egyptian control and Egyptian garrisons were placed in various Canaanite cities. Rameses II (c. 1290–1273 BC), the most famous king of the dynasty, fought a battle with the resurgent Hittites at Kedesh on the Orontes. This battle established the northern limits of Egyptian control and influence in southern Syria.

According to tradition the Exodus of the Israelites from Egyptian captivity occurred

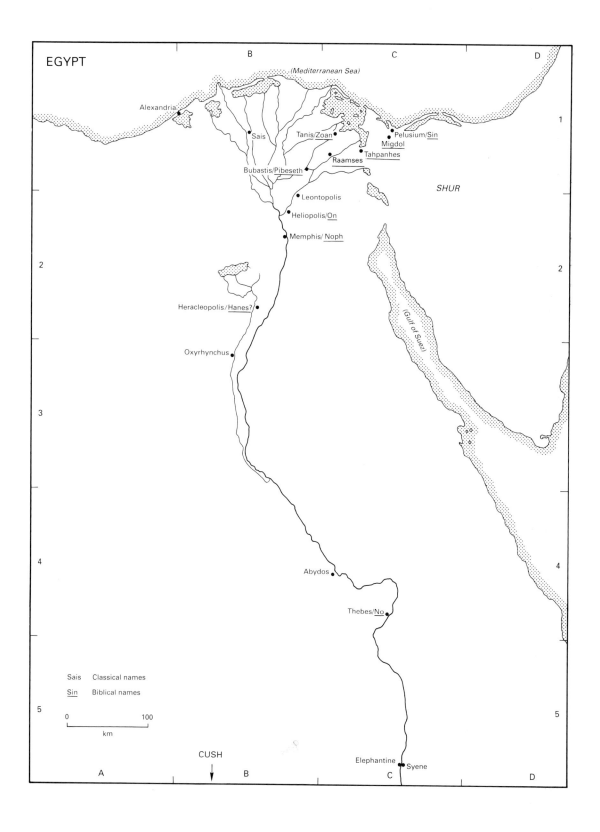

EGYPT

(Mediterranean Sea)

Alexandria

Sais

Tanis/Zoan   Pelusium/Sin
              Migdol
              Tahpanhes
       Raamses
Bubastis/Pibeseth

SHUR

Leontopolis

Heliopolis/On

Memphis/ Noph

Heracleopolis/Hanes?

(Gulf of Suez)

Oxyrhynchus

Abydos

Thebes/No

Sais   Classical names

Sin   Biblical names

0   100
     km

CUSH

Elephantine
        Syene

A   B   C   D

1

2

3

4

5

towards the last quarter of the second millennium BC during the reign of Raameses II. Thus the Book of Exodus relates: 'Therefore they did set over them taskmasters to afflict them with their burdens. And they built for Pharaoh store-cities, Pithom and Raamses.' As the greatest builder of the Nineteenth Dynasty New Kingdom Raameses engaged in building works at these two sites, employing vast numbers of slaves. Yet most scholars believe that the Israelites escaped during the reign of his successor Merneptah. A victory stele of this pharaoh dated 1220 BC relates that he won a battle in Canaan and mentions the defeated people as 'Israel'. Taken in conjunction with biblical evidence such as calculations based on I Kings 6:1 ('And it came to pass in the four hundred and eightieth year after the children of Israel were come out of the land of Egypt, in the fourth year of Solomon's reign over Israel, in the month Zif, which is the second month, that he began to build the house of the Lord'), it appears that the Exodus of the Israelite nation would have occurred by c. 1225 BC.

Moses and the Exodus

According to the Book of Exodus, a son was born to Amram of the House of Levi and his wife Jochebed. At the age of three months his parents hid him among the reeds along the banks of the Nile to save him from Pharaoh's decree that the first-born male Israelites be killed. When he was discovered by Pharaoh's daughter, she adopted him as her son Moses. Later as a grown man, Moses attacked and killed a taskmaster who was assaulting a Hebrew slave; in fear of his life he fled to the desert. There he sojourned with Jethro, a priest of Midian, marrying his daughter Zipporah. In Midian God revealed himself to Moses, commanding that he free the Israelite nation from Pharaoh's bondage: 'I am the God of your father, the God of Abraham, the God of Isaac, and the God of Jacob. I have seen the affliction of my people who are in Egypt, and have heard their cry because of their taskmasters. I know their sufferings ... Come, I will send you to Pharaoh that you may bring forth my people, the sons of Israel out of Egypt' (Exodus 3:6–7, 10).

In order to impel Pharaoh to let the people go, God sent ten plagues on to the Egyptians – the last involved the slaying of every first-born son in Egypt. The first-born of the Israelites, however, were spared: each family slaughtered a lamb and daubed its blood on the doorposts of their dwellings. When the angel of death observed this sign, he passed over the household. After the tenth plague, Pharaoh set the Israelites free, and they escaped without even waiting for their bread to rise. None the less, their perils had not come to an end. Changing his mind, Pharaoh sent his army in pursuit. When the Israelites arrived at the Red Sea, it appeared that there could be no escape. But miraculously Moses converted the water to dry land by a strong wind so that they could flee Pharaoh's army. The Egyptians, however, drowned as they pursued the Israelite nation:

> The Egyptians pursued, and went in after them into the midst of the sea, all Pharaoh's horses, his chariots, and his horsemen ... The waters returned and covered the chariots and the horsemen and all the host of Pharaoh that had followed them into the sea; not so much as one of them remained.
>
> (Exodus 14:23, 28)

The Israelites penetrated into the wilderness of Sinai, where Moses performed miracles so that they would have enough food and water (Exodus 16–17). After journeying for ninety days, they set up camp before Mt Sinai. There God commanded Moses to ascend the mountain and told him that if the nation would hearken to him and keep his covenant, they would become his special people. For two days the assembled gathering were to wash and purify themselves; on the third day they stood before the mountain

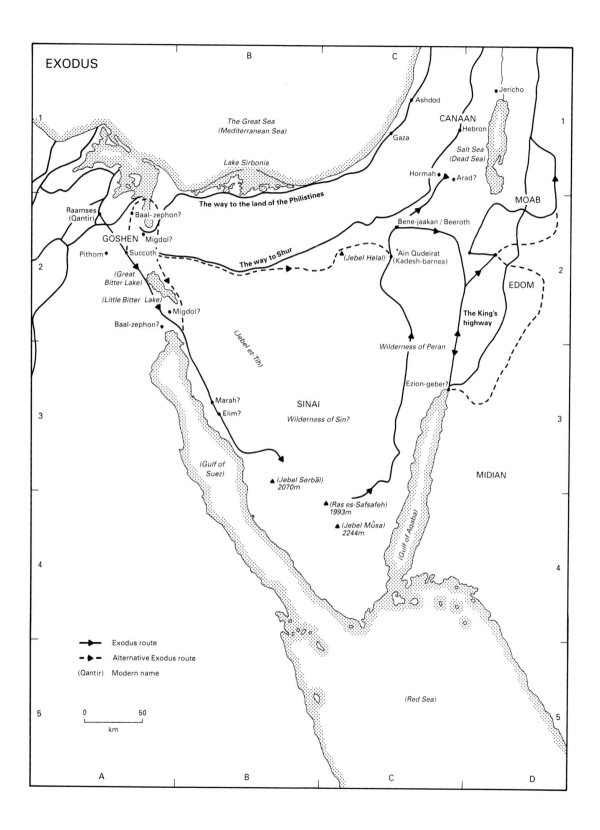

EXODUS

The Great Sea
(Mediterranean Sea)

Lake Sirbonis

The way to the land of the Philistines

Ashdod

CANAAN

Gaza

Hebron

*Salt Sea
(Dead Sea)*

Jericho

Raamses
(Qantir)

Baal-zephon?

GOSHEN   Migdol?

Pithom

Succoth

Hormah   Arad?

Bene-jaakan / Beeroth

MOAB

The way to Shur

(Jebel Helal)

'Ain Qudeirat
(Kadesh-barnea)

EDOM

(Great
Bitter Lake)

(Little Bitter Lake)

Migdol?

Baal-zephon?

(Jebel et-Tîh)

**The King's
highway**

Wilderness of Peran

Marah?

Elim?

SINAI

Wilderness of Sin?

Ezion-geber?

(Gulf of
Suez)

▲ (Jebel Serbâl)
2070m

MIDIAN

▲ (Ras es-Safsafeh)
1993m

▲ (Jebel Mûsa)
2244m

(Gulf of Aqaba)

➤ Exodus route

➤ Alternative Exodus route

(Qantir)   Modern name

(Red Sea)

0   50
km

Figure 2   Moses showing the tablets of the law to the people, Rembrandt (Gemaldegalerie, Staatliche Museen Preussischer Kulturbestz, Berlin)

amongst thunder, lightning and the sound of a ram's horn to hear God's voice. Alone Moses ascended the mountain, where he remained for forty days; at the end of this period he returned carrying two tablets of stone on which God's laws were inscribed. Yet on his return Moses discovered that the Israelites had abandoned him and their God. Furious at their disloyalty he smashed the tablets, only later carving new ones. In time the nation came to Kadesh-barnea near the border of Canaan. There Moses saw the Promised Land:

> And Moses went up from the plains of Moab to the top of Pisgah, which is opposite Jericho. And the Lord showed him all the land ... And the Lord said to him, 'This is the land of which I swore to Abraham, to Isaac, and to Jacob, I will give it to your descendants.' I have let you see it with your eyes, but you shall not go over there.'
>
> (Deuteronomy 34:1, 4)

Although the biblical account gives some indication of the location of these events, there is considerable uncertainty about the geographical details of the Exodus. According to some scholars, the crossing of the Red Sea (or Reed Sea), took place, not at the head of the Gulf of Suez (which is far from the Israelites' point of departure), but at one of the lakes now joined by the Suez Canal. Other scholars believe it occurred at the head of the Gulf of Aqaba, or alternatively Lake Sirbonis. The mountain where God appeared to Moses has traditionally been identified with Jebel Musa in the south of Sinai, but it has been objected that such a location would have taken the Israelites dangerously close to the route the Egyptians used to reach copper and turquoise mines in the region. Another suggestion is that the disturbances on the mountain suggest volcanic activity; however, since no mountain in the Sinai area is volcanic, it has been advanced that the site was in north-western Arabia. Thus, there is a lack of certitude about various features of the narrative describing the route of the Israelites in the wilderness.

Conquest and settlement

After Moses' death, God commanded Joshua the son of Nun to guide the children of Israel to the land he had promised to their ancestors. After crossing the River Jordan, Joshua conquered Ai and subsequently defeated the southern and northern kings. In order to embolden the people, he delivered speeches encouraging them to remain faithful to God. At the age of 110, Joshua died and the nation split into separate groups. Initially there were twelve tribes called after Jacob's sons: Joseph and Benjamin (the sons of Rachel), Levi, Simeon, Reuben, Judah, Issachar and Zebulun (the sons of Leah), Dan and Naphtali (the sons of Bilhah), and Gad and Asher (the sons of Zilpah). When Levi as a priestly group was excluded from this territorial partition, the tribe of Joseph was divided into two separate tribes: Ephraim and Manasseh.

The Book of Judges recounts the lives of national heroes who acted as judges of the Israelite nation after Joshua's death: Othniel, Ehud, Deborah, Gideon, Jephthah and Samson. These figures served as tribal rulers attached to specific regions, and their reign continued during the twelfth and eleventh centuries BC. During peaceful periods the tribes were administered by councils of elders, but at times of emergency the judges took control. Throughout the era of the judges, the Covenant between God and the Israelites was repeatedly proclaimed at national shrines such as Shechem.

As the nation became more settled, additional legislation was added to the Covenant. Originally Mosaic law consisted primarily of unconditional commandments, yet as time passed numerous other provisions were included. Many of these prescriptions were needed for an agricultural community and appear to date back to the time of the judges. At this time it also became increasingly clear to the Jewish nation that the

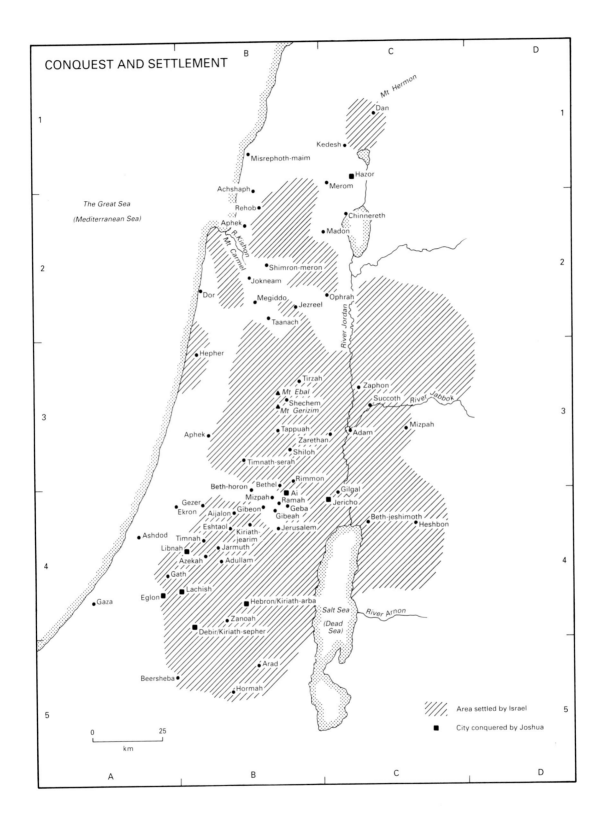

CONQUEST AND SETTLEMENT

Mt Hermon

Dan

Kedesh

Misrephoth-maim

Achshaph

■ Hazor

Merom

Rehob

Chinnereth

Aphek

R. Kishon

Madon

The Great Sea
(Mediterranean Sea)

Mt Carmel

Shimron-meron

Jokneam

Dor

Megiddo

Ophrah

Jezreel

Taanach

River Jordan

Hepher

Tirzah

Zaphon

▲ Mt Ebal

Succoth

River Jabbok

Shechem

▲ Mt Gerizim

Aphek

Tappuah

Mizpah

Zarethan

Adam

Shiloh

Timnath-serah

Rimmon

Beth-horon

Bethel

■ Ai

Gilgal

Mizpah

Ramah

■ Jericho

Gezer

Gibeon

Geba

Ekron

Aijalon

Gibeah

Beth-jeshimoth

Eshtaol

Jerusalem

Heshbon

Ashdod

Kiriath-
jearim

Timnah

■ Libnah

Jarmuth

Azekah

Adullam

Gath

■ Lachish

Eglon ■

Gaza

■ Hebron/Kiriath-arba

Salt Sea
(Dead Sea)

River Arnon

Zanoah

■ Debir/Kiriath-sepher

Arad

Beersheba

Hormah

0   25
km

///// Area settled by Israel

■ City conquered by Joshua

14

God of Israel was the providential Lord of human history: the Exodus and the conquest of the Promised Land were perceived as the unfolding of a divine scheme. Within this context numerous features of the Canaanite religion were rejected: unlike the Canaanites, who worshipped local gods, the people of Israel emphasized their indifference to place-related ties by revering a mobile tabernacle (which contained the sacred ark) which they carried from place to place. In addition, the Israelites condemned such Canaanite practices as fertility rituals, the making of idols, temple prostitution, and human sacrifice. Moreover, the Israelites reinterpreted various Canaanite celebrations to suit their own religious aims: the Spring festival was transformed into *Pesach* (Passover) to commemorate the Exodus from Egypt; the Autumn festival became *Succot* (Booths) to celebrate the dwelling in tents in the desert; and the Summer festival was changed to *Shavuot* (Weeks) to commemorate the revelation on Mt Sinai. These three festivals became institutionalized occasions to remind the Jewish nation of their oppression, deliverance, and dedication to the Covenant.

Although archaeological discoveries have not conclusively confirmed the biblical account of the conquest of the Land, they do cast light on various aspects of this period. The Tell-el-Amarna letters, for example, from the early fourteenth century, which were written by rulers in Canaan and Syria to Amunhotep III (1405–1367 BC) and his successor Akhenaton (1367–1350 BC), mention raiders (the *Habiru*) who devastated the countryside. Concerning the biblical claim that Joshua conquered various Canaanite cities, evidence from different sites such as Hazor illustrates that there was widespread destruction during the thirteenth century BC. Archaeological evidence also provides information about the Canaanite religion. The tell of Ras-esh-Shamra was the site of the citadel of Ugarit, which flourished in the fifteenth and fourteenth centuries BC. In the annex to the temple these archaeologists found a collection of thirteenth-century tablets describing the exploits of Baal and other Canaanite gods and goddesses. Such evidence casts important light on the history of the ancient Israelites and the development of their religion during the period of conquest and settlement in the Promised Land.

2 THE RISE OF MONARCHY AND THE TWO KINGDOMS

Monarchy

During the period of the judges the Israelites engaged in battles with their neighbours. In this conflict the people viewed God as the supreme ruler. As a consequence when some tribes recommended to Gideon that he become king, he replied that it was impossible for the nation to be ruled over by both God and a human monarch (Judges 8:22–3). Nevertheless the people became increasingly dissatisfied with tribal allegiance and simple trust in God. In addition, the nation was politically and militarily less well organized than its neighbours and was unable effectively to resist invading armies. After a defeat at Aphek, the leaders of the Israelites decided to ensure that God would be with them in battle. 'Let us bring the ark of the Covenant of the Lord here from Shiloh', they affirmed, 'that he may come among us and save us from the power of our enemies' (I Samuel 4:3). This plan, however, proved to be unsuccessful: the ark was captured, its shrine at Shiloh devastated, and the Israelite army defeated.

Although the ark was later returned, this conquest overwhelmed the nation and led to the desire for kingship; yet in Scripture the people's wish for a king is presented as a rejection of God's authority. According to the Book of Samuel, the king was chosen by means of a sacred lot at a national assembly summoned by Samuel – in this context Samuel warned against the dangers of kingly rule:

And now behold the king whom you have chosen, for whom you have asked; behold, the Lord has set a king over you. If you will fear the Lord and serve him and hearken to his voice and not rebel against the commandment of the Lord, and if both you and the king who reigns over you will follow the Lord your God, it will be well; but if you will not hearken to the voice of the Lord, but rebel against the commandments of the Lord, then the hand of the Lord will be against you and your king.

(I Samuel 12:13–15)

Samuel's predictions proved correct: Saul's regime as king was beset by numerous problems. His first difficulty was the loss of Samuel's support. When Saul was told to take neither prisoners nor spoil in a battle against the Amalekites, he did not strictly follow these orders. As a result, Samuel denounced the king and stated that Saul had been rejected by God (I Samuel 15). The second trouble concerned Saul's moods of gloom and violence. God's spirit came upon Saul after he was anointed king, and imparted to him prophetic frenzy and thereby enabled him to lead Israel to victory. For Saul such emotional activity had a devastating impact on his emotional equilibrium. To calm him, David joined his entourage so that he could bring relief by playing music. This, however, proved to be no remedy since Saul became jealous of David's popularity and success. Saul's reign hence began with military victory, but ended in madness and defeat.

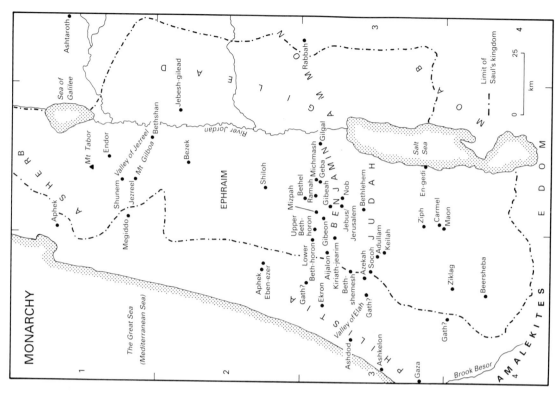

MONARCHY

Ashtaroth

Sea of Galilee

Jebesh-gilead

A S H E R

B

Mt Tabor

Endor

Shunem

Valley of Jezreel

Jezreel

Mt Gilboa

Bethshan

Megiddo

Bezek

Rabbah

River Jordan

G I L E A D

A M M O N

Limit of Saul's kingdom

0   25

km

Aphek

Shiloh

EPHRAIM

Mizpah

Upper Beth-horon

Bethel

Ramah

Geba

Michmash

Gibeah

Gibeon

Gilgal

BENJAMIN

Nob

Jebus/Jerusalem

J U D A H

Bethlehem

Salt Sea

Ziph

Carmel

Maon

En-gedi

Lower Beth-horon

Aijalon

Kiriath-jearim

Azekah

Beth-shemesh

Socoh

Adullam

Keilah

Gath?

Ekron

Beersheba

Ziklag

I S R A E L

Aphek

Eben-ezer

The Great Sea
(Mediterranean Sea)

Gath?

Valley of Elah

Gath?

Ashdod

Ashkelon

P H I L I S T I A

Gaza

Brook Besor

A M A L E K I T E S

E D O M

1   2   3   4

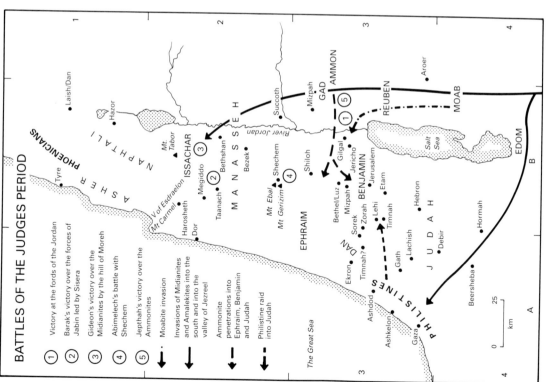

BATTLES OF THE JUDGES PERIOD

① Victory at the fords of the Jordan

② Barak's victory over the forces of Jabin led by Sisera

③ Gideon's victory over the Midianites by the hill of Moreh

④ Abimelech's battle with Shechem

⑤ Jepthah's victory over the Ammonites

⬇ Moabite invasion

⬇ Invasions of Midianites and Amalekites into the south and into the valley of Jezreel

⬇ Ammonite penetrations into Ephraim, Benjamin and Judah

⬇ Philistine raid into Judah

P H O E N I C I A N S

Tyre

A S H E R

N A P H T A L I

Laish/Dan

Hazor

Mt Tabor

ISSACHAR

③

Megiddo

②

MANASSEH

Taanach

Bezek

Succoth

Mizpah

GAD

AMMON

①

⑤

REUBEN

Aroer

MOAB

V of Esdraelon

Harosheth

Dor

Mt Carmel

Mt Ebal

④

Mt Gerizim

Shechem

Shiloh

Gilgal

Jericho

BENJAMIN

Jerusalem

Bethel/Luz

Mizpah

Salt Sea

EDOM

EPHRAIM

DAN

Ekron

Sorek

Zorah

Timnah?

Lehi

Timnah

Etam

J U D A H

Hebron

Gath

Lachish

Debir

Ashdod

Ashkelon

Gaza

P H I L I S T I N E S

The Great Sea

Beersheba

Hormah

0   25

km

A   B

1   2   3   4

Figure 3   David playing the harp before Saul.
Rembrandt (Mauritshuis – The Hague)

David and Solomon

After David (1010–970 BC) joined Saul's entourage, he gained a reputation as a successful warrior as reflected in the story of his victory over the giant Goliath. Subsequently he married Saul's daughter Michal, obtaining her hand with the foreskins of a hundred Philistines. Such military victories as well as David's popularity provoked Saul's hostility, and on the advice of Saul's son Jonathan he fled to the Cave of Adullam in the southern wilderness for safety. When both Saul and Jonathan were killed in battle on Mt Gilboa, David became the leader of the southern tribes and was anointed King of Judah at Hebron. Within the month, however, Saul's son Ishbaal was proclaimed king; later he was supplanted by David, who became king of the entire country. In an early victory as monarch, David vanquished the Jebusites in Jerusalem, which he announced as the new capital and subsequently transformed into a major administrative centre. Hiring foreign craftsmen, he built new fortifications and a palace. In addition he brought the ark of the Covenant to Jerusalem, thereby transferring power away from the tribes.

Despite David's glory as a military leader, Scripture despairs of David's immorality. After committing adultery with Bathsheba, he caused the death of her husband Uriah. Full of wrath, the prophet Nathan denounced David, demanding his repentance. Yet for all his iniquity, the king was assured that his dynasty would continue. As God proclaimed:

When your days are fulfilled and you lie down with your fathers, I will raise up your offspring after you, who shall come forth from your body, and I will establish his kingdom. He shall build a house for my name, and I will establish the throne of his kingdom for ever.

(II Samuel 7:12–14)

Near the end of David's life, rivals for the throne engaged in bitter conflict. Revolts led by his son Absalom and by Sheba from the tribe of Benjamin were crushed, and his son Adonijah

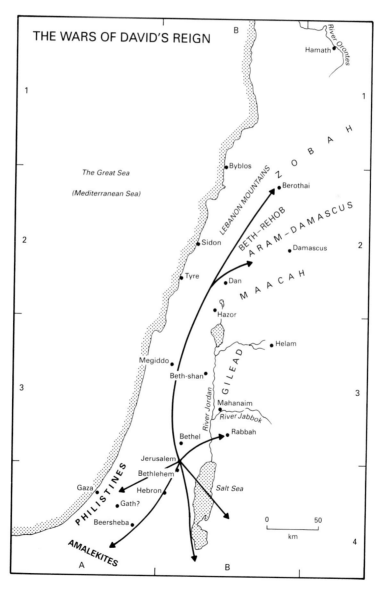

THE WARS OF DAVID'S REIGN

emerged as the likely successor. Although Adonijah was supported by both the priest Abiathar and the army-general Joab, another son Solomon (970–930 BC) was promoted by his mother Bathsheba as well as Nathan the prophet, Zadok the priest, and Benaiah, an army commander. In time Solomon triumphed; Adonijah and his supporters were put to death and Abiathar was sent into exile.

During Solomon's reign enormous resources were directed into a personal army of 12,000 men and horses and 1,400 chariots. In foreign affairs, Solomon engaged in trade with Arabia, Syria and Cilicia as well as north and east Africa. He also married an Egyptian princess, thereby linking himself with Egypt. One of Solomon's closest foreign links was with Hiram, the King of Tyre; by means of this Phoenician connection he was able to develop trade in the Red Sea and Indian Ocean. In addition, Solomon traded horses with

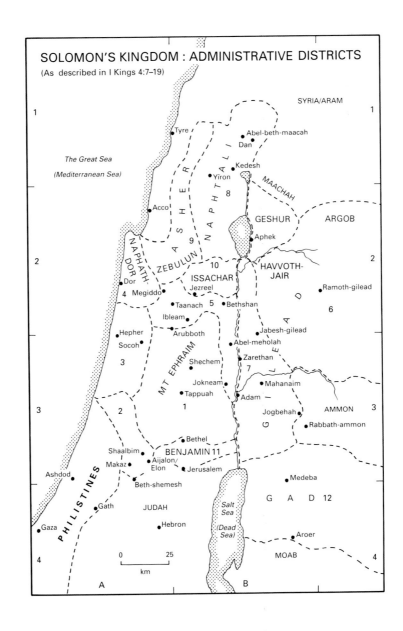

the Egyptians in the South and the Hittites in the North.

Through this activity Solomon was able to construct a new palace for himself, another for his Egyptian wife, a hall for state occasions, a judgement chamber, and the Temple itself. In addition to such architectural achievements, Solomon was widely respected as a wise ruler. As Scripture relates, Solomon's wisdom surpassed the wisdom of all the people of the East, and all the wisdom of Egypt (I Kings 4:30). Tradition records that he was able to recite 'three thousand proverbs; and his songs were a thousand and five. He spoke of trees, from the cedar that is Lebanon to the hyssop that grows out of the wall; he spoke also of beasts, and of birds, and of reptiles and of fish' (I Kings 4:32–3).

To support Solomon's many projects, an elaborate system of taxation was enforced – all twelve districts of the country were required to

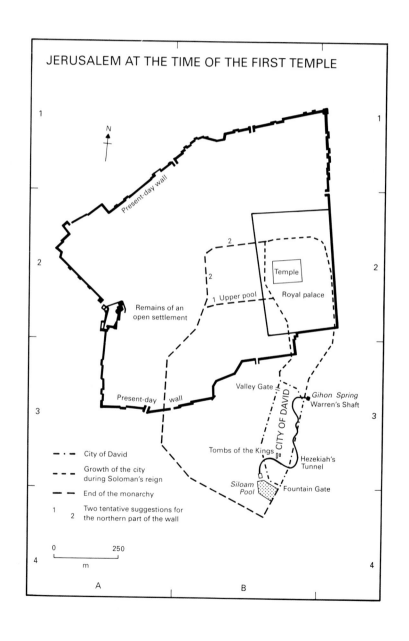

JERUSALEM AT THE TIME OF THE FIRST TEMPLE

Present-day wall

Temple

Royal palace

Upper pool

Remains of an open settlement

Present-day wall

Valley Gate

Gihon Spring
Warren's Shaft

CITY OF DAVID

Tombs of the Kings

Hezekiah's Tunnel

Siloam Pool

Fountain Gate

– · – City of David

– – – Growth of the city during Soloman's reign

– – End of the monarchy

1 2 Two tentative suggestions for the northern part of the wall

0   250
        m

A   B

support the royal court for one month a year. Such taxation evoked widespread discontent: the existence of a privileged elite supported by the general populace contradicted the egalitarian nature of tribal unity. Further, the fact that the Canaanites adopted a similar socio-economic system highlighted the foreignness of such an arrangement; none the less, even such a scheme of taxation proved insufficient to support Solomon's endeavours, and he instituted enforced labour. Solomon's policies provoked an unsuccessful revolt by the northern leader, Jeroboam. Yet despite this defeat, the northern tribes remained dissatisfied by what they perceived as a system of exploitation and political favouritism.

The kingdoms of Israel and Judah

After the death of Solomon, his son Rehoboam (930–908 BC) became king and appealed to the northern tribes for support. At a meeting in Shechem, they stipulated the terms on which they would accept the monarchy. Rehoboam, however, refused to comply, declaring: 'My father made your yoke heavy, but I will add to your yoke; my father chastised you with whips, but I will chastise you with scorpions' (I Kings 12:14). As a result, the northern tribes revolted against him and chose Jeroboam I as their king (930–910 BC): 'When all Israel heard that Jeroboam had returned, they sent and called him to the assembly and made him king over all Israel' (I Kings 12:20). Initially Shechem was Jeroboam's administrative centre, but later Tirzah became the capital.

After the division of the two kingdoms, a foreign aggressor, Shoshenk I, the first pharaoh of the Twenty-Second Dynasty, invaded the country, forcing Rehoboam to pay tribute. In the North this external danger was matched by an internal threat: the tribes were troubled by the loss of the Temple and wished to make pilgrimage to Jerusalem. To stem such sentiment, Jeroboam I established shrines at the old centres of Canaanite worship (Dan and Bethel), where he set up golden bulls in an attempt to reconcile the faith of Israel with Canaanite practices. After Jeroboam I's death, he was succeeded by his son Nadab (910–909 BC) and then Baasha (909–886 BC). Like Jeroboam I, Baasha encouraged a mixture of Canaanite and Israelite religions. When he died, Elah (886 BC) attempted to become king but was assassinated, and Zimri (886 BC), an army commander, usurped the throne. Zimri's reign lasted only seven days; he was followed by another general, Omri (885–874 BC), and later his son Ahab (874–852 BC). Under Omri and Ahab the position of the northern kingdom was made more secure – they ended the conflict with Judah, and an alliance between the two kingdoms was sealed by the marriage of Ahab's daughter to Jehoram (851–842 BC), the son of Jehoshaphat (875–851 BC) (King of Judah). In addition, Israel made peace with Phoenicia and Ahab himself married the Phoenician princess, Jezebel.

With Jezebel's encouragement, Ahab incorporated Canaanite religious features into the religion of Israel. As Scripture records: 'He did evil in the sight of the Lord more than all that were before him, and as if it has been a light thing for him to walk in the sins of Jeroboam ... and went and served Baal and worshipped him' (I Kings 16:31).

To combat such idolatrous practices, the prophet Elijah challenged 450 prophets of Baal and 400 prophets of Asherah to a contest on Mt Carmel, where an altar to the God of Israel had been replaced by a shrine to Baal. There both he and the Canaanite prophets prepared sacrifices and prayed to their respective gods to ignite the offerings. The prophets of Baal and Asherah cried aloud and cut themselves with swords – yet no answer was forthcoming. But, as Scripture relates, Elijah's plan was successful:

The fire of the Lord fell, and consumed the

THE KINGDOMS OF ISRAEL AND JUDAH

◉ Capital city

■ Town fortified by Rehoboam

--- Territorial boundary

The Great Sea
(Mediterranean Sea)

P H O E N I C I A

L E B A N O N

A R A M

G A L I L E E

I S R A E L

P H I L I S T I A

J U D A H

HAVVOTH-JAIR

AMMON

MOAB

Sidon
Zarephath
Damascus
Tyre
Abel-beth-maachah
Dan
Kedesh-naphtali
Hazor
Chinnereth
Gath-hepher
Jokneam
Shunem
Beth-arbel
Ramoth-gilead
Dor
Megiddo
Jezreel
Taanach
Beth-shean
Ibleam
Dothan
River Cherith
Socoh
Tirzah
◉ Shechem
Succoth
Penuel
Mahanaim
Tappuah
Zarethan
Joppa
Shiloh
Ephron
Rabbath-ammon
Beth-horon
Bethel
Jabneel
Ekron
Shaalbim
Mizpah
Gilgal
Gezer
Geba
Jericho
Elealeh
Gibbethon
Aijalon
Gibeon
Ramah
Heshbon
Libnah
Zorah
Kiriath-jearim
Ashdod
◉ Jerusalem
Medeba
Moresheth-gath
Azekah
Bethlehem
Baal-meon
Socoh
Etam
Adullam
Tekoa
Mareshah
Beth-zur
Ataroth
Lachish
Hebron
Adoraim
Ziph
En-gedi
Dibon
Salt
Sea
Beersheba
Nimrim
Kir-hareseth

Mt Carmel

River Jordan

River Abana
Mt Hermon
River Pharpar

0   25
km

A   B   C   D
1   2   3   4   5

23

burnt offering, and the wood and the stones, and the dust and licked up the water that was in the trench. And when all the people saw it, they fell on their faces, and they said, 'The Lord, he is God; the Lord, he is God.'

(I Kings 18:38–9)

Despite this triumph, Jezebel persuaded Ahab to observe Phoenician customs; since she regarded the life and property of all subjects as belonging to the king, she insisted that the Israelite Naboth be killed so that her husband could seize his property. In response, the prophet Elijah rebuked the king for his unscrupulousness; not even the royal family was above God's law.

Ahab was followed by his two sons Ahaziah (852–850 BC) and Joram (850–842 BC), but those loyal to the faith of Israel rebelled. Inspired by the prophet Elisha, these devotees chose an army officer Jehu (842–815 BC) as King of Israel, who assassinated Joram, Ahaziah, the King of Judah (842 BC), and Jezebel; when Jehu appealed to the city rulers of Samaria to pay allegiance to him, they presented him with the heads of seventy members of Ahab's family. Yet despite this victory, Jehu lost the loyalty of Phoenicia as well as the southern kingdom. In Judah, Ahab's sister Athaliah (842–837 BC) seized control and killed all claimants for the throne except for one child, Joash (837–800 BC), who was rescued by the priest Jehoiada. After reigning for six years, Athaliah was deposed and Joash became king. During this period Israel became almost a province of Syria under Jehu's son Jehoahaz (815–801 BC). However, by the time Jehu's grandson Jehoash (801–786 BC) became king, Assyria had grown in power, as Scripture relates: 'The Lord gave Israel a saviour so that they were saved from the hands of the Syrians' (II Kings 13:5).

Figure 4 *King Jehu presenting tribute to Shalmaneser III on the Black Obelisk from the Assyrian city of Nimrud* (British Museum)

The rise of Assyria gave the northern king Jehoash an opportunity to recover Israel's territory; Amaziah, the King of Judah (800–783 BC) was similarly able to take back land. At this stage Amaziah declared war on the northern kingdom; when Judah was defeated, Jehoash invaded Jerusalem. As a result, King Amaziah was assassinated and replaced by his son Uzziah (783–742 BC).

Jeroboam II to the fall of the northern kingdom

With Uzziah in Judah and Jeroboam II (786–746 BC) in Israel, the nation flourished during the next forty years. Uzziah repaired the defences in Jerusalem, reorganized and equipped the army with new weapons, initiated advanced agricultural methods, and reopened Solomon's copper refineries. In the North Jeroboam II erected new buildings and participated in international trade. Such prosperity encouraged the people to become more religious – they were convinced their affluence was the result of God's favour. None the less some critics argued that the desire for riches was incompatible with God's Covenant.

Near the end of Jeroboam II's reign, the prophet Amos distanced himself from the cultic prophets, declaring that Israelite society had become morally corrupt. Many had become rich at the expense of the poor. Israel sinned, he stated:

> because they sell the righteous for silver and the needy for a pair of shoes, they that trample the head of the poor into the dust of the earth, and turn aside the way of the afflicted.
>
> (Amos 2:6–7)

The shrines were full of worshippers, but such ritual practice was without merit. According to Amos, the 'day of the Lord' would be a time of punishment for those who sinned:

> Woe to you who desire the day of the Lord ... It is darkness and not light ... I hate, I despise your feasts, and I take no delight in your solemn assemblies. Even though you offer me your burnt offerings and cereal offerings, I will not accept them ...

> Therefore I will take you into exile beyond Damascus, says the Lord, whose name is the God of Hosts.
>
> (Amos 5:18, 21–2, 27)

These dire predictions were repeated by the prophet Hosea. Israel, he proclaimed, had gone astray and would be punished. Through his own personal tragedy – the infidelity of his wife Gomer – Hosea was able to offer a message of condolence and hope. Just as his love for Gomer had been repudiated, so God's love for his chosen people had been rejected. Yet despite the coming disaster, God would not cease to care for Israel. As Hosea was unable to give up his wife, so God would not abandon the Israelite nation: 'How can I hand you over, O Israel!... My heart recoils within me, my compassion grows warm and tender' (Hosea 11:8).

Within a short time these prophecies of destruction were fulfilled. During the reign of Menahem, King of Israel (746–738 BC), King Tiglath-Pileser III of Assyria embarked on a policy of expansion. For two years Menahem's son Pekahiah (738–737 BC) reigned as the northern king by paying tribute to the Assyrian ruler. In 737 BC he was overthrown by Pekah (737–732 BC). This new Israelite leader formed an alliance with the King of Syria against the Assyrians, and these two monarchs attempted to persuade the King of Judah, Jotham (742–735 BC), to join them. However, when he refused, they declared war on the southern kingdom. Aware of this danger the southern prophet Isaiah warned Jotham's successor, Ahaz (735–715 BC), that this threat would not be fulfilled since both Israel and

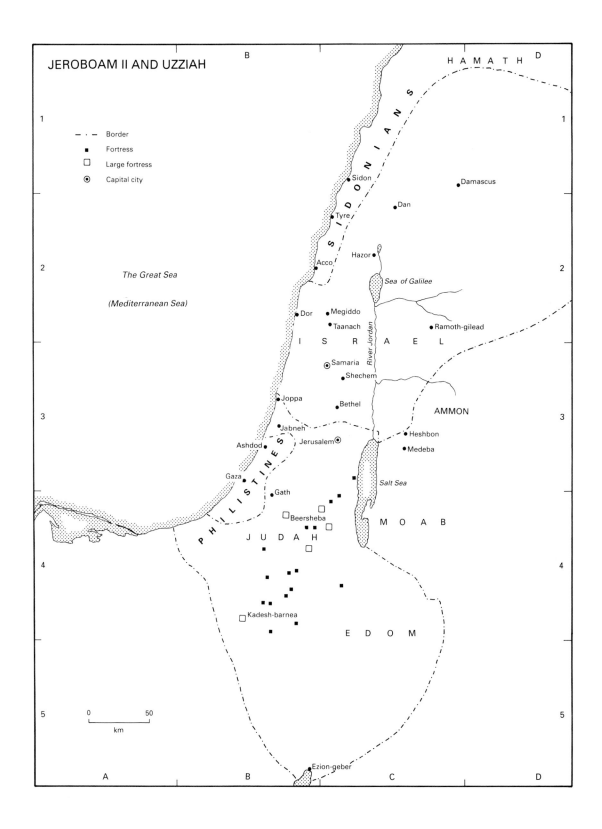

JEROBOAM II AND UZZIAH

Border
Fortress
Large fortress
Capital city

HAMATH

S I D O N I A N S

The Great Sea

(Mediterranean Sea)

Sidon

Damascus

Dan

Tyre

Hazor

Acco

Sea of Galilee

Dor

Megiddo

Taanach

Ramoth-gilead

I S R A E L

River Jordan

Samaria

Shechem

Joppa

Bethel

AMMON

Jabneh

Heshbon

Ashdod

Jerusalem

Medeba

Gaza

Salt Sea

Gath

M O A B

Beersheba

J U D A H

Kadesh-barnea

E D O M

0   50
km

Ezion-geber

26

Syria would collapse. Subsequently Ahaz attempted to placate the Assyrians, travelling to Damascus, which had just been conquered by the Assyrians, to pay homage to Tiglath Pileser III. On his return, he planned for an altar to be set up in the Temple as a symbol of Judah's submission. In the North, Pekah's position deteriorated as the Assyrians advanced, and he was assassinated by Hoshea (732–722 BC), who surrendered to the Assyrians. In 727 BC Shalmaneser V replaced Tiglath-Pileser III and overwhelmed Israel's capital Samaria after a siege of two years. According to the annals of Shalmaneser's successor Sargon II, 27,290 Israelites were deported as a result of this victory. This marked the end of the northern kingdom.

Ahaz and Hezekiah

With the destruction of the northern kingdom, Judah came under threat. To placate Assyria, the southern king Ahaz (735–715 BC) offered tribute and promoted the worship of Assyrian gods. In opposition to such practices, the prophet Isaiah declared that the collapse of Israel was God's punishment for the nation's sinfulness. Judah, he believed, would suffer a similar fate, and he warned that God was not satisfied with empty ritual:

> What to me is the multitude of your sacrifices? says the Lord. I have had enough of burnt offerings of rams and the fat of fed beasts; I do not delight in the blood of bulls, or of lambs, or of he-goats.
>
> (Isaiah 10:11)

Echoing this message, his contemporary the prophet Micah also predicted destruction:

> Hear this, you heads of the house of Jacob and rulers of the house of Israel, who abhor justice and pervert all equity … because of you Zion shall be plowed as a field; Jerusalem shall become a heap of ruins.
>
> (Micah 3:9,12)

Trusting in his own political machinations, Ahaz ignored these words. The southern kingdom, he believed, was secure from danger.

By the time Ahaz was succeeded by Hezekiah (715–687 BC), the King of Assyria, Sargon II, directed his attention to other parts of the empire; this gave Egypt and Philistia an opportunity to rebel against Assyrian oppression. The Philistine ambassadors attempted to secure Hezekiah's support, but the prophet Isaiah warned against such an alliance. Assyria, he maintained, could not be stopped; to dramatize the inevitable destruction, he walked naked around Jerusalem. 'So', he stated, 'shall the king of Assyria lead away the Egyptian captives, and the Ethiopian exiles, both the young and the old, naked and barefoot, with buttocks uncovered, to the shame of Egypt' (Isaiah 20:4). Fortunately for the southern kingdom, Hezekiah heeded Isaiah's words as Assyria conquered the Philistine and Egyptian nations.

After the Assyrian victory Hezekiah endeavoured to establish his independence from Assyrian domination by reforming the nation's religious practices: he removed the altar to Assyrian gods in the Temple, closed down local shrines in order to centralize the Jerusalem cult, and sent a message to those residing in the former northern kingdom urging them to worship in the South. In addition, the King prepared the country for an Assyrian advance. He established new defences, reorganized the army, created new store cities, and rationalized the civil service. In Jerusalem he constructed the Siloam Tunnel so as to provide a water supply if the city were besieged.

With the death of Sargon II, the Kings of Babylon and Egypt pleaded with Hezekiah for assistance in overthrowing the Assyrians. Wary of such political involvement, Isaiah cautioned against joining this alliance; Hezekiah, however, paid no attention to the prophet's warning.

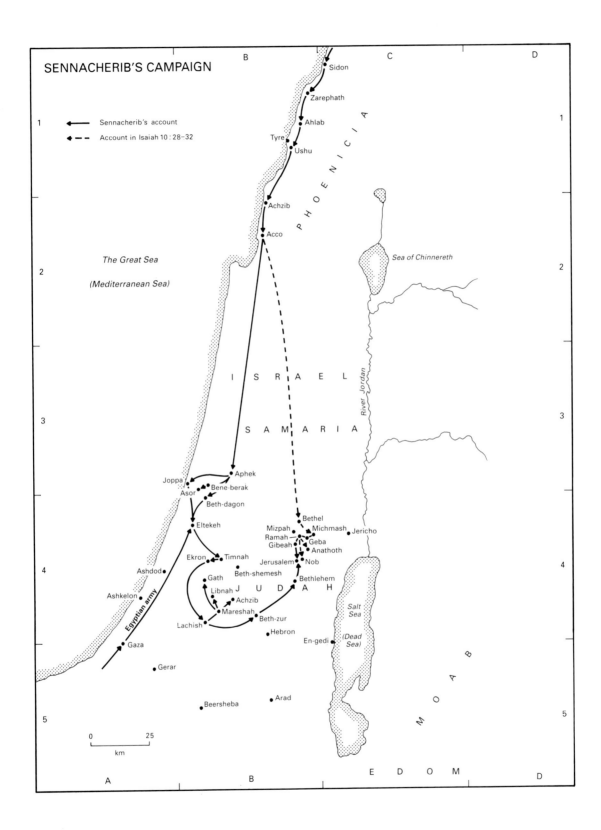

SENNACHERIB'S CAMPAIGN

Sennacherib's account
Account in Isaiah 10 : 28–32

Sidon
Zarephath
Ahlab
Tyre
Ushu
Achzib
Acco

PHOENICIA

The Great Sea

(Mediterranean Sea)

Sea of Chinnereth

ISRAEL

SAMARIA

River Jordan

Joppa
Aphek
Bene-berak
Asor
Beth-dagon
Eltekeh
Bethel
Mizpah
Michmash
Jericho
Ramah
Geba
Gibeah
Anathoth
Ekron
Timnah
Jerusalem
Nob
Ashdod
Beth-shemesh
Gath
Bethlehem
Ashkelon
Libnah
J U D A H
Achzib
Mareshah
Beth-zur
Egyptian army
Lachish
Hebron
Salt
Sea
Gaza
En-gedi
(Dead
Sea)
Gerar

M O A B

Beersheba
Arad

0   25
km

E   D   O   M

Anxious to suppress this revolt, Sargon's successor Sennacherib subdued Babylon, Phoenicia and Philistia, and then invaded the kingdom of Judah in 701 BC. The annals of Sennacherib record that the Assyrian army besieged and captured forty-six of Hezekiah's 'strong walled cities as well as the small cities in their neighbourhood'. The next stage of the Assyrian campaign was the assault of Jerusalem. According to Sennacherib's records, the Judaean king was shut up in the city like a bird in a cage; seeing no means of escape, Hezekiah offered gold and silver as a tribute to the Assyrian king, who was encamped at Lachish. Yet according to the Book of Kings, this siege ended in failure: the Assyrian army were stationed outside the city, but just as their victory seemed imminent, they withdrew.

3 CAPTIVITY AND RETURN

From Manasseh to Babylonian captivity

After the conquest of Judah, Sennacherib was killed and succeeded by Esarhaddon, who became a successful ruler. Once he died, his empire was divided between two sons: Ashur-bani-pal, who ruled in Nineveh, and Shamash-Shanakin, who resided in Babylon. At this time Assyria became the ascendant power in Mesopotamia. Under Ashur-bani-pal Nineveh became a great cultural centre where artists created magnificent works and scribes collected together the literary products of Mesopotamian culture. During this period Hezekiah's successor in Judah, Manasseh (687–642 BC), was dominated by Assyria, and pagan practices again became prevalent. Like Ahaz, Manasseh was compelled to worship Assyrian gods as a sign of submission, and his son and successor Amon (642–640 BC) continued this policy.

Yet despite Assyria's prominence, the empire came under increasing threat from Lydia in the North-West, the Medes in the East, and the Scythians in the North. This lessening of Assyrian dominance brought about a nationalistic revival in Judah; none the less the prophet Jeremiah cautioned that the southern kingdom would be overwhelmed by foreign nations. However, the new king Josiah (640–609 BC) was convinced he could restore the nation to its previous glory through territorial conquest and religious reform. As a consequence he banned the symbols of Assyrian control in the former northern kingdom, destroyed the sanctuary at Bethel set up by

Jeroboam I, and eliminated many local shrines as well as their priests. In addition, during his reign the Book of Deuteronomy was found in the Temple: this work insisted that a single God should be worshipped in a central place by a united congregation. This discovery had a powerful effect on the people. In a solemn ceremony, the nation dedicated themselves to God:

> And the king stood by the pillar and made a covenant before the Lord, to walk after the Lord and to keep his commandments and his testimonies and his statutes, with all his heart and all his soul, to perform the words of this covenant that were written in this book; and all the people joined in the covenant.
>
> (2 Kings 23:3)

As these events unfolded in Judah, the Babylonians attacked the Assyrians, capturing all the empire's main cities. Some time after Josiah's reforms, the Assyrians made a final assault on the town of Harran. Josiah attempted to halt the Egyptian army which had been summoned by the Assyrians to come to their aid; in the ensuing battle he was mortally wounded, and Judah came under Egyptian dominance. Subsequently, however, the Assyrian empire collapsed, and the Babylonians conquered the Egyptians at Carchemish in 605 BC. When this occurred King Jehoiakim (609–598 BC), who was established as the monarch by the Egyptians, transferred his

Figure 5   Nebuchadnezzar's army attacking the Temple, Jean Fouquet (Bibliothèque Nationale)

allegiance to King Nebuchadnezzar II of Babylon. During Jehoiakim's reign, the prophet Jeremiah predicted disaster. Jerusalem and the Temple, he proclaimed, would be devastated. This prediction was echoed by his contemporary: the prophet Habakkuk declared that God would use foreign nations to punish the southern kingdom. Undeterred by this message, Jehoiakim was convinced he could assert his independence from foreign rule.

Some years later Babylon was defeated by Egypt, and Jehoiakim believed the time was ripe for rebellion. Such resistance was met by an Assyrian onslaught on Judah: Nebuchadnezzar invaded the country and conquered Jerusalem. In this siege Jehoiakim was killed and succeeded by his son Jehoiachin (597 BC), who was taken captive. Other important citizens were also led into captivity and the treasures of the palace and Temple plundered. In the same year a new king, Zedekiah (597–586 BC) was set on the throne by Nebuchadnezzar. Jeremiah attempted to persuade the king to accept Babylonian rule, but he decided instead to join a rebellion led by Egypt. After eighteen months of siege, Jerusalem was conquered in 586 BC: all the main buildings were

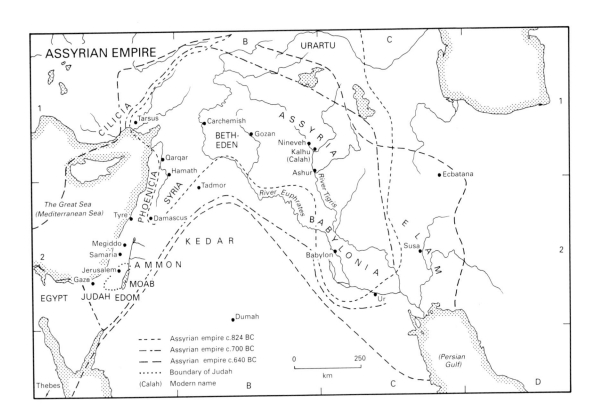

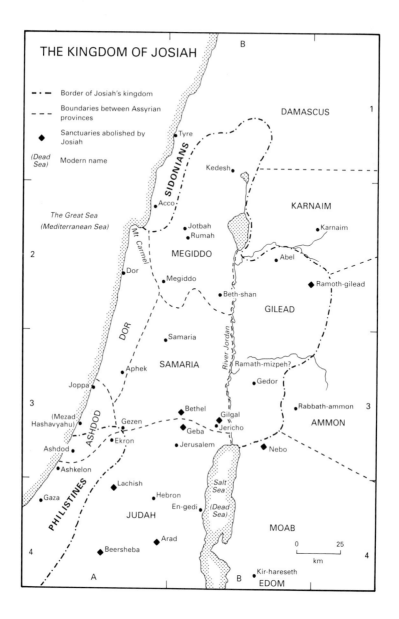

THE KINGDOM OF JOSIAH

- —·—·— Border of Josiah's kingdom
- — — — Boundaries between Assyrian provinces
- ◆ Sanctuaries abolished by Josiah
- *(Dead Sea)* Modern name

The Great Sea (Mediterranean Sea)

SIDONIANS

B

DAMASCUS

1

Tyre

Kedesh

KARNAIM

Acco

Jotbah
Rumah

Karnaim

MEGIDDO

Abel

2

Mt Carmel

Dor

Megiddo

◆ Ramoth-gilead

Beth-shan

GILEAD

DOR

Samaria

SAMARIA

River Jordan

Ramath-mizpeh?

Aphek

Joppa

Gedor

3

(Mezad Hashavyahu)

Gezen

◆ Bethel

◆ Gilgal

Rabbath-ammon

3

Ashdod

Ekron

◆ Geba
Jericho

AMMON

ASHDOD

Jerusalem

◆ Nebo

Ashkelon

Salt Sea

◆ Lachish

Hebron

En-gedi

(Dead Sea)

Gaza

MOAB

PHILISTINES

JUDAH

Arad

0   25

km

◆ Beersheba

4

A

B

Kir-hareseth

EDOM

devastated and Zedekiah was blinded and taken into exile in Babylon. The final days of Judah just before this conquest are depicted in a collection of potsherds written by Hoshayahu, the officer in charge of a military outpost to the north of Lachish.

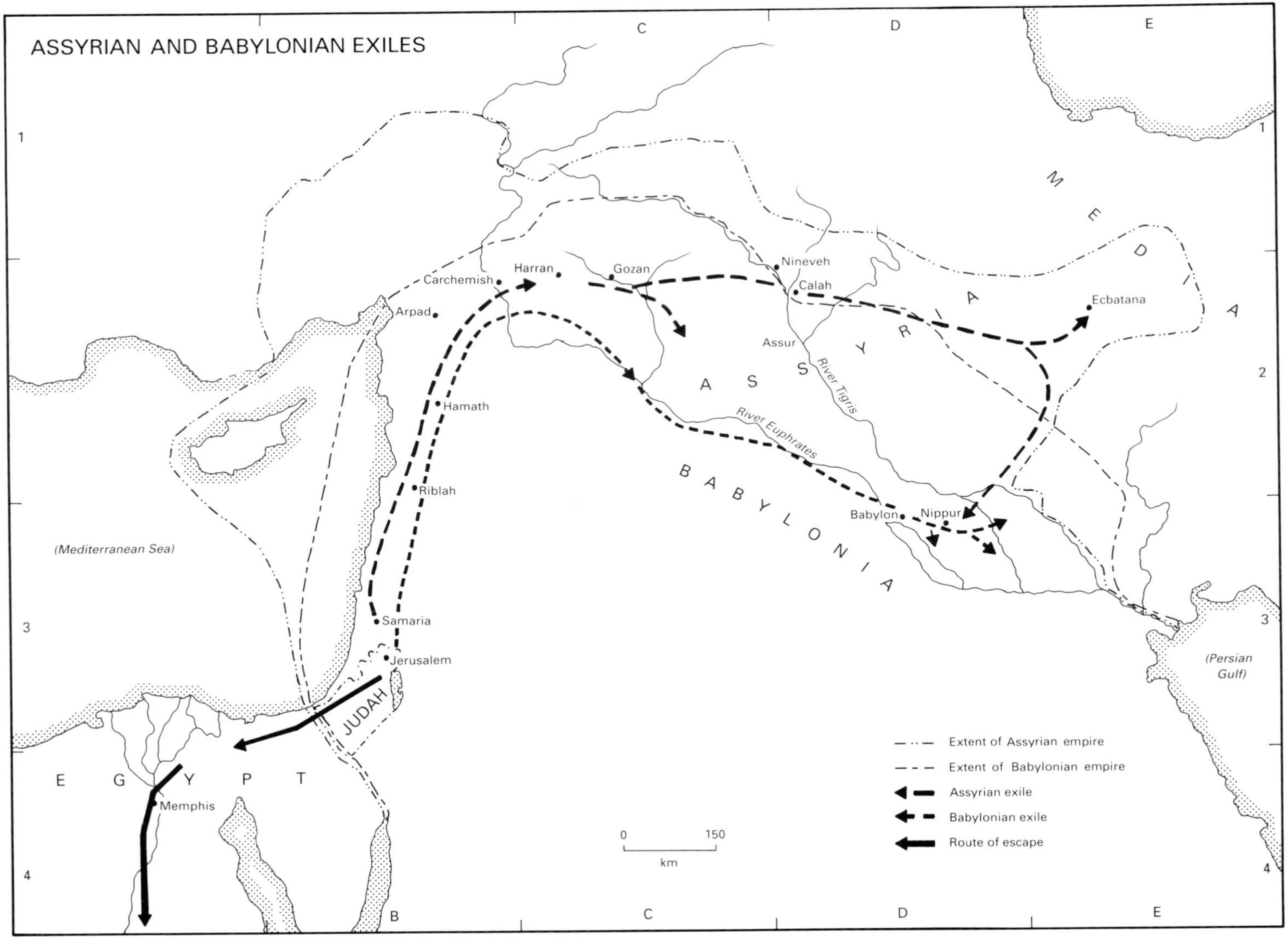
ASSYRIAN AND BABYLONIAN EXILES
MEDIA
ASSYRIA
BABYLONIA
EGYPT
JUDAH
Carchemish
Harran
Gozan
Nineveh
Calah
Assur
Ecbatana
Arpad
Hamath
Riblah
Samaria
Jerusalem
Babylon
Nippur
Memphis
River Tigris
River Euphrates
(Mediterranean Sea)
(Persian Gulf)
Extent of Assyrian empire
Extent of Babylonian empire
Assyrian exile
Babylonian exile
Route of escape
0
150
km

Aftermath of the fall of Judah

The Book of Lamentations records the despair of the people after the Babylonian conquest:

> How lonely sits the city that was full of people!
> How like a widow she has become
> She that was great among the nations!...
> The roads to Zion mourn,
> for none come to the appointed feasts;
> all her gates are desolate,
> her priests groan;
> her maidens have been dragged away
> and she herself suffers bitterly.
>
> (Lamentations 1:1,4)

In 586 BC a palace official, Gedaliah, was established as governor of Judah with his capital at Mizpah, but he was subsequently assassinated by Ishmael, a member of the former royal family. Yet fearing Babylonian retaliation, the supporters of this revolt escaped to Egypt with Jeremiah as a hostage. In their exile these rebels were convinced that the destruction of their country was the fault of prophets like Jeremiah who had criticized the nation for worshipping foreign deities. What was required, they maintained, was a return to the worship of Caanite deities:

> But we will do everything that we have vowed, burn incense to the queen of heaven and pour our libations to her ... since we left off burning incense to the queen of heaven and pouring our libations to her, we have lacked everything and have been consumed by the sword and the famine.
>
> (Jeremiah 44:17–18)

Jeremiah viewed such an attitude with horror – it was just such worship that had caused the fall of the southern kingdom. Eventually Jeremiah's outlook became the basis for reconstructing Jewish life, and it appears that the Books of Deuteronomy, Joshua, Judges, Samuel and Kings were collected together at this time to form an epic history of the Jewish nation based on this vision of God's dealings with his chosen people.

Those exiles who remained in Babylon prospered, keeping their faith alive in the synagogues. As Scripture relates, the Babylonian king Nebuchadnezzar's successor Amel-Marduk freed Jehoiachin from prison in Babylon and granted him a position in the Babylonian court. Yet despite their well-being, the exiles bemoaned the loss of their homeland. As Psalm 137 records:

> In the waters of Babylon, there we sat down and wept, When we remembered Zion ... How shall we sing the Lord's song in a foreign land?
>
> (Psalm 137:1, 4).

The prophet Ezekiel, however, encouraged the people not to despair. God, he stated, would deliver the fallen nation and gather them up again:

> I will rescue them from all places where they have been scattered on a day of clouds and thick darkness. And I will bring them out from the peoples, and gather them from the countries, and will bring them into their own land.
>
> (Ezekiel 34:12–13)

In the years that followed, Babylonia was ruled by a series of weak and inept rulers. According to the Bible, this was a particularly difficult time for the Jewish community. The Book of Daniel, for example, recounts the story of Daniel and his friends, who were subjected to cruel treatment by Belshazzar, the King of Babylon.

When the Babylonian empire began to disintegrate, the kingdom of Persia emerged as a powerful force in the region. In 539 BC Cyrus of Persia conquered Babylon. Fortunately for the Jewish people, this Persian ruler adopted a liberal policy toward other nations. Although he worshipped the god Marduk, Cyrus thought all peoples should be allowed to pray to their own deities and live wherever they wished. In consequence of this attitude, he allowed the Jewish population to return to their homeland. As the Book of Ezra recounts:

> Concerning the house of God at Jerusalem, let the house be rebuilt, the place where sacrifices are offered and burnt offerings are brought ... let the gold and silver vessels of the house of

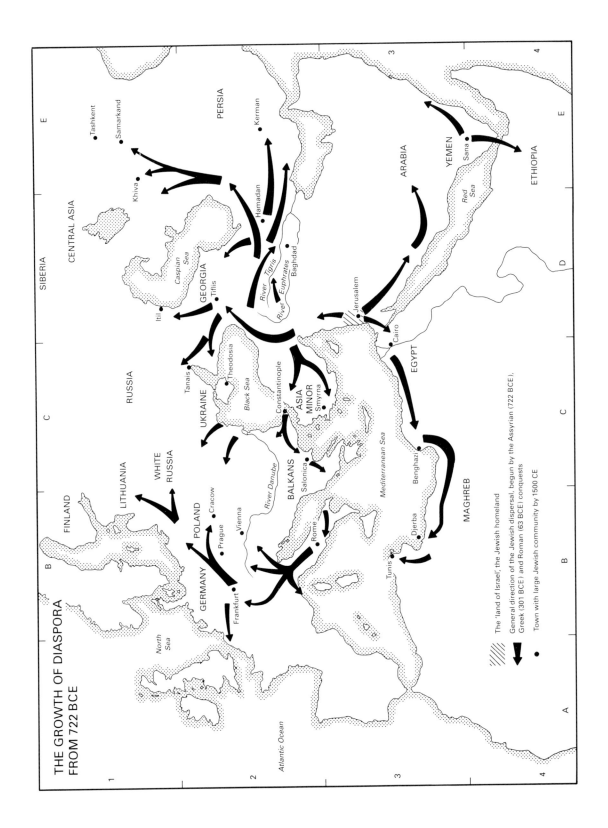

THE GROWTH OF DIASPORA
FROM 722 BCE

SIBERIA

CENTRAL ASIA

• Tashkent
• Samarkand
Khiva •

PERSIA
Kerman •

Itil •
Caspian Sea
GEORGIA
Tiflis •
Hamadan •

River Tigris
River Euphrates
Baghdad •

ARABIA

YEMEN
Sana •
Red Sea

ETHIOPIA

RUSSIA

UKRAINE
Tanais •
Theodosia •
Black Sea
Constantinople •
ASIA MINOR
Smyrna •

Jerusalem

Cairo •
EGYPT

FINLAND

LITHUANIA

WHITE RUSSIA

POLAND
• Cracow
Prague •
Vienna •

River Danube

BALKANS
Salonica •

Mediterranean Sea

Benghazi •

MAGHREB

GERMANY
Frankfurt •

Rome •

Tunis •
Djerba •

North Sea

Atlantic Ocean

The 'land of Israel', the Jewish homeland

General direction of the Jewish dispersal, begun by the Assyrian (722 BCE),
Greek (301 BCE) and Roman (63 BCE) conquests

• Town with large Jewish community by 1500 CE

God which Nebuchadnezzar took out of the Temple that is in Jerusalem and brought to Babylon, be restored and brought back to the Temple which is in Jerusalem ... let the governor of the Jews and the elders of the Jews rebuild this house of god on its site.

(Ezra 6:3–7)

In the book of Isaiah, this return is depicted as leading to a universal deliverance of all people in which Israel would have a pre-eminent role: 'I will give you as a light to the nations, that my salvation may reach to the end of the earth' (Isaiah 49:6).

Return and restoration

To implement Cyrus' policy of repatriation, the Persians appointed Shesbazzar governor of Judah. He was joined by other returning exiles including Joshua the priest and Zerubbabel (the grandson of Jehoiachin), who administered the repair and reconstruction of the Temple. The Book of Jeremiah relates that after Nebuchadnezzar's invasion worshippers continued to make pilgrimages to the Temple site. These individuals offered to help Zerubbabel, but he refused their assistance since he regarded them as of uncertain racial origin. Aware that the returning exiles were intent on forming a state in which they would have no role, these Judaean inhabitants as well as the people of Samaria persuaded the Persian officials responsible for the western empire that the plans for restoration were illegal: this postponed work on the Temple for over a decade.

Despite this setback Zerubbabel and Joshua were encouraged in their labours by the prophets Haggai and Zechariah. Haggai insisted that the rebuilding of the Temple become a major priority; once it was restored, he proclaimed, a new era in Jewish history would commence. Zerubbabel, he believed, was God's chosen ruler in this task of rebuilding:

On that day, says the Lord of Hosts, I will take you, O Zerubbabel, my servant, the son of Shealtiel ... and make you like a signet-ring; for I have chosen you.

(Haggai 2:23)

Similarly Zechariah urged that the Temple be rebuilt; he too insisted that God was with Zerubbabel:

Moreover the word of the Lord came to me, saying, 'The hands of Zerubbabel have laid the foundation of this house: his hands shall also complete it. Then you will know that the Lord of Hosts has sent me to you'.

(Zechariah 4:8–9)

In 515 BC the Temple was completed; nevertheless, according to the Book of Malachi, in the years that followed there was a general disregard of Temple worship and social evil became widespread. In consequence, the prophet Malachi warned that God would eventually punish those who had become corrupt. In addition, he lamented that Jewish men were marrying women of mixed racial origins. By the middle of the fifth century BC Nehemiah and Ezra attempted to reform the life of the Jewish population. When Nehemiah (who had been appointed governor of Judah by the Persian king Artaxerxes I) arrived in the country, he found that Jews had intermarried with peoples of other races and that the rich were oppressing the poor. To deter such religious and moral laxity Nehemiah insisted that the community purify itself by concentrating Jewish life within the boundaries of Jerusalem, and he encouraged the rebuilding and fortification of the city. This policy was opposed by Sanballat (the governor of Samaria), Tobiah (an important Ammonite), and others who feared that Israelites of mixed ancestry would be excluded from such plans. Yet despite such resistance, Nehemiah triumphed and Jerusalem was restored.

In these endeavours Nehemiah was joined by

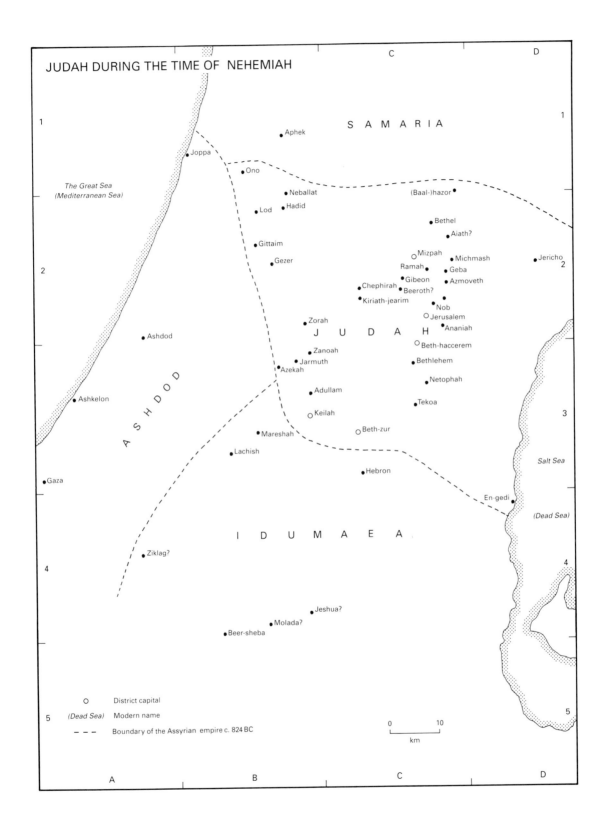

JUDAH DURING THE TIME OF NEHEMIAH

S A M A R I A

The Great Sea
(Mediterranean Sea)

• Aphek

• Joppa

• Ono

• Neballat

(Baal-)hazor •

• Lod • Hadid

• Bethel

• Gittaim

• Aiath?

○ Mizpah

• Gezer

Ramah •

• Michmash

○ Mizpah

Geba •

• Gibeon

Azmoveth •

• Chephirah • Beeroth?

• Kiriath-jearim

• Nob

• Zorah

○ Jerusalem

J U D A H

• Ananiah

• Ashdod

○ Beth-haccerem

• Zanoah

• Jarmuth

• Bethlehem

Azekah •

A S H D O D

• Adullam

• Netophah

• Ashkelon

• Tekoa

○ Keilah

3

• Mareshah

○ Beth-zur

Salt Sea

• Lachish

• Hebron

En-gedi •

• Gaza

(Dead Sea)

I D U M A E A

• Ziklag?

4

• Jeshua?

• Molada?

• Beer-sheba

5

○   District capital

5   (Dead Sea)   Modern name

– – –   Boundary of the Assyrian empire c. 824 BC

0   10

km

A   B   C   D

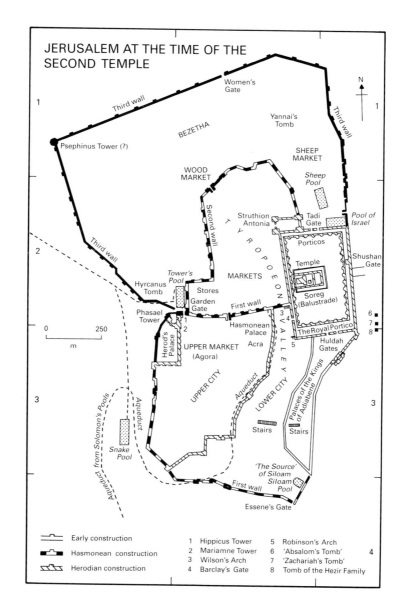

JERUSALEM AT THE TIME OF THE SECOND TEMPLE

N

Women's Gate

Third wall

BEZETHA

Yannai's Tomb

SHEEP MARKET

Psephinus Tower (?)

Sheep Pool

WOOD MARKET

Second wall

Struthion Antonia

Tadi Gate

Pool of Israel

TYROPOEON

Porticos

Temple

Shushan Gate

Tower's Pool

MARKETS

Hyrcanus Tomb

Stores

Garden Gate

First wall

Soreg (Balustrade)

Phasael Tower

Hasmonean Palace

The Royal Portico

Herod's Palace

UPPER MARKET (Agora)

Acra

Huldah Gates

VALLEY

UPPER CITY

Aqueduct

LOWER CITY

Palaces of the Kings of Adiabene

Aqueduct from Solomon's Pools

Aqueduct

Stairs

Stairs

Snake Pool

'The Source' of Siloam

Siloam Pool

First wall

Essene's Gate

0   250
m

Early construction
Hasmonean construction
Herodian construction

1 Hippicus Tower
2 Mariamne Tower
3 Wilson's Arch
4 Barclay's Gate
5 Robinson's Arch
6 'Absalom's Tomb'
7 'Zachariah's Tomb'
8 Tomb of the Hezir Family

the priest Ezra. Like Nehemiah, Ezra was a Persian state official who had been authorized to return to Judah. Together with other returning exiles he was determined to revive Jewish life; to bring about this renewal, Ezra insisted on reading the law to the people (which was subsequently translated by the priests, since the inhabitants of the land spoke only Aramaic, the official language of the Persian empire). When the people heard these words, they were profoundly moved and promised to observe the religious

practices and festivals of their ancestors such as the pilgrim festivals, the New Year celebration and the Day of Atonement.

In the years following Ezra's reforms, the inhabitants of Judah renewed Jewish life (even though the Books of Ruth and Jonah were composed as propaganda against his xenophobic policies). The Books of Chronicles support such Jewish nationalism; harking back to the reigns of David and Solomon as a golden age, they blame later disasters on the corruption of later kings. In the wake of these nationalist aspirations, the peoples of Samaria came to see that they would be banned from Temple worship; as a result, they developed their own beliefs and culture, building their own temple on Mt Gerizim. In 333 BC the Persian king Darius III Codomannus was defeated in battle by the Macedonian king Alexander the Great. After this conquest Alexander advanced toward Egypt, and he founded the city of Alexandria on the Nile delta. In 323 he died of a fever, and a power struggle took place among his generals. Subsequently both Egypt and Judah (by then called Judaea) came under the jurisdiction of the Ptolemaic dynasty.

Under the Seleucids

After the defeat of Alexander the Great, Judaea came under the jurisdiction of the Ptolemaic dynasty, which endured from 320 BC until 198 BC. Although Ptolemy was victorious in securing Judaea, another of Alexander's generals, Seleucus, was dissatisfied with this situation. Throughout the third century BC his successors attempted to attain sovereignty over the country. Eventually the issue was resolved in 198 BC, when the Seleucid king, Antiochus III, vanquished Scorpus, the general of the Egyptian king, Ptolemy V. At first Antiochus III adopted a positive attitude toward the Jewish population; however, he later reversed this policy. In 190 BC the Seleucid king was defeated in a battle with the Romans at Magnesia; in the peace treaty he was forced to relinquish his territory in Asia Minor. A year later he was killed while plundering the Temple and was succeeded by his son Seleucus IV.

During the reign of the Seleucids in the second century BC, two Jewish families engaged in rivalry: the Tobiads and the Oniads. In 175 BC, Seleucus IV was murdered, and succeeded by Antiochus IV Epiphanes. At this time Jason, a member of the Oniad family, bribed the Seleucid king to make him High Priest instead of his brother Onias. Once appointed to this position, Jason attempted to Hellenize Jerusalem, but a large segment of the Jewish population was shocked by his violations of traditional sensibilities, and Jason was deposed and replaced by Menelaus, a member of the Tobiad family. While this internal struggle took place in Judaea, Antiochus IV engaged in battle and defeated the Egyptian king Ptolomy VI; on his return he robbed the Temple in Jerusalem. Again in 168 BC Antiochus IV invaded Egypt, but this time his advance was repulsed by the Romans. In Jerusalem the rumour spread that Antiochus IV had been killed, and Jason attempted to remove Menelaus as High Priest. However, Antiochus acted quickly to quell this rebellion: he conquered Jerusalem, and led away some of the people as slaves. In addition he banned circumcision, Sabbath observance and Torah reading; he also declared that the Temple should be dedicated to the worship of the god Zeus, that pigs should be sacrificed on the altar, and that non-Jews as well as Jews should be permitted to worship in the Temple.

Not surprisingly the Jewish community was deeply offended by these policies, and many Jews were willing to die as martyrs rather than violate Jewish law. Eventually a rebellion was led by a priest, Mattathias, and his five sons. After his death, this revolt was spearheaded by his son Judas. Some Jews (Hasideans) were unwilling to engage in armed struggle against the Seleucids and fled to the Judaean desert; there they were slaughtered by the Seleucid forces when they refused to fight on the Sabbath. This incident drew other Jews to the side of the rebels, and after a number of battles they emerged victorious. As a result, Jewish law was reinstated, and the Temple was rededicated on 14 December 164 BC. This victory enabled Judas' clan (the Hasmoneans) to become the ruling family in Judaea.

After his defeat of the Seleucids, Judas made a treaty with the Romans; however, in 160 BC he died in battle and was succeeded by Jonathan, his brother. When the High Priest died, Jonathan

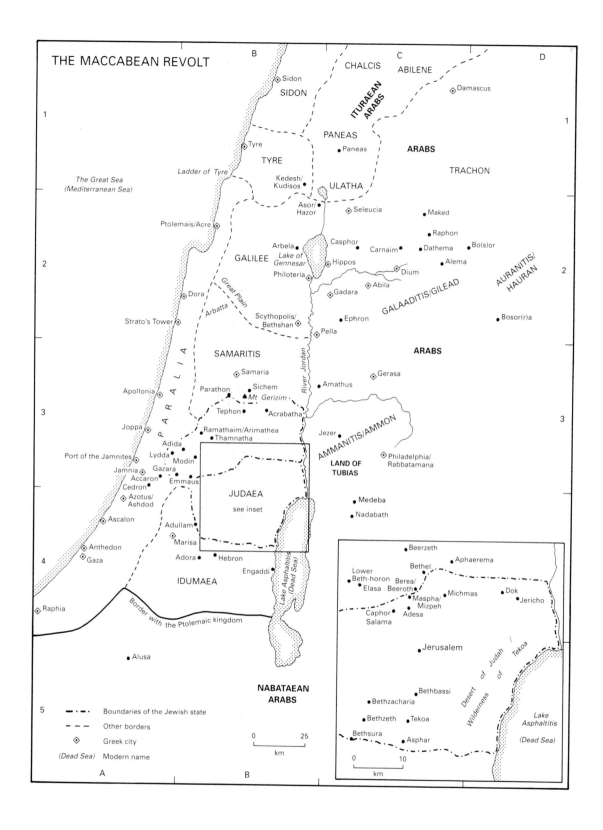

THE MACCABEAN REVOLT

CHALCIS ABILENE

⊗ Sidon
SIDON

⊗ Damascus

ITURAEAN ARABS

PANEAS

ARABS

• Paneas

⊗ Tyre
TYRE

The Great Sea
(Mediterranean Sea)

Ladder of Tyre

Kedesh/
Kudisos •
ULATHA

TRACHON

Asor/
Hazor •

• Maked

⊗ Ptolemais/Acre

⊗ Seleucia

• Raphon

Arbela •
GALILEE
Lake of
Gennesar

Casphor •
• Carnaim

• Dathema
• Bo(s)or

⊗ Hippos

AURANITIS/
HAURAN

Philoteria ⊗
• Alema

⊗ Dora
Great Plain

⊗ Abila

• Dium

⊗ Gadara

GALAADITIS/GILEAD

Strato's Tower ⊗

Arbatta

Scythopolis/
Bethshan

• Ephron

• Bosor(r)a

⊗ Pella

SAMARITIS

ARABS

⊗ Samaria

• Gerasa

Apollonia ⊗

Parathon •
• Sichem
▲ Mt Gerizim

• Amathus

Tephon •
• Acrabatha

Joppa •

Ramathaim/Arimathea •
• Thamnatha

Adida •

Lydda •
Gazara •

• Jezer

AMMANITIS/AMMON

⊗ Philadelphia/
Rabbatamana

Modin •

Port of the Jamnites ⊗
Emmaus •

LAND OF
TUBIAS

Jamnia ⊗
Accaron •
Cedron •

JUDAEA
see inset

• Medeba

⊗ Azotus/
Ashdod

• Nadabath

⊗ Ascalon

Adullam •

⊗ Anthedon

⊗ Marisa

Adora •
• Hebron

⊗ Gaza

Engaddi •
Lake
Asphaltitis
(Dead Sea)

IDUMAEA

⊗ Raphia

Border with the Ptolemaic kingdom

• Alusa

NABATAEAN
ARABS

5

—·—·— Boundaries of the Jewish state

— — — Other borders

⊗ Greek city

(Dead Sea) Modern name

0   25
km

River Jordan
PARALIA

Inset:

• Beerzeth
• Aphaerema

Bethel •

Lower
Beth-horon •
Berea/
Beeroth •
• Michmas
• Dok
• Jericho

Elasa •
Maspha/
Mizpeh •

Caphor
Salama •
Adesa •

Jerusalem •

Desert of Judah / Tekoa

Wilderness

Lake
Asphaltitis

• Bethbassi

• Bethzacharia

(Dead Sea)

• Bethzeth
• Tekoa

Bethsura •
• Asphar

0   10
km

A   B   A   B

41

was appointed supreme pontiff, and was later formally recognized as governor of Judaea. In time the last surviving brother, Simon, Jonathan's successor, asserted independence from the Seleucids: he expelled the Seleucid garrison from the Jerusalem citadel in 142–141 BC, seized the fortress of Gazara, and forced the Seleucid monarch to acquiesce. After this act Simon took on the hereditary title of ethnarch (a designation which denotes the ruler of an *ethnos* (nation)).

In 135 Simon was killed in a palace intrigue and was succeeded by his son John Hyrcanus I (134–104 BC), who became ethnarch as well as High Priest. In the early part of his reign the Seleucids attacked Jerusalem; as a result John Hyrcanus I was compelled to relinquish some territory and join the Seleucid king in a campaign against the Parthians. Eventually John Hyrcanus I captured large tracts of land in Transjordan and Samaria, where he razed the Samaritan temple on Mt Gerizim. In addition he conquered Idumaea and compelled the inhabitants to become Jewish converts. The conquest of Galilee was later completed by one of his sons, Aristobulus I (104–103 BC), and his second son, Alexander Janneus (102–76 BC), annexed various Hellenized cities of the coastal region and northern Transjordan.

Hellenism and Roman rule

During the first century BC the Jewish community in Judaea was fragmented into a variety of sects. As the Jewish historian Josephus relates, the three most important groups were the Sadducees, the Pharisees and the Essenes. The Sadducees were composed of prominent individuals who were in charge of the Temple cult in Jerusalem. These Jews maintained that there was no reason to expand the written law contained in the Torah, and they also rejected belief in an afterlife. The Pharisees, on the other hand, believed in the resurrection of the body and the world to come. Further, they attempted to make biblical law relevant to contemporary circumstances by interpreting the Torah text. This oral procedure, they believed, was communicated by God to Moses on Mt Sinai when he received the written law. Unlike the Sadducees, who supervised Temple worship, the Pharisees centred their activities on the synagogue. Yet despite their differences in outlook both the Pharisees and the Sadducees were members of the Great Sanhedrin, the central religious and legislative body of the Judaean Jewish community.

The third major sect were the Essenes (who may have been an offshoot of the Hasideans). These pious individuals believed that the Hellenizers and the Sadducees had abandoned the Covenant; despising town life, they congregated in semi-monastic communities. According to most scholars, it was this sect who produced the Dead Sea Scrolls. These texts were composed by a devoted community based near the Dead Sea who wrote about an ideal leader, the Teacher of Righteousness. Believing themselves to be the sole members of the new covenant prophesied by Jeremiah, they anticipated a cataclysmic end of the world involving a struggle between good and evil in which Israel would emerge victorious.

During Alexander Jannaeus' reign, a number of Pharisees rebelled against his policy of Hellenization. Seizing Jerusalem and the royal mint, they issued coins of their own in the name of the Council of Elders. When this revolt was crushed many of these rebels lost their lives. Eventually Salome Alexandra (76–67 BC) succeeded her husband Alexander Jannaeus and reversed his religious policies, treating the Pharisees with favour. When she died her two sons John Hyrcanus II and Aristobulus struggled for power. In this conflict Antipater, a chieftain from Idumaea, assisted John Hyrcanus II by inviting his allies the Nabataeans to advance against Jerusalem. However, it was left to the Roman leader Pompey to decide the matter of the Hasmonean succession. When he marched into Jerusalem, he killed many of the inhabitants and entered the Holy of Holies in the Temple. Under

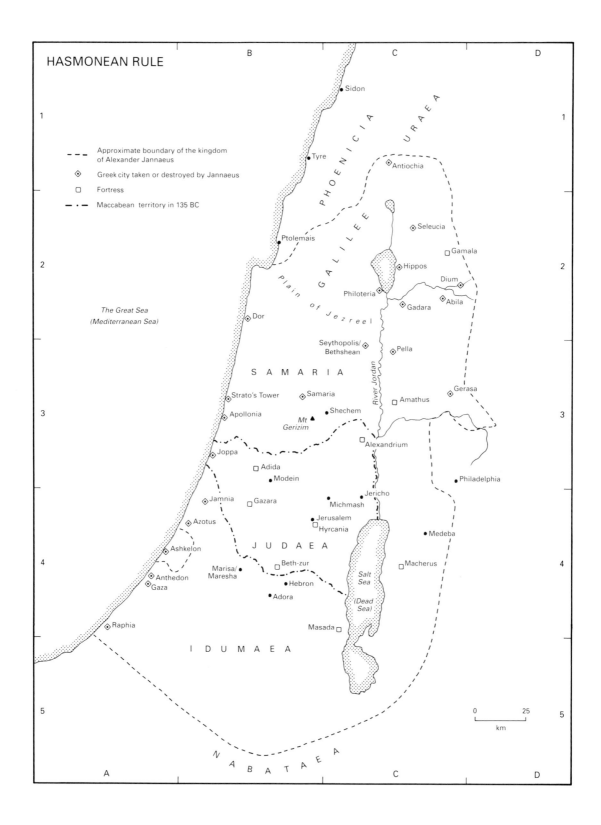

HASMONEAN RULE

Legend:

- – – – Approximate boundary of the kingdom of Alexander Jannaeus
- ◇ Greek city taken or destroyed by Jannaeus
- ☐ Fortress
- –·–·– Maccabean territory in 135 BC

The Great Sea
(Mediterranean Sea)

Sidon

Tyre

PHOENICIA

ITURAEA

Antiochia

Seleucia

Gamala

Ptolemais

Hippos

Dium

GALILEE

Philoteria

Gadara

Abila

Plain of Jezreel

Dor

Pella

Seythopolis/
Bethshean

River Jordan

SAMARIA

Gerasa

Strato's Tower

Samaria

Amathus

Apollonia

Mt
Gerizim

Shechem

Alexandrium

Joppa

Philadelphia

Adida

Modein

Jamnia

Gazara

Jericho

Michmash

Azotus

Jerusalem

Hyrcania

Medeba

JUDAEA

Ashkelon

Salt
Sea

Anthedon

Marisa/
Maresha

Beth-zur

Macherus

Gaza

Hebron

Adora

(Dead
Sea)

Raphia

Masada

IDUMAEA

0   25
km

NABATAEA

43

Pompey Judaea became a client state of Rome, and John Hyrcanus II was appointed High Priest as well as ethnarch of Judaea and Galilee. In addition, John Hyrcanus II was granted authority over matters relating to the Jewish communities in the diaspora. However, after five years, he was deposed as ethnarch, and the country was divided into five districts administered by courts of local dignitaries drawn largely from the Sadducees. In this new arrangement Antipater was placed in charge of Idumaea, but he still retained special powers in Jerusalem.

In 48 BC Pompey died, and John Hyrcanus II and Antipater assisted Julius Caesar in his battle with Egyptian forces. As a reward for this assistance Caesar enlarged John Hyrcanus II's former state, and recognized Antipater as chief minister. In addition, Caesar introduced several measures to protect the security of Jewish communities outside Judaea: they were granted freedom of religious observance, permission to send gifts to the Jerusalem Temple, exemption from military duty and the right to their own jurisdiction. Further, Antipater's son Phasael was appointed governor of Jerusalem, and his other son was made governor of Galilee. However, when Herod suppressed a Galilean revolt, the Great Sanhedrin censured him for his brutality and he was forced to leave Judaea. None the less the new governor of Syria gave him an important military command, as did Cassius when Caesar was assassinated. In time when Mark Antony and Octavian avenged Caesar's death, they appointed Phasael and Herod as tetrarchs (subordinate rulers) of Judaea, despite the disapproval of the Jewish population. In the subsequent Parthian invasion of Roman Asia Minor, Syria and Judaea, John Hyrcanus II was dethroned in favour of Antigonus, his nephew; Phasael was killed; and Herod was forced to flee.

4 FROM HEROD TO REBELLION

The kingship of Herod

Once the Parthians were victorious, Herod went to Rome to meet Mark Antony, who had obtained the eastern provinces from Octavian in the division of the Roman empire. Through Mark Antony's influence Herod was established as King of Judaea; by this means the Romans hoped to depose Antigonus, the nominee of the Parthians. Advancing against Judaea, Herod conquered the country with the aid of a Roman army. After a siege lasting five months Jerusalem succumbed in 37 BC. Herod then unified the country (by incorporating Samaria), replaced the Council of Elders by an advisory body, and executed forty-five members of the Great Sanhedrin, including many Sadducees who supported the Hasmonean dynasty.

Because Herod was an Iduamite (a descendant of the Edomites who had been converted to Judaism by the Hasmoneans), he was ineligible for the office of High Priest. Thus he granted this position to Hananel, a Babylonian Jew who was a descendant of the Zadokite house. According to Herod, Hananel's claims for this office were better than those of any Hasmonean ruler; however, his mother-in-law Alexandra (daughter of John Hyrcanus II) protested to the Egyptian queen Cleopatra about this nomination. In consequence Herod was compelled to appoint Alexandra's younger son Aristobulus, but he soon died and was replaced by Hananel.

When Antony and Cleopatra were defeated by Octavian's admiral Marcus Agrippa in 31 BC, Herod pledged his loyalty to Octavian (Augustus). This declaration was accepted, and he was granted back most of the territory that Pompey had taken from Judaea in 63 BC. In addition, Herod received two Greek cities across the Jordan: Hippos and Gadara. At this time Alexandra and her daughter, Herod's wife Mariamne, were put to death for plotting against Herod. For the next three decades Herod served as Augustus' agent: he initiated games in honour of Augustus' victory, built a Greek theatre and amphitheatre in Jerusalem, transformed Samaria into a Graeco-Samaritan city, and constructed the port Caesarea. Further, he established citadels and palaces at various strategic points such as Jericho, Herodium and Masada. The greatest triumph of his reign was the rebuilding of the Jerusalem Temple, which was open to all people and served as a meeting place, market centre, and platform for preachers. All that remains of the Temple are the foundations of the Western Wall, leading to the court of the gentiles. Inside the court of the gentiles was another gateway reserved for Jews; this opened into the court of women. Beyond this stood the court of priests, where the Sadducees offered sacrifices. The most sacred place in the Temple was the Holy of Holies; this was only entered by the High Priest on the Day of Atonement.

During his reign, Herod obtained two large regions of southern Syria from Augustus. In addition, he intervened with the Romans to prevent Greek cities from withholding those privileges to which Jews in the diaspora were

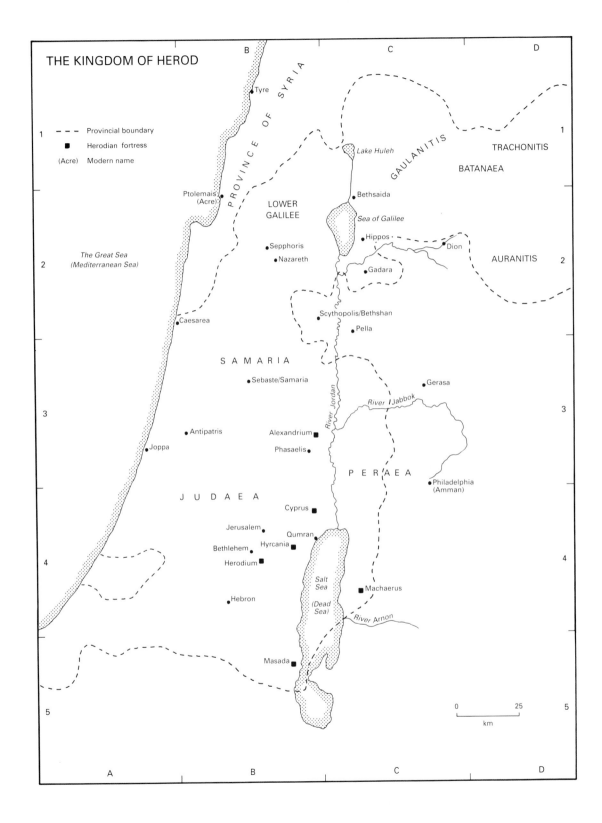

THE KINGDOM OF HEROD

- - - Provincial boundary
■ Herodian fortress
(Acre) Modern name

PROVINCE OF SYRIA

Tyre

1

GAULANITIS

TRACHONITIS

BATANAEA

Lake Huleh

Ptolemais (Acre)

LOWER GALILEE

Bethsaida

Sea of Galilee

The Great Sea (Mediterranean Sea)

Sepphoris

Nazareth

Hippos

Dion

AURANITIS

2

Gadara

Caesarea

Scythopolis/Bethshan

Pella

S A M A R I A

Sebaste/Samaria

Gerasa

River Jabbok

3

Antipatris

Alexandrium ■

Joppa

Phasaelis

P E R A E A

Philadelphia (Amman)

J U D A E A

Cyprus ■

Jerusalem

Qumran

Bethlehem

Hyrcania ■

Herodium ■

Salt Sea (Dead Sea)

Machaerus ■

4

Hebron

River Arnon

Masada ■

0   25
km

5

A   B   C   D

entitled. Yet despite such successes, Herod enraged Augustus by executions of those he suspected of intrigue as well as by his onslaught on the Nabataeans. In order to pacify the emperor, Herod declared that all Jews in Judaea must swear an oath of loyalty to both the Roman ruler and himself. Fearing that such an act might involve worship of the emperor's statues, a number of Pharisees refused to comply. Increasingly these objectors became convinced that the period of messianic redemption was at hand and engaged in messianic speculation. At this time,

several Pharisees persuaded Bagoas, a royal court official, that he would be the father of the messianic king. Herod, however, regarded such talk as treasonable, and he executed Bagoas and others in 5 BC. In the next year, a number of Pharisaic scholars demonstrated against the erection of an eagle over the main gate of the Temple; these rioters pulled it down and as a consequence were put to death. In the same year Herod died, to the great relief of the Jewish population.

Rebellion against Rome

After Herod's death, Judaea was divided between his three sons: Archelaus (4 BC–AD 6) ruled the central region of Judaea including Samaria; Herod Antipas (4 BC–AD 39) received Galilee; Philip (4 BC–AD 34) as tetrarch ruled over lands in southern Syria. Following the period of tetrarchs, Judaea became a Roman province administered by governors with the title of prefect (later procurator). When the Romans made a census of the population, they evoked Jewish antipathy since census-taking was contrary to Jewish law. In response, a resistance movement (the Zealots) under Judas the Galilean gathered force; in addition a number of messianic aspirants emerged who were viewed with mistrust by the Roman authorities. Despite such hostility toward Rome, the Sadducees collaborated with the Romans, who continued to appoint High Priests from their ranks, and under the prefects the Sanhedrin was reinstituted and played an important role in the administration of the country.

When Tiberius became emperor in AD 14, he came to rely increasingly on the advice of Sejanus, the commander of his bodyguard. Sejanus had been ill-disposed to the Jewish population since two Jews, Hasinai and Hanilai, established an autonomous community at Nehardea in Parthian Babylonia; Sejanus feared that such aspirations might spread to Judaea. The fourth prefect of Judaea, Pontius Pilate (AD 25–36),

also had difficulties with the Jewish population, who viewed his military standards bearing medallions of the emperor as idolatrous. After demonstrations in Jerusalem, a group of protestors encamped in front of Pilate's residence at Caesarea Martima and subsequently in the stadium. In addition, Pilate caused considerable distress when he plundered a Jewish religious fund to pay for an aqueduct, and again when he set up gilded shields bearing his and the emperor's names in Herod's former palace.

Under Tiberius' successor Caligula (AD 37–41), the Jews of Alexandria were also involved in a conflict with the Roman authorities. These Jews had put forward a claim for full citizenship rights, thereby evoking a hostile reaction from the gentile community. In consequence, Greek mobs broke into synagogues and set up statues of the emperor.

In addition the Roman governor of Egypt (Aulus Avillius Flaccus) decreed that thirty-eight members of the Jewish Council be flogged in the theatre, while Jewish women were commanded to eat pork. To calm the situation, Agrippa I recalled Avillius Flaccus. Subsequently both the Greek and Jewish communities sent delegates to Rome to put their case before Caligula. According to an account written by the leader of the Jewish delegation, the Alexandrian Neo-Platonic philosopher Philo, Caligula viewed the Jews' unwillingness to recognize his divinity as

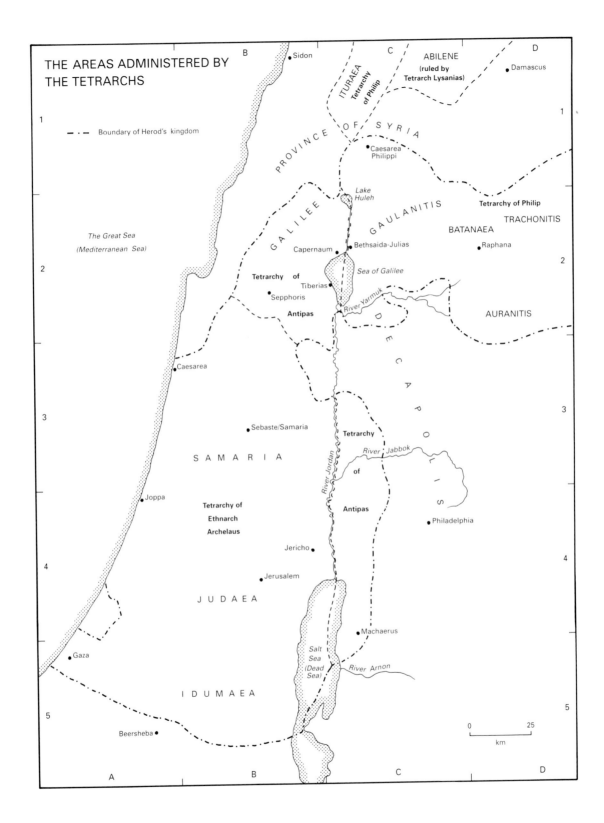

THE AREAS ADMINISTERED BY
THE TETRARCHS

–·–· Boundary of Herod's kingdom

• Sidon

PROVINCE OF SYRIA

ITURAEA
Tetrarch
of Philip

ABILENE
(ruled by
Tetrarch Lysanias)

• Damascus

•Caesarea
Philippi

Lake
Huleh

GALILEE

GAULANITIS

Tetrarchy of Philip

BATANAEA

TRACHONITIS

The Great Sea
(Mediterranean Sea)

Capernaum •

• Bethsaida-Julias

•Raphana

Tetrarchy of
Tiberias•
• Sepphoris

Sea of Galilee

River Yarmuk

AURANITIS

Antipas

D
E
C
A
P
O
L
I
S

•Caesarea

Tetrarchy

SAMARIA

• Sebaste/Samaria

River Jabbok

of

•Joppa

Tetrarchy of
Ethnarch
Archelaus

River Jordan

Antipas

• Philadelphia

Jericho •

• Jerusalem

JUDAEA

• Machaerus

•Gaza

Salt
Sea
(Dead
Sea)

River Arnon

IDUMAEA

0   25

km

Beersheba •

madness. Meanwhile at Jamnia the Greek community set up an altar in honour of Caligula; this act was viewed by the Jewish community there as a deliberate provocation, and they demolished it. In response, the emperor and his advisers revived the anti-Jewish policy of Antiochus IV Epiphanes: all Jewish places of worship were to be transformed into shrines of the imperial cult. Orders were therefore given to the governor of Syria (Publius Petronius) to create a statue of Caligula in the guise of Jupiter to be set up in Jerusalem. However, Agrippa I persuaded him not to carry out these plans on condition that the Jewish population cease attempting to prevent gentiles from participating in imperial worship. A short time later Caligula was murdered, an event celebrated by the Jews with a joyful feast.

Caligula's successor Claudius (AD 41–54) was compelled to deal with renewed conflict between Jews and Greeks in Alexandria. In a letter to both groups, he urged tolerance; specifically, he encouraged the Jews not to be contemptuous of the gods of other peoples. In Judaea, Claudius eliminated direct Roman rule and granted the country the status of a self-governing client kingdom. Further, Agrippa I was allowed to add the Roman province of Judaea to the lands he had previously been given where he reigned as king. Agrippa I's death in AD 44, however, ended this period of relative tranquillity. Judaea reverted to the status of a Roman province, and under the rulers that followed numerous difficulties arose: tensions developed between the rich and the poor; rebels, prophets and holy men roamed the country; and insurrections took place throughout the land. Moreover, the procurator Tiberius Julius Alexander (AD 46–8) had to cope with extensive famine; Ventidius Cumanus (AD 48–52) experienced riots, a massacre at the Temple and friction between Samaritans and Galileans; and Antonius Felix (AD 52–60) was confronted by freedom fighters who advanced the cause of Jewish nationalism and miracle workers who preached about the coming of the Messiah.

Jewish war and aftermath

For two decades after the death of Agrippa I there was constant conflict between Roman rulers and the Jewish population in Judaea. Under the procurator Florus (AD 64–6) fighting occurred between the Greek population and Jews in Caesarea. Adopting an anti-Jewish stance, the procurator permitted his troops to riot in Jerusalem as well as execute a number of prominent Jews. When Florus returned to Caesarea, the small Roman legion of Judaea as well as Jews who supported the Roman authorities were massacred by Jewish rebels. In addition, sacrifices on behalf of the Roman people and the emperor were banned. To check this revolt the governor of Syria and an army advanced toward Jerusalem, where he began a siege of the Temple, but they were met with resistance and retreated to the sea coast. In consequence the Roman military presence in Judaea was replaced by a provisional government.

In response to this rebellion, the general Vespasian assembled an army in AD 67 in the North. In Galilee Sepphoris refused to participate in the revolt against Rome, and the Jewish rebels were unable to stand against the Roman legions. The fortress of Jodepath held out for over a month, but it eventually fell and most of the population was killed by the Romans. In the winter of AD 67–8 the Zealots overthrew the moderate government in Jerusalem; those Jews suspecting of aiding the Romans were arrested or killed, and anti-Roman groups seized control of the city. However, in March 67 Vespasian vanquished Transjordan, western Judaea, Idumaea, Samaria and Jericho. The only sections of Judaea remaining in Jewish hands were Jerusalem as well as several Herodian fortresses.

After the emperor Nero committed suicide in June 68 Roman armies in different parts of the empire elevated three generals to the throne. In

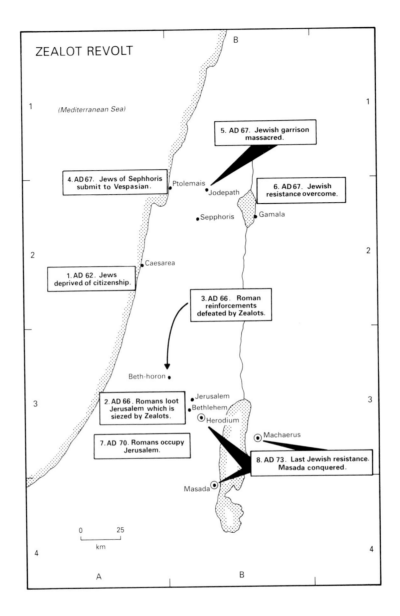

ZEALOT REVOLT

(Mediterranean Sea)

5. AD 67. Jewish garrison massacred.

4. AD 67. Jews of Sephoris submit to Vespasian.

6. AD 67. Jewish resistance overcome.

Ptolemais
•Jodepath
•Sepphoris   •Gamala

•Caesarea

1. AD 62. Jews deprived of citizenship.

3. AD 66. Roman reinforcements defeated by Zealots.

Beth-horon •

•Jerusalem
•Bethlehem
⊙Herodium

⊙Machaerus

2. AD 66. Romans loot Jerusalem which is siezed by Zealots.

7. AD 70. Romans occupy Jerusalem.

8. AD 73. Last Jewish resistance. Masada conquered.

Masada⊙

0   25
km

July 69 the eastern provinces proclaimed Vespasian, who put his son Titus in charge of the Judaean campaign. In April 70 Titus encamped outside Jerusalem; the next month the Roman army occupied part of Jerusalem north of the Temple; by the end of July they seized control of the citadel adjacent to the Temple; on 6 August the sacrifices ceased. A week later the porticos around the Temple courtyards were burned, and on 28 August the Temple was set alight during the fighting. After another month the Roman forces captured the upper city west of the Temple. Following these defeats, all resistance ceased, and Titus decreed that Jerusalem should be destroyed except for the towers of Herod's palace. During this year of Roman victory Titus held celebrations in various parts of the Near East; Jewish prisoners were thrown to wild animals or forced to fight with gladiators. In 71 Titus and Vespasian conducted a triumphal procession in which ritual objects and rebel leaders were displayed – this event is recorded on

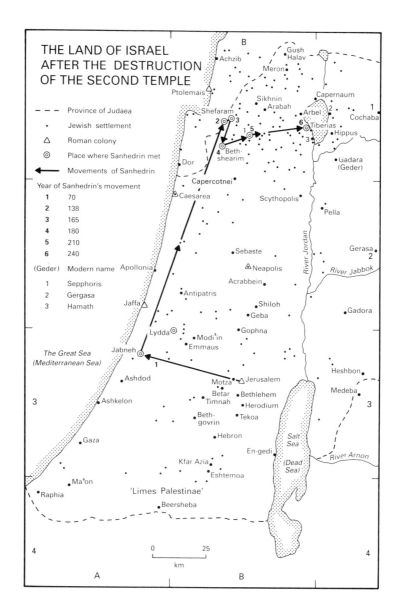

THE LAND OF ISRAEL
AFTER THE DESTRUCTION
OF THE SECOND TEMPLE

- - - - Province of Judaea
•   Jewish settlement
△   Roman colony
◎   Place where Sanhedrin met
◀—   Movements of Sanhedrin

Year of Sanhedrin's movement
1   70
2   138
3   165
4   180
5   210
6   240

(Geder) Modern name
1   Sepphoris
2   Gergasa
3   Hamath

The Great Sea
(Mediterranean Sea)

0   25
km

the Arch of Titus in Rome. Over the next few years the Romans captured the few remaining fortresses occupied by Jewish rebels such as Masada, which fell in April 74.

The Roman conquest brought about enormous devastation as well as the enslavement of thousands of Jews. None the less reconstruction of the country began immediately, and the Jews continued to be the largest population in Judaea. Though they were heavily taxed, the Jewish community were allowed to practise their faith

and were exempt from emperor worship as well as other religious obligations. In the post-Roman war years, the Sadducees and Essenes ceased to play a role in Jewish life; in their place the Pharisees became the dominant religious group. In Jamnia Johanan ben Zaccai, who escaped from Jerusalem during the siege, assembled a group of Pharisaic scholars (known as Tannaim) who engaged in the development of the legal tradition. Under Johanan ben Zaccai and later Rabban Gamaliel II, the rabbinical assembly

51

(Sanhedrin) compiled the teachings of the earlier schools of Hillel and Shammai, determined the canon of Scripture, organized the daily prayers, transferred to the synagogue some of the observances of the Temple, and instituted a procedure of rabbinical ordination.

Although this body was presided over by a head, the rabbis as a group reached decisions binding on the entire people. Its members were drawn from throughout society and attracted a large number of students to hear their teachings. The first generation of sages included such figures as Eliezar ben Hyrcanus, Elazar ben Azaria and Joshua ben Haninah; this was followed by a second generation of sages such as Tarphon and Ishmael ben Elisha. In the first decades of the second century the most important scholar was Akiva ben Joseph who was an exegete, mystic, legal systematizer and pioneer of scriptural interpretation.

The rise of Christianity

Following the years of unrest after Herod's death in 4 BC a Jewish sect of Christians emerged in Judaea. Convinced that Jesus of Nazareth was the promised Messiah, these believers anticipated the fulfilment of human history. According to the New Testament, Jesus spent most of his life in Galilee where he was a healer, exorcist and preacher who announced the coming of God's Kingdom. After associating with John the Baptist, he drew to himself disciples from the most marginalized sectors of society. His activity, however, aroused the opposition of the Jewish authorities, and he was put to death in about AD 30 during the reign of Pontius Pilate. Subsequently he appeared to his followers as the risen Christ and promised to bring about the period of messianic redemption.

According to the Acts of the Apostles, a considerable number of Jews accepted Jesus as the messianic deliverer in the 30s and 40s: these individuals worshipped in the Temple and observed Jewish laws. In time Paul, a diaspora Jew from Tarsus, travelled to scattered communities in Asia Minor and Greece and spread faith in Jesus. In his epistle to the Galatians, he declares that he was previously a Pharisee who had persecuted Christians until he received a revelation from God which transformed him into a disciple of Christ.

For you heard of my former life in Judaism, how I persecuted the church of God violently and tried to destroy it; and I advanced in Judaism beyond many of my own age among my people, so extremely zealous was I for the traditions of my fathers. But when he who set me apart before I was born, and had called me through his grace, was pleased to reveal his son to me, in order that I might preach him among the gentiles ...

(Galatians 1:13–16)

In his writings Paul proclaims that a new era is at hand, yet he differentiates between the period before Christ and the time afterwards in terms of two states. The first, fleshly state is the realm of death, bondage and sin; in contrast the second, spiritual state is a condition of eternal life, freedom and the right relation to God. For Paul the crucifixion and resurrection represent the inbreaking of the eschaton; even though the period of final judgement has not yet occurred, those who receive Christ are redeemed from sin. Jesus was sent to conquer death – as God's son, he humbled himself so that everyone could come to the Father. Fundamental to this view is the distinction between 'works' and 'faith'. According to Paul, faith is a gift – the sign of divine grace. It is impossible to attain salvation by observing the law, but 'he who through faith is righteous shall live' (Galatians 3:11).

In his writings Paul distinguishes life in Christ from licentiousness as well as from the conviction that all things are permitted to those who believe. On the basis of this conviction, Paul emphasizes the significance of love; it is the supreme spiritual

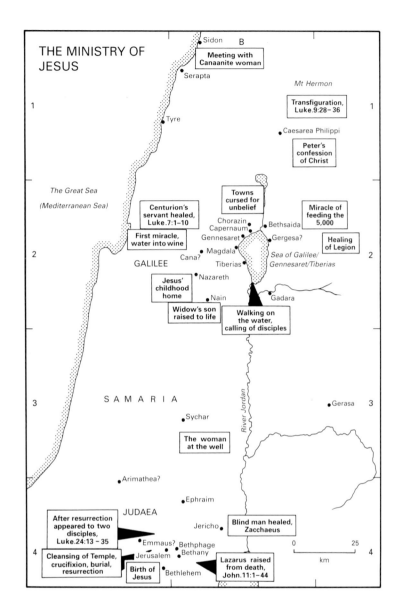

THE MINISTRY OF JESUS

B
Meeting with Canaanite woman

Mt Hermon

Transfiguration, Luke.9:28–36

• Caesarea Philippi

Peter's confession of Christ

• Sidon
• Serapta

1

• Tyre

The Great Sea (Mediterranean Sea)

Towns cursed for unbelief

Miracle of feeding the 5,000

Centurion's servant healed, Luke.7:1–10

Chorazin •
Capernaum •
Gennesaret •
• Bethsaida

First miracle, water into wine

Cana? •
• Magdala
Tiberias •
• Gergesa?

Healing of Legion

Sea of Galilee/ Gennesaret/Tiberias

GALILEE

2

Jesus' childhood home

• Nazareth

Widow's son raised to life

• Nain

Walking on the water, calling of disciples

• Gadara

River Jordan

SAMARIA

3

• Gerasa

• Sychar

The woman at the well

• Arimathea?

• Ephraim

JUDAEA

After resurrection appeared to two disciples, Luke.24:13–35

Jericho •

Blind man healed, Zacchaeus

0   25

km

Cleansing of Temple, crucifixion, burial, resurrection

• Emmaus?
Jerusalem

Bethphage
Bethany

Birth of Jesus

• Bethlehem

Lazarus raised from death, John.11:1–44

gift. A second motif in Paul's letters is his repudiation of the demands of the Mosaic law. It is not necessary, he maintains, for Christians to undergo circumcision or observe Jewish food laws. Underlying this belief was Paul's vision of an apocalyptic history of salvation. By means of Adam's disobedience, sin and death entered the world. Abraham's trust in God demonstrates that faith is more important than law. For Paul Mosaic legislation was only temporarily signifi-

cant – it cannot by itself bestow justification. The more one struggles to follow the law, the greater one is conscious of sin. Therefore God made Christ available to overcome the human propensity to evil. In this regard Paul interprets Abraham's sons – Ishmael and Isaac – allegorically. Ishmael represents the old Covenant; Isaac symbolizes the new dispensation.

In the years following Paul's death, traditions about Jesus circulated and in time served as the

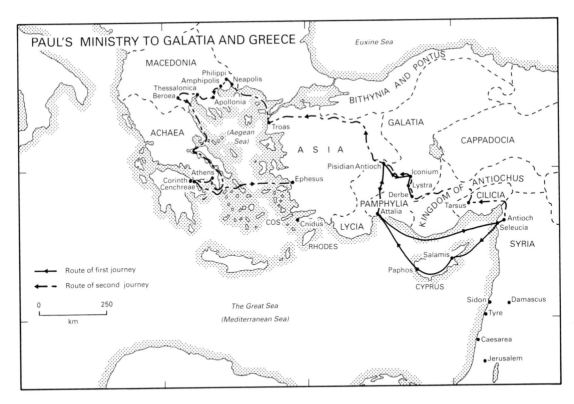

PAUL'S MINISTRY TO GALATIA AND GREECE

Euxine Sea

MACEDONIA

Philippi
Amphipolis · Neapolis
Thessalonica
Beroea
Apollonia

BITHYNIA AND PONTUS

GALATIA

ACHAEA

Troas

CAPPADOCIA

(Aegean Sea)

A S I A

Pisidian Antioch

Iconium

Athens
Corinth
Cenchreae

Ephesus

Lystra

KINGDOM OF ANTIOCHUS

COS

Cnidus

Derbe

PAMPHYLIA

Attalia

Tarsus

CILICIA

Antioch
Seleucia

LYCIA

SYRIA

RHODES

Salamis

Paphos

Sidon · Damascus

Tyre

━━━◄━━━ Route of first journey

CYPRUS

Caesarea

- - -◄- - - Route of second journey

Jerusalem

0   250
━━━━━━━━
km

The Great Sea
(Mediterranean Sea)

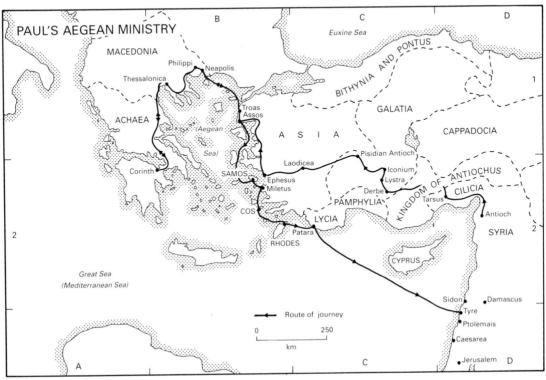

PAUL'S AEGEAN MINISTRY

B   C   D

Euxine Sea

MACEDONIA

BITHYNIA AND PONTUS   1

Philippi   Neapolis

Thessalonica

GALATIA

ACHAEA

Troas
Assos

CAPPADOCIA

(Aegean Sea)

A S I A

A

2

Corinth

Laodicea

Pisidian Antioch

Iconium
Lystra

KINGDOM OF ANTIOCHUS

SAMOS

Ephesus
Miletus

Derbe

CILICIA

COS

PAMPHYLIA

Tarsus

Antioch

LYCIA

SYRIA   2

Patara

RHODES

CYPRUS

Great Sea
(Mediterranean Sea)

Sidon · Damascus

Tyre

━━━◄━━━ Route of journey

Ptolemais

Caesarea

0   250
━━━━━━━━
km

Jerusalem

A   C   D

Figure 6   Caricature of Christ and the Jews, Jeroen Bosch (Museum voor Schone Kunsten Gent)

basis of the Synoptic Gospels and Acts which were written down in the last quarter of the first century AD. Each gospel reflects different religious intentions and concerns. Most scholars believe that Mark is the earliest and portrays Jesus as a divinely appointed figure whose task is to inaugurate God's Kingdom on earth. In Matthew, by contrast, Jesus is presented as a lawgiver offering the people moral instruction. The Gospel of Luke and the Acts of the Apostles describe Jesus as the fulfilment of scriptural teaching and depict the subsequent transference of the Church to the gentiles of the Graeco-Roman world. Finally the Fourth Gospel depicts Jesus as the divine Logos who is 'the way, the truth, and the life'. Although this message of deliverance attracted both Jewish and gentile converts, the majority of Jews rejected such claims and anathematized the Church for its false teaching.

Figure 7   *The Apostle Paul*, Rembrandt (National Gallery of Art at Washington)

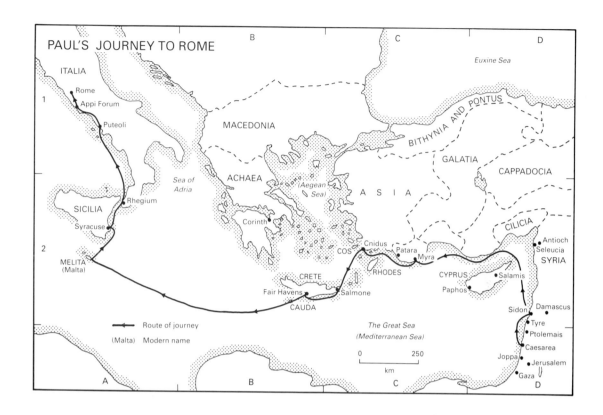

PAUL'S JOURNEY TO ROME

Jews in the Roman empire

Although the Romans had secured a devastating victory against the Jewish revolt, Jews continued to rebel against the empire. When the emperor Trajan (AD 98–117) invaded the East, Babylonian Jewry protested. In addition, riots took place throughout the Roman diaspora. According to the fourth-century writer Eusebius, many Jews were massacred in these uprisings:

> In Alexandria and the rest of the east, and in Cyrene as well ... [the Jews] rushed into a faction fight against their Greek fellow citizens ... against them the emperor sent Marcius Turbo with land and sea forces, including a contingency of cavalry. He pursued the war against them relentlessly in a long series of battles, destroying many thousands of Jews.
> (*The History of the Church*, trans. G.S. Williamson (Baltimore: Penguin, 1965), pp. 154–5)

In the second decade of the second century Jewish centres in Alexandria, Cyrenaica, Egypt and Cyprus were devastated. However, after Trajan's death, his successor (Hadrian 117–38) gave up the drive to extend the empire eastward; as a consequence, Jews in Babylonia were free from Roman rule.

In AD 132 a messianic revolt was led in Judaea by Simon bar Kosiba (also called Bar Kochba), who was aided by Akiva as well as other scholars from Jamnia in opposition to Hadrian's espousal of Hellenization. These Jewish rebels believed that God would empower the Jews to regain control of their homeland and rebuild the Temple. Although the rebels fought valiantly against the occupying forces, the Romans crushed the revolt. According to an account by the third-century historian Dio Cassius, hundreds of thousands of Jews were massacred and Judaea was almost completely destroyed. The rebellion came to an end in AD 135 with the fall of Bethar, south-west of Jerusalem. According to legend, this event took place on the 9th of Av, the same day as the destruction of both the first and second Temples. During the course of this campaign, Bar Kochba was killed, and Akiva was flayed alive as a martyr.

After the Bar Kochba war, Hadrian outlawed Judaism, but after his death in 138 prohibitions against the Jewish faith were rescinded. Regarding the Jews, their defeat under Bar Kochba led to a conciliatory policy toward the Romans, resulting in the flourishing of rabbinic scholarship. The centre of Jewish life was transferred to Galilee, where the Sanhedrin reassembled (at Usha). Among the outstanding scholars of this period were Simeon ben Gamaliel II, Elazar ben Shammua, Jose ben Halafta, Judah bar Illai, Simeon bar Yohai and Meir. These scholars ensured that the Sanhedrin became the decisive force in Jewish life; through its deliberations the legal decisions of previous generations

were systematized and disseminated throughout the Jewish world.

In time the economic conditions in Galilee improved, and the Jewish population established a harmonious relationship with the Roman administration. The Severan dynasty of Roman emperors granted the *nasi* the authority to appoint judges for Jewish courts, collect taxes and send representatives to diaspora communities. The most illustrious sage of this epoch was Judah ha-Nasi (the son of Simeon ben Gamaliel II), who served as the redactor of the Mishnah. This single volume consists of the discussions and rulings of scholars. Divided into six sections (or orders), this legal work contains a series of chapters on specific subjects.

The first order (Seeds) begins with a discussion of benedictions and continues with other sections dealing with legal matters such as the tithes of the harvest to be given to priests, Levites and the poor. The second order (Set Feasts) deals with the Sabbath, Passover, the Day of Atonement and

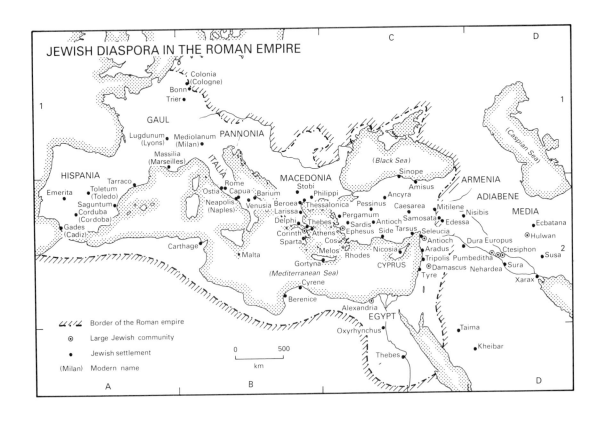

JEWISH DIASPORA IN THE ROMAN EMPIRE

Colonia (Cologne)
Bonn
Trier
GAUL
Lugdunum (Lyons)
Mediolanum (Milan)
PANNONIA
Massilia (Marseilles)
ITALIA
HISPANIA
Tarraco
Toletum (Toledo)
Emerita
Saguntum
Corduba (Cordoba)
Gades (Cadiz)
Carthage
Rome
Ostia Capua
Neapolis (Naples)
Barium
Venusia
Malta
(Black Sea)
MACEDONIA
Stobi
Philippi
Beroea
Larissa
Thessalonica
Delphi
Thebes
Corinth
Athens
Sparta
Melos
Gortyna
Rhodes
Pergamum
Sardis
Ephesus
Cos
Nicosia
CYPRUS
(Mediterranean Sea)
Cyrene
Berenice
Alexandria
Oxyrhynchus
EGYPT
Thebes
Sinope
Amisus
Ancyra
Pessinus
Caesarea
Mitilene
Antioch
Side Tarsus
Seleucia
Antioch
Aradus
Tripolis
Damascus
Tyre
Samosata
Edessa
ARMENIA
ADIABENE
Nisibis
MEDIA
Ecbatana
Hulwan
Dura Europus
Ctesiphon
Pumbeditha
Nehardea
Sura
Xarax
Susa
Taima
Kheibar
(Caspian Sea)

C
D
1
2
A
B
D

Border of the Roman empire
⊙ Large Jewish community
• Jewish settlement
(Milan) Modern name

0   500
km

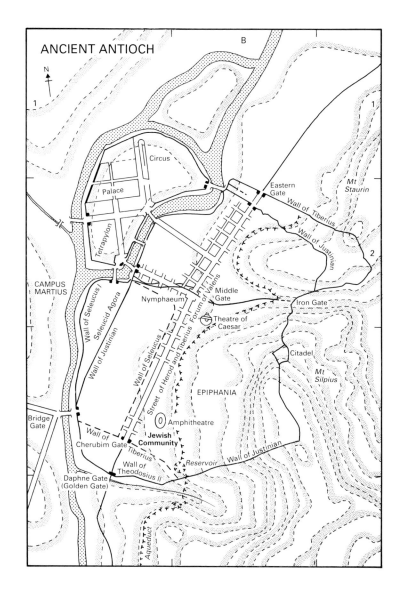

ANCIENT ANTIOCH

other festivals as well as shekel dues and the proclamation of the New Year. In the third section marriage matters as well as other issues affecting women are explored. The fourth section (Damages) deals with civil law, and contains a collection of moral maxims (Sayings of the Fathers). The final section (Purifications) treats various types of ritual uncleanliness and methods of purification.

The Sanhedrin, which had been fundamental in the compilation of this legal work, met in Galilee, but later settled in Tiberius. The *nasi* continued to serve as head of this body, but other scholars established their own schools in other parts of the country. In their teachings they applied the Mishnah to everyday life together with other rabbinic teachings (*beraitot*) which had not been included in the Mishnah.

5 JEWRY IN PALESTINE AND BABYLONIA

Palestinian Jewry

In the first few decades of the third century AD the Romans faced numerous problems, including inflation, population decline and the absence of technological development to support the army. In time rival generals fought against one another for power, and the government became increasingly inefficient. During this period of chaos and decline, the Jewish community was beset with famine, epidemic and plunder. By the end of the century the emperor Diocletian (AD 284–305) instigated reforms to strengthen the empire. Under his leadership an absolutist structure replaced the republican veneer of Roman rule, and a complex system of prices, offices and occupations was inaugurated to arrest economic decline. Further, Diocletian instituted measures to halt the spread of the Christian faith, which had become a serious challenge to the official religion of the empire.

Diocletian's successor Constantine the Great (AD 306–37) reversed his predecessor's antipathetical stance toward Christianity and extended official toleration to the Christian community in 313. By this stage the Christian religion had gained a considerable number of adherents from among the urban population. Eventually Constantine himself became interested in Church affairs, and before his death he was baptized. The Christianization of the empire continued throughout the century, and by the early part of the next century Christianity had become the state religion. Although this merger of the Roman government and the Church did not alter the legal rights of Jews, it did provide an important channel for anti-Jewish sentiment.

By the first half of the fourth century Jewish scholars had collected the teachings of generations of rabbis in the academies of Tiberius, Caesarea and Sepphoris – these discussions of the Mishnah became the Palestinian Talmud. This work treats thirty-nine Mishnaic tractates and contains approximately 750,000 words. The text itself consists largely of summaries of rabbinic debates: a phrase of Mishnah is interpreted, discrepancies resolved and redundancies explained. In this multi-volume compilation conflicting opinions of the earlier *Tannaim* are compared, unusual words explained and anonymous opinions identified. Frequently individual sages cite specific cases to support their views, and hypothetical eventualities are examined to produce a solution. Debates among outstanding scholars in one generation are frequently cited, as are differences of opinion between contemporary members of an academy or a teacher and his pupils. The range of exploration is much more extensive than in the Mishnah itself and includes rabbinic teachings about such subjects as theology, philosophy and ethics. The views of these Palestinian teachers (*Amoraim*) had an important influence on scholars in Babylonia despite the fact that this Talmud never had the same prominence in Jewish life as the Babylonian Talmud.

Although Jewish scholarship prospered in Palestine, the Jews there were confronted with

PALESTINIAN JEWRY

◇◇◇◇ Judaea at the beginning of independence under Simon, 142 BC

— · — Boundary of Hasmonean kingdom, 76 BC

◇ Greek city

■ Fortress

PHOENICIA

◇ Tyre

◇ Antiochia

● Gischala

◇ Seleucia

Ptolemais ◇

Sea of Galilee

● Garaba
● Tarichaea
● Arbela
■ Gamala

● Asochis

◇ Hippus

◇ Dium

Geba ●

● Sepphoris
● Sennabris
◇ Philoteria
◇ Abila

GALILEE

■ Mt Tabor

◇ Gadara

(Mediterranean Sea)

◇ Dor

GALAADITIS

● Capercotnei

◇ Scythopolis

Strato's Tower ◇

◇ Pella

● Narbata

SAMARIA

◇ Samaria

◇ Gerasa

● Apollonia

Mt Gerizim

■ ● Shechem

■ Ammathus

● Pegae

● Acrabeta

● Gerasa

■ Alexandrium

■ Gedor

Joppa ◇

ARAMATHEA

● Aramathea

PERAEA

◇ Philadelphia

Lydda ■

● Apherema

Jamnia ●

● Adida

JUDAEA

● Docus ■

Gazara ■

● Emmaus

● Jericho

● Samaga

Azotus ◇

● Accaron

● Jerusalem

■ Hyrcania

● Esbus

◇ Ascalon

● Medeba

◇ Anthedon

■ Beth-zur

(Dead Sea)

● Lemba

◇ Gaza

◇ Marisa

● Hebron

■ Machaerus

● Adora ● Aristobulias

● Orda

● Gerar

IDUMAEA

● En-gedi

◇ Raphia

● Masada ■

MOABITIS

● Beer-sheba

● Eglaim

● Malatha

● Rhinocorura

● Oronaim

● Elusa

NABATAEANS

● Zoar ● Gabalis

River Jordan

0   25
km

61

new difficulties. When Christianity emerged as the dominant religion of the Roman empire, Judaism came to be viewed as legally inferior. Thus imperial laws of the middle of the fourth century prohibited conversion to the Jewish faith as well as intermarriage between Jews and Christians. At the beginning of the fifth century Jews were barred from positions within the government: this exclusion continued throughout the rest of the century and was formally enforced through the decrees of the emperor Justinian (AD 525–65). The official position of the Church was that Jews should be converted to the true faith. The continued existence of Judaism and the Jewish people was seen as testimony to the truth of Scripture – in the eyes of the Church the Jews would eventually accept Jesus' messiahship and sovereignty.

Jews in Babylonia

After Nebuchadnezzar deported Jews from their homeland in the sixth century BC, Babylonia became a major centre of Jewish life. By the second century AD the Persian king (who ruled as an overlord in Mesopotamia) recognized the ethnarch as the leader of the Jewish community. This figure, who claimed descent from the kings of Judah who were originally deported, was responsible for collecting taxes, supervising the judiciary and representing the Jewish community at Persian court. By the middle of the century, rabbinic Judaism had spread to the east, and a number of Palestinian scholars took refuge in Babylonia during the Bar Kochba revolt and the Hadrianic persecutions.

In time Babylonian Jews travelled to centres of scholarship in Galilee to study under leading Pharisaic sages; the codification of the Mishnah

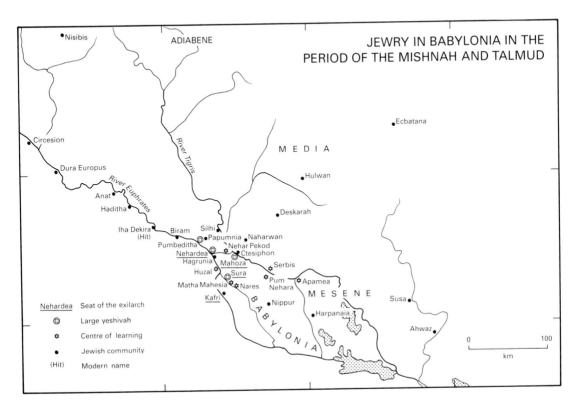

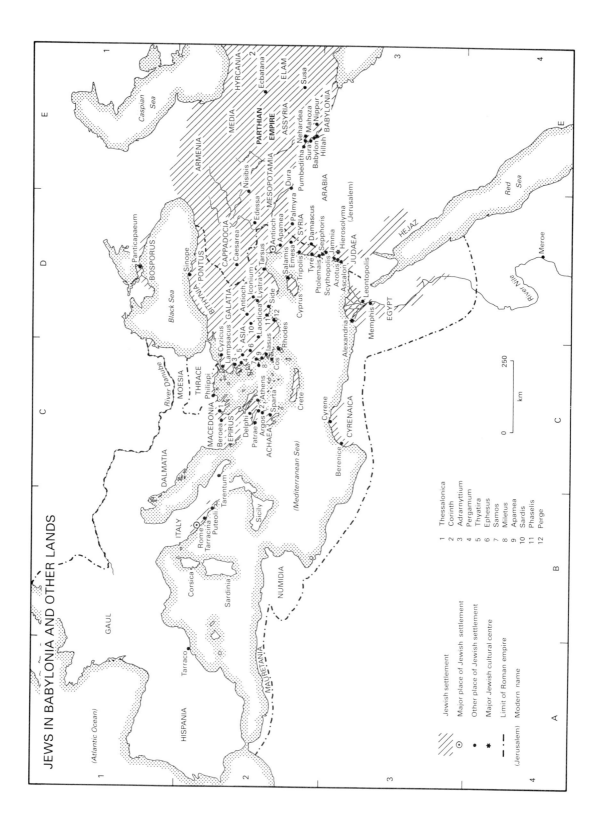

JEWS IN BABYLONIA AND OTHER LANDS

(Atlantic Ocean)

GAUL

HISPANIA

Tarraco

Corsica

Sardinia

ITALY
Rome
Tarracina
Puteoli
Tarentum

Sicily

NUMIDIA

MAURETANIA

DALMATIA

MOESIA
River Danube

THRACE
Philippi
MACEDONIA
Beroea
EPIRUS
Delphi
Patrae
Argos
ACHAEA
Sparta

Athens

Crete

(Mediterranean Sea)

CYRENAICA
Cyrene
Berenice

Black Sea

Panticapaeum

BOSPORUS

Sinope
BITHYNIA
PONTUS
CAPPADOCIA
Caesarea
Cyzicus
Lampsacus GALATIA
Antioch
Iconium
Laodicea Lystra Tarsus
ASIA
Side

Rhodes
Cos

Cyprus

EGYPT
Alexandria
Memphis
Leontopolis

Caspian Sea

ARMENIA

MEDIA
HYRCANIA
Ecbatana
ELAM
Susa
PARTHIAN
EMPIRE
ASSYRIA
Nehardea
Sura Mahoza
Pumbeditha Nippur
Babylon BABYLONIA
Hillah

Nisibis
Edessa
MESOPOTAMIA
Antioch
Apamea Dura
Palmyra
Emesa SYRIA
Damascus
Tripolis Sepphoris
Tyre
Ptolemais Jamnia
Salamis Scythopolis
Azotus Hierosolyma
Ascalon (Jerusalem)
JUDAEA

ARABIA

HEJAZ

Red Sea

River Nile

Meroe

0   250

km

1 Thessalonica
2 Corinth
3 Adramyttium
4 Pergamum
5 Thyatira
6 Ephesus
7 Samos
8 Miletus
9 Apamea
10 Sardis
11 Phaselis
12 Perge

Jewish settlement

Major place of Jewish settlement

Other place of Jewish settlement

Major Jewish cultural centre

Limit of Roman empire

(Jerusalem) Modern name

Figure 8   Silver gilt bust of a Sassanian King, probably Shapur II (Metropolitan Museum of Art, New York

served as head of another academy at Nehardea. When in AD 259 Nehardea was destroyed in an invasion, the school at Pumbeditha also became an important centre of rabbinic learning.

Some years previous to these developments (in AD 226), the Arsacid dynasty was overthrown by the Sassanians, who established a more centralized administration of the Persian empire with greater governmental supervision. They also established a revised form of Zoroastrianism as the official state religion with its own priestly hierarchy. This priestly class attempted to proselytize the Jewish community during the reign of Ardashir (AD 226–40), the first Sassanian king. His successor Shapur I (AD 240–71) allowed religious freedom for non-Zoroastrians and recognized the Jewish exilarchate in Babylonia. None the less Jewish leaders were forced to accept the authority of Persian state law: this arrangement was enshrined in the formula: *Dina demalkhuta dina* ('the law of the government is the law'). In Israel there had never existed an equivalent recognition of Roman law, but this formula provided a basis for permitting Jewish law to be superseded everywhere by non-Jewish civil law (as long as it did not conflict with Jewish religious rituals and ceremonies).

Under the Sassanian dynasty Babylonian Jews came into contact with a variety of religious sects such as the Manichaeans, yet they remained loyal to the faith of their fathers. Their religious leaders were renowned for their scholarship, and the academies they founded became major centres of learning. Carrying on the Galilean tradition of disputation, these sages developed and expanded Jewish law; in the fourth century Abbaye (AD 278–338) and Rava (AD 229–352) taught at Pumbeditha and were considered the most outstanding scholars of the period. As Jewish institutions declined in Israel, Babylonia emerged as the great centre of Jewish learning.

With the rise of Christianity as the official religion of the Roman empire, Christians rather than Jews were subject to persecution by the Sassanian dynasty, since Rome was perceived as an enemy. Throughout the fourth and fifth centuries, clergy, monks and lay persons were subject to attack. In contrast only for a short

by Judah ha-Nasi further stimulated such interchange. As a result of this efflorescence of learning, the exilarch encouraged the development of Babylonian scholarship and appointed the leading proponents as administrators and judges. During this period post-Mishnaic scholars in both Palestine and Babylonia engaged in a debate about the application of Jewish law. In the third century Rav founded an academy at Sura in central Mesopotamia; his contemporary Samuel

period in the fifth century (AD 445–75) was hostility directed toward the Jewish population: the exilarchate was suspended, synagogues and academies closed and the Torah banned. However, by the sixth century a period of tranquillity had begun – at this time the Babylonian Talmud was redacted (an editorial task begun by Rav Ashi (AD 335–427) at Sura).

Paralleling the Palestinian Talmud, this work is largely a summary of the Amoraic discussions that took place in the Babylonian academies. Although this Talmud deals with slightly fewer tractates than the Palestinian Talmud, it is nearly four times the size (approximately 2,500,000 words).

The Babylonian academies

The emergence of academies in Babylonia was the result of a large influx of refugees from Palestine during the period of the Bar Kochba revolt (AD 132–5) as well as at the time of subsequent persecution. These individuals included a number of the most outstanding scholars of the time. In addition Babylonian sages travelled to Palestine to study Torah; on their return they made a major impact on Babylonian Jewish society. Among such scholars was Rav; on

his return he went to Sura – which contained a significant Jewish population – where he founded an academy. In addition, another academy was founded at Nehardea, and under the leadership of Samuel became a major centre of learning. There Rav introduced the study of the Mishnah and employed the Palestinian system of study. However, since Samuel did not regard himself as subject to the rulings of the Palestinian authorities, his academy adopted a different curriculum.

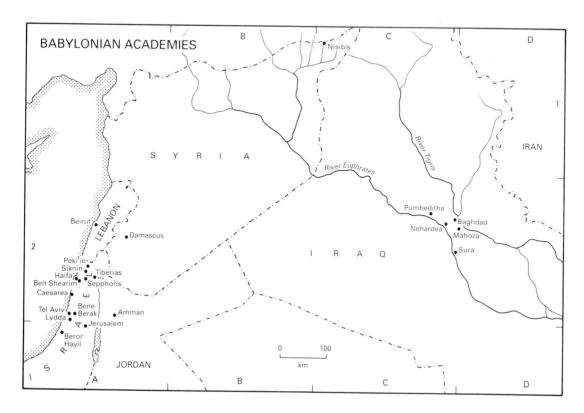

With the founding of these two academies, Jewish Babylonia was divided into two groups: some towns were under the influence of Sura and adopted its rulings, while others took their lead from Nehardea. At Sura approximately 1,200 students were engaged in the study of Jewish law in Rav's time. This was the era in which the custom of *yarhei kallah* was established: during the two months of the year in which work in the field ceased (in *Adar* and *Elul*), thousands of Jews went to these two centres of learning to study. In subsequent centuries these academies continued to serve as the chief source of the spiritual life. At times Sura was more important that Nehardea: while in other periods Nehardea became the leading academy. Eventually alternative academies were founded; none the less Sura and Pumbeditha – the successor to Nehardea – remained the pre-eminent academies of Babylonian Jewry.

Over the centuries developments in Jewish law – based on the Mishnah – took place in the Babylonian academies in the form of discussions that expanded and supplemented statements in the Mishnah. These were largely oral traditions that varied from academy to academy. During the presidency of Ashi at Sura (371–427), they were summarized and edited in the form of the Babylonian Talmud which follows the order of the tractates and chapters of the Mishnah. The text of the Babylonian Talmud contains evidence of this editing and reflects centuries of religious thought and experience. Unlike the Mishnah, which is composed primarily of deliberations about the *halakhah*, the Babylonian Talmud contains a vast amount of aggadic material.

This talmudic work is constructed on the same pattern as its Jerusalem counterpart – both have much in common since they are based on the same foundation and also because of the close connections between the two centres of Jewish life. Nevertheless there are a number of differences between these two repositories of learning. The first concerns language: those passages of the Jerusalem Talmud that are not in Hebrew are in western Aramaic with a significant addition of Greek words. The Babylonian Talmud, on the other hand, contains eastern Aramaic with far fewer Persian terms. Second, the Jerusalem Talmud is more concise and incorporates less detailed legal discussions than many parts of the Babylonian Talmud. Finally, the two Talmuds at times reach different conclusions, and Mishnaic passages are often interpreted in different ways because of variations between Palestinian and Babylonian customs or varying socio-economic and political conditions. As time passed, the Jerusalem Talmud gained little currency outside of Israel; instead the Babylonian Talmud became pre-eminent and exerted a primary influence on later Jewish history.

The final edition of the Babylonian Talmud dates from the fifth century; it was completed during the time of Jose of Pumbeditha, and Ravina (the last leader of Sura). The era following the conclusion of the Talmud until shortly before the Arab conquest is known as the Savoraite era. According to Jewish tradition, the scholars (*savoraim*) who lived during this period were concerned with explaining Jewish law; the Babylonian Talmud includes a number of their sayings even though they are designated as *savoraim*. These sages included Jose, Rahumi, Asha of Bei Hattim, Huna the exilarch and Samuel, the son of Abahu.

The revolt of Mar Zutra

During the reign of Yazdigar III (440–57), the priesthood of the magi gained greater influence; this change resulted in a wave of religious persecution throughout Persia. Christians were attacked more severely than Jews since they were suspected of sympathizing with Byzantium. None the less the general ban on religious practices caused great distress within the Jewish community. In 455 an edict was promulgated which abolished the Sabbath. The consternation

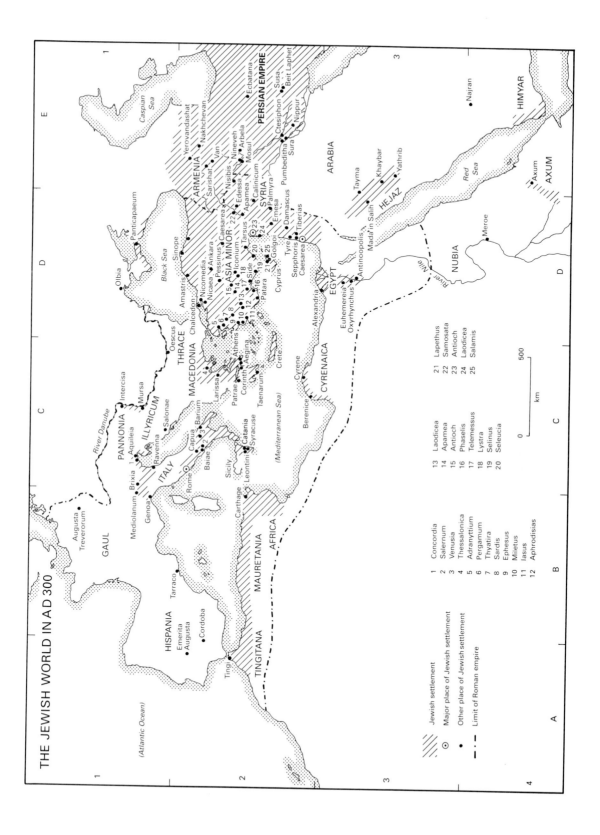

THE JEWISH WORLD IN AD 300

Key

⫽⫽	Jewish settlement		
⊙	Major place of Jewish settlement		
•	Other place of Jewish settlement		
—··—	Limit of Roman empire		

1 Concordia
2 Salernum
3 Venusia
4 Thessalonica
5 Adranyttium
6 Pergamum
7 Thyatira
8 Sardis
9 Ephesus
10 Miletus
11 Iasus
12 Aphrodisias

13 Laodicea
14 Apamea
15 Antioch
16 Phaselis
17 Telemessus
18 Lystra
19 Selinus
20 Seleucia

21 Lapethus
22 Samosata
23 Antioch
24 Laodicea
25 Salamis

GAUL · Augusta Treverorum · Mediolanum · Genoa · Brixia · Aquileia · Ravenna · ITALY · Rome ⊙ · Baiae · Capua · Barium · Salernum · Leontini · Catania · Syracuse · Sicily · Carthage · AFRICA · MAURETANIA · TINGITANA · HISPANIA · Emerita Augusta · Cordoba · Tarraco · Tingi · (Atlantic Ocean)

PANNONIA · Intercisa · Mursa · Salonae · ILLYRICUM · River Danube · Oescus · THRACE · MACEDONIA · Larissa · Corinth · Patrae · Athens · Aegina · Taenarum · Crete · (Mediterranean Sea) · CYRENAICA · Cyrene · Berenice

Panticapaeum · Olbia · Black Sea · Sinope · Amastris · Chalcedon · Nicomedia · Nicaea · Ankara · Pessinus · ASIA MINOR · Iconium · Side · Tarsus · Patara · Cyprus · Golgoi · Caesarea

Caspian Sea · ARMENIA · Yerovandashat · Nakhchevan · Sarishat · Van · Nisibis · Nineveh · Edessa · Mosul · Apamea · Arbela · Callinicum · SYRIA · Palmyra · Emesa · Damascus · Tyre · Sepphoris · Tiberias · Caesarea ⊙

PERSIAN EMPIRE · Ecbatana · Susa · Beit Laphet · Ctesiphon · Pumbeditha · Sura · Nippur · ARABIA · Tayma · Khaybar · Yathrib · HEJAZ · Mada'in Salih · Najran · HIMYAR · Axum · AXUM · Red Sea · NUBIA · Meroe · River Nile · EGYPT · Alexandria · Antinopolis · Oxyrhynchus · Euhemereia

500 0 km

caused by this act is reflected in an account of its repeal: 'And the rabbis proclaimed a fast, and the Holy One Blessed Be He sent a crocodile unto him in the night which swallowed him as he lay on his couch, and the decree was invalidated.' Under Yazdigar's son Piruz (458–85), the Jewish population continued to suffer persecution: synagogues and Torah schools were banned. Jews were compelled to stand trial in Persian law courts, and Jewish children were seized from their parents to be educated by the magi. In addition several scholars were cast into prison and executed.

Amidst this distress the exilarch founded a Jewish kingdom on Babylonian territory. A report of this event depicts how widespread the Jewish population in Babylonia was as well as the power of its leaders even during the time of persecution. Further, it illustrates that the exilarchate and the academies conflicted about such issues as the appointment of judges. Thus Huna, the exilarch, offended his father-in-law Haninah (the president of the academy) by refusing to confirm a judge nominated by him. However, once Huna had been put to death by the Persian authorities, Haninah raised the exilarch's son, Mar Zutra, and confirmed upon him the office of the exilarchate when it was usurped by relatives.

In 495 disorders occurred throughout the Persian empire, and King Kabad I (488–531) was deposed and put in prison. Taking advantage of such confusion and instability, Mar Zutra drew together an army and established a kingdom with Mahoza as its capital. In addition, he levied taxes and engaged in warfare against the Persians. In 502 Mar Zutra as well as Haninah were killed on the bridge of Mahoza. Once the Jewish rebellion was suppressed, institutions within the Jewish community were closed. In response the heads of the Jewish community along with the presidents of the academies escaped to the river Saba and founded an academy there beyond the control of the Persian government. Subsequently a son of Mar Zutra was raised in secret; at the age of 18 he travelled to Israel, where he was appointed head of the Sanhedrin.

After these events discrimination against the Jewish population lessened. A number of Jews served in the Persian army; at one of the battles with the Byzantine general Belisarius, the Persian commander asked his adversary to cease fighting during Passover for the sake of his Jewish soldiers. Eventually in the sixth century Babylonian Jewry re-established its institutions including the office of the exilarch and the tradition of *yarhei kallah*.

During the reign of Hormizd IV the magi again gained considerable power at the royal court; this initiated another period of Jewish persecution. The major Jewish institutions were closed, and the heads of the academy of Pumbeditha went to Piruz-Shapur near Nehardea – there the king's power had little influence. However, in the last years of the Persian empire under Khusroe II (590–628) and the twelve years of confusion following his death, Jewish institutions again came into operation: the academies reopened and the exilarch operated as before. Yet despite this resurgence of Jewish life, it was not until the time of the Arab conquest (628–39) that Babylonian Jewry was able to liberate itself from the harsh rule of the Persian kings.

The geonim

After the period of the *savoraim*, the geonim were recognized as the religious authorities in Babylonia. These leaders emerged at the end of the sixth century, when the academies regained their prominence. During the previous talmudic period the heads of Sura and Pumbeditha were appointed by scholars of the academies, but subsequently the geonim were chosen by the exilarchs. Usually these individuals rose through the hierarchies in the academies; as a result not all geonim were outstanding figures, since the exilarchs frequently appointed men of inferior qualities whom they expected to be subservient. Thus it is recorded that the exilarch rejected the

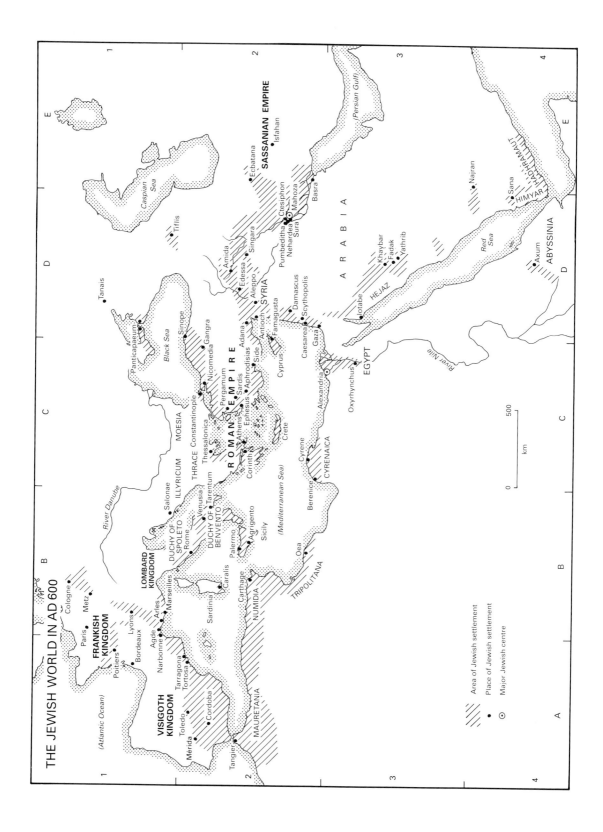

THE JEWISH WORLD IN AD 600

(Atlantic Ocean)

FRANKISH KINGDOM

Cologne
Metz
Paris
Lyons
Poitiers
Bordeaux
Agde
Narbonne
Arles
Marseilles

VISIGOTH KINGDOM

Toledo
Merida
Cordoba
Tarragona
Tortosa
Tangier
Caralis
Sardinia

MAURETANIA
NUMIDIA
Carthage

TRIPOLITANA

Oea

Sicily
Palermo
Agrigento

LOMBARD KINGDOM

DUCHY OF SPOLETO
Rome
DUCHY OF BENEVENTO
Tarentum
Venusia
Salonae

ILLYRICUM
MOESIA
THRACE
River Danube

Tanais

Black Sea
Panticapaeum
Sinope

Constantinople
Thessalonica
Nicomedia
Gangra
Pergamum
Sardis
Athens
Ephesus
Aphrodisias
Corinth
Side
Adana
Crete

R O M A N   E M P I R E

(Mediterranean Sea)

Cyrene
Berenice
CYRENAICA

Cyprus
Famagusta
Antioch
Scythopolis
Caesarea
Gaza
Damascus

SYRIA
Aleppo
Edessa
Amida
Singara

Alexandria
Oxyrhynchus
EGYPT

River Nile

Tiflis
Caspian Sea

Ecbatana

SASSANIAN EMPIRE

Isfahan

Ctesiphon
Mahoza
Nehardea
Pumbeditha
Sura
Basra

(Persian Gulf)

A R A B I A

Iotabe
HEJAZ
Khaybar
Fadak
Yathrib

Red Sea

Najran
Sana
HIMYAR
HADHRAMAUT

Axum
ABYSSINIA

Area of Jewish settlement
Place of Jewish settlement
Major Jewish centre

500
km
0

outstanding scholar Aha of Shabha; instead he selected his disciple Natronai Kahana to the gaonate in Pumbeditha. None the less after the authority of the exilarchs weakened in the ninth century, scholars came to play a greater role in the appointment of the gaon, particularly at Pumbeditha.

During the period of the gaonate the Babylonian academies served as the cultural centres for Jews throughout the world. At Sura and Pumbeditha the sages interpreted the Talmud in the form in which they received it from the *savoraim* in order to ensure that it was accepted as the universal code of Jewish law. In addition, the geonim made the academy a supreme court as well as a source of teaching for Jewry. Because of the prominence of these institutions, thousands of Jews assembled in these centres in the *kallah* months of *Elul* and *Adur* to attend lectures on Jewish law. During this time the gaon would also answer questions sent to him from diaspora communities. Further, the geonim exercised jurisdiction over the courts in all the districts of Babylonia. Yet despite this influence, judges were appointed by the exilarch with the consent of the geonim. (It was only under Hai Gaon that the supreme court of Pumbeditha was given authority to appoint judges.) Regarding the law, the geonim made new regulations covering contemporary needs based on talmudic precedent. Their *takkanot* ('ordinances') were considered authoritative because the geonim were viewed as presidents of the Sanhedrin in their generation.

In order to accomplish these tasks the academies employed large staffs consisting of scribes, directors of *kallah* assemblies and other officials. The finances of the academies were obtained through taxes levied on districts as well as through contributions from communities which addressed questions to the geonim. In some cases the geonim themselves requested financial

Figure 9 Dura Europos Synagogue painting of the *Consecration of the Temple* (Yale University Art Gallery)

support. Toward the end of the gaonic period, such requests for support increased, and candidates for the office of gaon increasingly had to possess administrative abilities in addition to Jewish learning. Descent was also an important factor in the selection of the geonim – most of the geonim of Sura and Pumbeditha were drawn from six or seven leading families. When a gaon was appointed, a festive ceremony took place in which scholars of the two academies as well as Jewish dignitaries in Babylonia headed by the exilarch participated.

Alongside the exilarch the gaonate had specific political and communal duties. Only once did the geonim represent the Jewish community, but they frequently attempted to influence governmental policy toward Babylonian Jewry. Nevertheless their particular achievement was their success in ensuring that the Talmud was accepted as the authoritative basis for Jewish life in all lands. Through their writings they made a significant impact on Jewish life and thought. Their importance is attested by a statement of Zemah b. Hayyim, the gaon of Sura, in a response to the community in Kairouan:

And when Eldad said that they pray for the scholars of Babylonia and then for those in the Diaspora, they are right. For the major scholars and prophets were exiled to Babylonia, and they established the Torah and founded the academy on the Euphrates under Jehiachin, king of Judah, until this day, and they were the dynasty of wisdom and prophecy and the source of Torah for the entire people.

In time, however, the academies began to decline. From the late ninth century most geonim ceased to live in Sura and Pumbeditha; rather they resided in Baghdad, the residence of the exilarch. One of the reasons for the loss of importance of these great centres was the competition between Sura and Pumbeditha. In addition the quarrels in the academies regarding the appointment of the gaon had a decisive influence. Further, the emergence of new centres for talmudic studies and the appearance of great scholars throughout the diaspora had an important impact. As a consequence, Jewish intellectual life gradually shifted to other areas in the Jewish world.

6 JUDAISM UNDER ISLAM IN THE MIDDLE AGES

Judaism and the rise of Islam

In the sixth and seventh centuries Arabs in the Arabian peninsula were polytheists who lived in nomadic tribes and urban centres. At the beginning of the seventh century Muhammed (a caravan merchant from Mecca) condemned their religious practices. Convinced that the one true God had revealed his will to him, he initially preached that biblical figures such as Abraham and Moses were sent by God to warn humankind to forsake their idolatrous ways. In this light he cautioned the Meccans that each person would be judged on the final day of judgement: 'When the sky is rent asunder; when the stars scatter and the oceans roll together, when the graves are hurled about; each soul shall know what it has done and what it has failed to do.'

Muhammed declared that those who refuse to heed this message would be destroyed except for Jews and Christians who had passed on the revelations given in the Torah and the gospels. These early revelations, Muhammed believed, were superseded by a new revelation which God had transmitted to him as his prophet. In 622 Muhammed left Mecca and settled in Yathrib, 280 miles to the north. After a number of conflicts with the Meccans, Muhammed and his supporters re-entered Mecca in 630. By 632 — when Muhammed died — the shrine of Mecca was purified of pagan deities and became the chief holy centre of the religion Muhammed founded.

At the beginning of his ministry Muhammed attempted to convert the Jewish community, but they refused to accept him as prophet. In response Muhammed denounced the Jewish nation:

> To Moses We (i.e. God) gave the Scriptures and after him We sent other apostles. We gave Jesus the son of Mary veritable signs and strengthened him with the Holy Spirit. Will you then scorn each apostle whose message does not suit your fancies, charging some with imposture and enslaving others?
>
> They (the Jews) say: 'Our hearts are sealed.' But Allah has cursed them for their unbelief. They have but little faith. And now that a Book confirming their Scriptures has been revealed to them by Allah, they deny it, although they know it to be the truth and have long prayed for help against the unbelievers. May Allah's curse be upon the infidels!
>
> (Sura 2:87–91)

According to Muhammed, the Jews have distorted Allah's words, and their Scriptures contain untruths. The Koran, however, both proves the Torah and corrects it. Islam is therefore superior to Judaism because it is a restoration of the original form of monotheism. Abraham was the first Muslim, but Muhammed is the 'Seal of the Prophets'. For Muslims, then, Judaism is legitimate, but incomplete — the Jews are blind and dangerous in so far as they refuse to accept the truth which is offered them by Allah's true prophet. As a consequence of this teaching, by 626 two Jewish tribes had been expelled from Medina and a third exterminated (except for

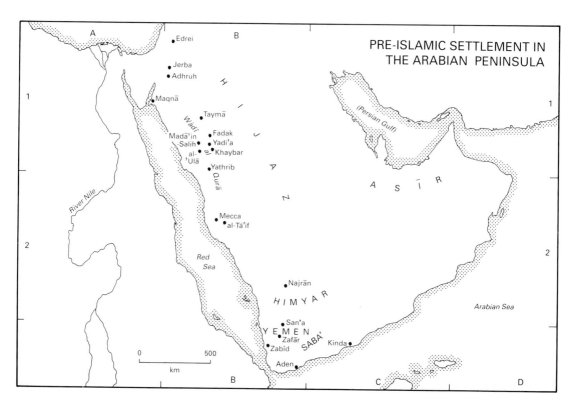

PRE-ISLAMIC SETTLEMENT IN THE ARABIAN PENINSULA

Edrei

Jerba
Adhruh

Maqnā

Taymā

H I J A Z

Wādi'

Madā'in
-Salih   Fadak
al-   Yadi'a
'Ulā   al-   Khaybar
        Qura'
        Yathrib

(Persian Gulf)

A S Ī R

Mecca
al-Tā'if

Red
Sea

Najrān

H I M Y A R

San'a
Y E M E N
Zafār
Zabīd   SABA'   Kinda

Aden

Arabian Sea

River Nile

0   500
km

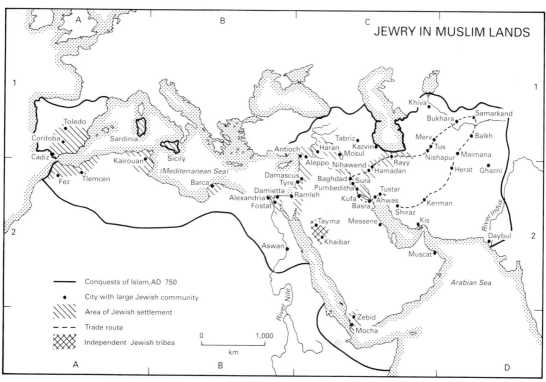

JEWRY IN MUSLIM LANDS

Khiva

Toledo   Samarkand
                                    Bukhara
Cordoba   Sardinia   Merv   Balkh
Cadiz   Sicily   Antioch   Haran Tabriz Kazvin Tus Maimana
        Kairouan   (Mediterranean Sea) Aleppo Mosul Nishapur
Fez   Tlemcen   Damascus Nihawend Rayy Herat Ghazni
                        Barca   Tyre   Hamadan
                              Damietta Baghdad Sura
                        Alexandria Ramleh Pumbeditha Tustar
                              Fostat   Kufa Ahwas Kerman
                                    Basra Shiraz
                              Tayma   Messene Kis
                              Khaibar Daybul

Aswan   Muscat

                                    Arabian Sea

River Nile

Zebid
Mocha

Conquests of Islam, AD 750
City with large Jewish community
Area of Jewish settlement
Trade route
Independent Jewish tribes

0   1,000
km

women and children, who were taken away as slaves). Two years later Muslims conquered the Jewish oasis of Khaybar; there the Jewish population were subsequently allowed to remain if they gave half of their produce as a tribute to Muslims.

By 644 Muslim soldiers occupied Syria, Israel, Egypt, Iraq and Persia; in the next sixteen years the Ummayad dynasty of caliphs had consolidated their control of the Islamic empire. Yet despite these conquests, the Arab world was plagued by unrest over the right of leadership. In 750 the Ummayads were replaced by the Abbasid dynasty of caliphs, who transferred the capital from Damascus to Baghdad.

In the following century the Abbasid caliphate flourished; the Islamic post-scriptural oral tradition was formed, and Muslim jurisprudence, theology and science made significant advances. Initially conversion to Islam was not encouraged – Jews as well as Christians were regarded as Peoples of the Book and guaranteed religious freedom and judicial autonomy. In turn they were compelled to recognize the supremacy of the Islamic state. According to the Pact of Omar from about 800 Jews were restricted in various areas: they were not permitted to build new synagogues, make converts, carry weapons or ride horses. Further, they were required to wear distinctive garments and pay a yearly poll tax. Under such conditions, Jewish life prospered. In many urban centres Jews worked in crafts such as tanning, dyeing, weaving, silk manufacture and metalwork; others engaged in interregional trade.

During this period a number of Jews migrated from Babylonia to other parts of the diaspora. Some of these émigrés created new centres of Jewish life, and even penetrated outside the Islamic empire to conduct trade. It was just such merchants who converted the kings of the Turkish people on the Volga, the Khazars, to Judaism. In the former Byzantine provinces Jews welcomed the Muslim regime. In place of previous centuries of Christian persecution, they were granted a defined legal standing as protected subjects of the state.

Jewry under Arab rule

The Arab conquerors did not encourage Jewish conversion to Islam; rather Jews were recognized as a People of the Book as their Scriptures were based on divine revelation. For this reason they were guaranteed religious toleration, judicial autonomy, exemption from military service, and security of life as well as property. In turn, Jewry was compelled to recognize the political authority of the Islamic state. However, during the first two centuries of Muslim rule, a major change took place in Jewish life: Jews became an urbanized people since excessive land taxes made it impossible for them to remain farmers and peasants. With the revival of old cities and the creation of new urban centres, they engaged in alternative occupations. With the expansion of the empire, military camps (such as Basra, Kufa, Fostat-Cairo and Kairouan) and the Abbasid capital in Baghdad flourished as commercial and administrative centres – this change in Islamic society provided new economic opportunities for Jews who engaged in a wide variety of crafts such as tanning, dyeing, weaving, silk manufacture and metal-work. In addition, the Jewish upper classes participated in interregional trade.

This political and economic framework enabled Jews to migrate from Babylonia to outlying regions. Some even travelled outside the Muslim empire to conduct trade; in time this migration led to an overall geographical redistribution of Jewry. Another result of Arab conquest was the abandonment of Aramaic and Greek for Arabic. By adopting Arabic as their spoken language Jews came into contact with Islamic thought – this linguistic development resulted in a new phase of Jewish intellectual and literary activity. Arab expansion also fostered the spread of the Islamic faith. In consequence both Zoroastrianism and Orthodox Christianity experienced a serious decline. Jews, however, welcomed

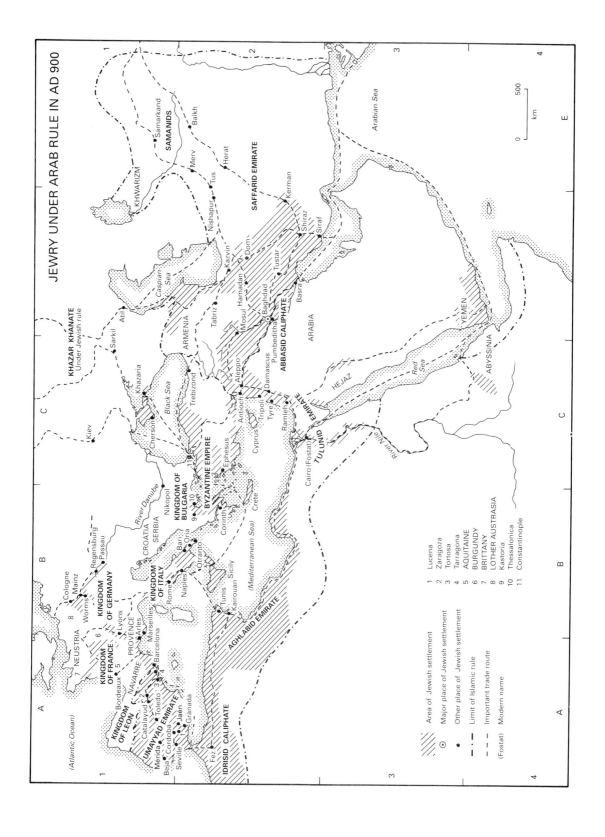

JEWRY UNDER ARAB RULE IN AD 900

Key:
- Area of Jewish settlement
- ⊙ Major place of Jewish settlement
- • Other place of Jewish settlement
- — · — · Limit of Islamic rule
- — — — Important trade route
- (Fostat) Modern name

1 Lucena
2 Zaragoza
3 Tortosa
4 Tarragona
5 AQUITAINE
6 BURGUNDY
7 BRITTANY
8 LOTHER AUSTRASIA
9 Thessalonica
10 Kastoria
11 Constantinople

(Atlantic Ocean)

KINGDOM OF LEON
NAVARRE
UMAYYAD EMIRATE
Bordeaux
Catalayud
Toledo
Merida
Beja
Cordoba
Seville
Jaén
Granada
Fez
IDRISID CALIPHATE

KINGDOM OF FRANCE
NEUSTRIA
Cologne
Mainz
Worms
Regensburg
Passau
KINGDOM OF GERMANY
Lyons
Arles
PROVENCE
Marseilles
Barcelona
Tarragona

KINGDOM OF ITALY
CROATIA
SERBIA
Rome
Naples
Bari
Oria
Otranto
Sicily
Tunis
Kairouan
AGHLABID EMIRATE
(Mediterranean Sea)

KINGDOM OF BULGARIA
Nikopol
Corinth
Crete
BYZANTINE EMPIRE
Ephesus
Thessalonica
Constantinople

River Danube

KHAZAR KHANATE
Under Jewish rule
Kiev
Sarkil
Khazaria
Cherson
Black Sea
Atil
Caspian Sea
ARMENIA
Trebizond
Tabriz

Samarkand
SAMANIDS
Balkh
Merv
KHWARIZM
Tus
Herat
Nishapur
SAFFARID EMIRATE
Kerman
Kazvin
Dom
Shiraz
Siraf
Tustar
Hamadan
Mosul
Baghdad
Basra
ABBASID CALIPHATE
Pumbeditha
Aleppo
Antioch
Damascus
Tripoli
Tyre
Ramleh
Cyprus
Cairo (Fostat)
TULUNID EMIRATE
River Nile
HEJAZ
ARABIA
Red Sea
YEMEN
ABYSSINIA
Arabian Sea

0   500
km

the Arab conquests since these new invaders brought relief from the persecution they experienced from the Christian population. Although they were regarded as second-class citizens, they were protected by the state.

As far as Jewish institutions were concerned, the Arabs confirmed the authority of the exilarch when they conquered Babylonia. During the period when the reign of the Ummayad caliphs was at its height, the exilarch became the most important Jewish official. An ancient account of the installation of the exilarch illustrates his pre-eminence in the community.

> On Thursday they assembled in the synagogue, blessed the exilarch, and placed their hands on him. They blew the horn, that all the people, small and great, might hear. When the people heard the proclamation every member of the community sent him a present, according to his power and means.... When he arose on Sabbath morning to go to the synagogue, many of the prominent men of the community met him to go with him to the synagogue. At the synagogue a wooden pulpit had been prepared for him.... When all the people were seated, the exilarch came out from the place where he was concealed. Seeing him come out, all the people stood up, until he sat on the pulpit which had been made for him. Then the head of the academy of Sura came out after him, and after exchanging courtesies with the exilarch he sat down on the pulpit. Then the head of the academy of Pumbeditha came out, and he, too, made a bow, and sat down at his left.

> (*Post-Biblical Hebrew Literature: An Anthology*, trans. B. Halpen (Philadelphia: Jewish Publications Society, 1921), pp. 64–7)

By the Abbasid period the exilarch was compelled to share his authority with the geonim. Initially the exilarch dominated the academies and appointed their heads, but later in the eighth century the heads became more important and claimed the right to nominate the exilarch. In addition taxes from districts in Iraq and Persia were sent directly to the academies rather than the exilarch. Such a three-way division of power and income frequently created conflict. Gradually the authority of the exilarch diminished so that by the eleventh century the office of exilarch became simply an honorific one.

Karaites

In the eighth century messianic movements flourished in the Persian Jewish community, a development which led to armed uprisings against the Muslim authorities; these revolts, however, were quickly suppressed. Yet an even more serious threat to Jewish stability was posed by the emergence of an anti-rabbinic sect in the middle of the eighth century. This group, the Karaites, was headed by Anan ben David, who had been passed over as exilarch. According to Anan, Jewish practices must be governed by scriptural precedent. The central interpretative principle formulated by Anan, 'Search thoroughly in Scripture and do not rely on my opinion', served to highlight the overriding importance of the Torah itself as the sole source of law.

For Anan religious observances must conform to biblical precedent rather than rabbinic ordinances. Such a stance was not intended to encourage leniency; on the contrary, the Karaites were often more strict than the rabbis. Thus Anan did not permit lights or fire in Jewish households during the Sabbath although they were allowed by rabbinic law (as long as they were kindled previously). Further, he promulgated a seventy-day fast (which resembled Ramadan in the Muslim tradition), extended the prohibited degrees of marriage far beyond rabbinic law, introduced more complicated regulations for circumcision, and interpreted the prohibition of work on the Sabbath in stricter terms than the rabbis.

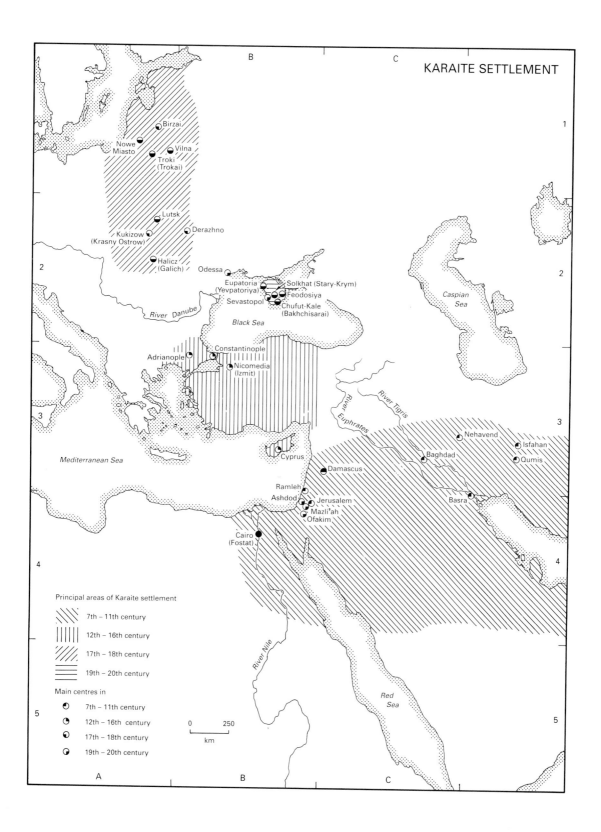

KARAITE SETTLEMENT

Birzai

Nowe Miasto
Vilna
Troki (Trokai)

Lutsk
Kukizow (Krasny Ostrow)
Derazhno

Halicz (Galich)
Odessa

Caspian Sea

Eupatoria (Yevpatoriya)
Solkhat (Stary-Krym)
Feodosiya
Sevastopol
Chufut-Kale (Bakhchisarai)

River Danube

Black Sea

Adrianople
Constantinople
Nicomedia (Izmit)

River Euphrates
River Tigris

Nehavend
Isfahan
Baghdad
Qumis

Mediterranean Sea

Cyprus
Damascus
Basra

Ramleh
Ashdod
Jerusalem
Mazli'ah
Ofakim

Cairo (Fostat)

River Nile

Red Sea

Principal areas of Karaite settlement

7th – 11th century

12th – 16th century

17th – 18th century

19th – 20th century

Main centres in

7th – 11th century

12th – 16th century

17th – 18th century

19th – 20th century

0   250
km

77

After Anan's death, new sects appeared within the Karaite movement. The followers of Anan were referred to as the 'Ananites' and remained few in number. In the early part of the ninth century Ishamel of Ukbara founded the Ukbaraite sect. Some years later two other sects were established in Ukbara by Mishawayh Al-Ukbari and his contemporary, Abu Imram Al-Tiflisi. In Israel yet another sect was formed by Malik Al-Ramli. By the end of the century Karaism had split into a variety of groups advocating different anti-rabbinic stances. None the less these groups were short-lived, and in time the Karaites merged into a uniform movement.

The major representative of mainstream Karaism was Benjamin ben Moses Nahavendi, who fostered a policy of free and independent study of Scripture – this became the dominant ideology of later Karaism. By the tenth century Karaite communities were established in Israel, Iraq and Persia. These groups rejected rabbinic legislation and formulated their own laws. Eventually a Karaite rabbinical academy was founded in Jerusalem; there the Karaite community produced some of the most distinguished sages of the period, who produced legal handbooks, composed biblical commentaries, engaged in philosophical and theological reflection, and wrote about Hebrew philology.

In the first centuries of its history Karaism was known for its asceticism, longing for an end to exile, rejection of rabbinic Judaism, individualistic biblical exegesis, and increasing interest in rationalistic criticism of rabbinism. Antagonistic to the closed character of the Babylonian yeshivot, the Karaites defied the established Jewish leadership. In addition, they attacked the Talmud itself. Thus a Karaite author of the tenth century, Jacob al-Kirkisani, wrote a history of the movement in which he linked Karaism to the Sadducees of the Second Temple. Like this ancient sect the Karaites wished to restore the Judaism of biblical times. According to al-Kirkisani, both groups believed themselves to be adherents of the only authentic form of Judaism.

The growth of Karaism stimulated the rabbis to attack it as a heretical movement. The first prominent rabbinic authority to engage in anti-Karaite polemic was Saadiah Gaon. In the first half of the ninth century he composed a book attacking Anan. This work was followed by other anti-Karaite polemics by eminent rabbinic scholars. In the First Crusade the Jerusalem Jewish community was devastated; as a result Karaite scholarly activity shifted to the Byzantine empire. From there Karaites founded other communities in the Crimea, Poland and Lithuania. However, by the eleventh century the movement diminished in importance in the Jewish world.

Jewry in Muslim lands

In 750 the Abbasid caliphs overthrew the Ummayads. In time the Abbasids began to lose control of outlying territories such as Morocco (780), Tunisia (c. 800), large areas of Persia (c. 820) and Egypt (c. 860). After 850 the Abbasid caliphs increasingly became captives of their Turkish troops. Eventually in 909 the Fatimids (a Shiite dynasty) seized control of north Africa, and in the latter part of the century the Fatimids conquered Egypt and Palestine. By the end of the tenth century, the Islamic world was divided into a number of smaller states. None the less, there was an active exchange of goods and trade throughout the entire area extending as far as India and China. Within this context Jews engaged in trade, and worked as small manufacturers as well as bankers and physicians.

With the disintegration of the Islamic empire, rabbinic Judaism underwent a process of decentralization. The geonic academies lost their previous pre-eminence, and in many lands new yeshivot were founded. In these centres of learning the Talmud was studied along with the responsa and other legal sources. The creation of such yeshivot led to the emergence of distinguished scholars whose prominence was based on

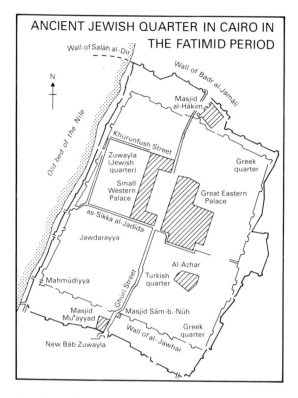

ANCIENT JEWISH QUARTER IN CAIRO IN THE FATIMID PERIOD

N

Wall of Salāh al-Dīn

Wall of Badr al-Jamālī

Old bed of the Nile

Masjid al-Hākim

Khurunfush Street

Zuwayla (Jewish quarter)

Greek quarter

Small Western Palace

Great Eastern Palace

as-Sikka al-Jadīda

Jawdarayya

Mahmūdiyya

Ghūrī Street

Al-Azhar

Turkish quarter

Masjid Mu'ayyad

Masjid Sām-b.-Nūh

Greek quarter

Wall of al-Jawhar

New Bāb Zuwayla

During this period Egyptian Jewry underwent an economic and intellectual revival. The most important rabbinic figure of the tenth century was an Egyptian Jew, Saadiah ben Joseph al-Fayyumi, who opposed Karaism and championed the Babylonian yeshivot. He was the first gaon of a Babylonian academy not to be appointed from the local Babylonian academies. Generally Jewish life flourished in Egypt under the Fatimids, and by the end of the tenth century a yeshivah was founded in Fostat. In addition, in Fostat, Alexandria and other towns in Egypt synagogues were founded by immigrants from Palestine and Babylonia.

By the tenth century Kairouan had also become an important Jewish centre. There academies were created by talmudists, and Jewish merchant families supported Jewish scholars and scientists. At this time Fez too became a centre of Jewish scholarship. There one of the most important talmudists of the eleventh century, Isaac Alfasi, produced a compendium of Jewish law which was a major contribution to post-geonic legal scholarship.

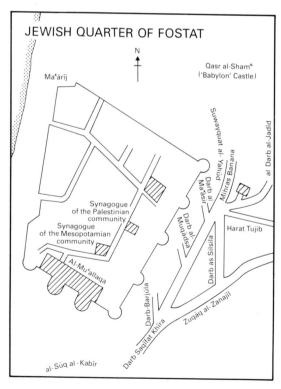

JEWISH QUARTER OF FOSTAT

N

Qasr al-Sham' ('Babylon' Castle)

Ma'ārij

Suwayquat al-Yahūd

al-Darb al-Jadīd

Darb al-Ma'āsir

Mihras Banana

Synagogue of the Palestinian community

Synagogue of the Mesopotamian community

Darb al-Muqadsa

Harat Tujib

Al-Mu'allaqa

Darb as Silsila

Darb-Barjūla

Darb Saqīfat Khīra

Zuqāq al-Zanajil

al-Sūq al-Kabīr

their learning rather than their status as head of one of the Babylonian academies. Further, Jewish learning broadened to include such secular subjects as natural science, philosophy, philology and poetry.

The most important region outside of Babylonia where local rabbis began to gain prominence was Palestine. Although Jews were persecuted in the Christian Roman empire in the fifth and sixth centuries, a rabbinic academy flourished in Tiberias. This was the centre of Masoretic learning. Here Masoretes established the standard tradition (*masorah*) of the Bible by vocalizing and punctuating the Hebrew text of Scripture. However, by the ninth century the academy of Tiberias was transferred to Ramleh and eventually to Jerusalem. Although the Jerusalem academy never attained the prominence of the Babylonian academies, it was sustained by the Jews of Egypt, Yemen and Syria when the Fatimid dynasty ruled Egypt and Palestine. Only when Palestine was invaded by Turks and Christians in the eleventh century did it undergo decline.

Jews in Muslim Spain and other lands

In the late Roman empire, a sizeable Jewish community lived in the Iberian peninsula. When the German visigoths came to power in the seventh century this population was bitterly persecuted. However, when the area was conquered by an Arab-Berber army at the beginning of the eighth century, the situation of Jews radically improved. As time passed Spanish Jewry was augmented by Middle Eastern and north African immigrants – eventually it became the largest Jewish settlement outside Babylonia. Under these favourable conditions Jews were active in a wide range of economic activities.

The Muslim authorities viewed the Jewish population as especially useful. Thus in the tenth century the Ummayad caliphs Abd al-Rahman III and Hakam II employed Hisdai ibn Shaprut as court physician, administrator of customs, and diplomat. In this capacity he acted as head of the Jewish community and became a patron of Jewish writers and scholars. During this period Cordoba served as the capital of the Ummayad caliphate and became a centre of Jewish scholarship. An important yeshivah was established there, and the city attracted Hebrew grammarians and poets.

In the next century the Ummayad caliphate began to disintegrate; in its place many small principalities emerged and engaged in conflict. A number of the rulers of these states employed Jewish courtiers such as Samuel ibn Nagrela of Granada. This distinguished Jewish figure was knowledgeable about mathematics, philosophy and literature and served as an accomplished statesman. For three decades he was Prime Minister of Granada and led its armies into battle. Other important Jewish courtiers resided in Seville, Saragossa, Cordoba, Toledo and Calatayud.

Of particular importance at this time was the city of Lucena, which was famed for its talmudic academy. There Isaac Alfasi trained a group of followers who became among the most famous halakhists of the age.

In 1086 the life of Spanish Jewry was disrupted when the Almoravides from North Africa penetrated into Spain to lead an onslaught on the Christian communities in the North; simultaneously they persecuted the Jewish population. None the less, Jews gained their former secure position.

In the next generation Jewish poets, philosophers, biblical commentators, rabbinic authorities and theologians played an important role in Spanish Jewish life. Yet in the middle of the twelfth century this golden age of Spanish Jewry ended. Fearing a Christian conquest, the Almohades (a Berber dynasty from Morocco) conquered the country and simultaneously devastated the Jewish community. Jews were compelled to convert to Islam, and academies and synagogues were shut. In response some Jews practised Judaism in secret while others fled to the Middle East or migrated to Christian Spain. The dominance of the Almohades ended at the beginning of the thirteenth century, however, when Christian kingdoms seized control of most of the former Spanish Muslim territories.

In other parts of the Muslim empire Jews also faced changing circumstances during these centuries. In the mid-twelfth century during the Almohade persecution, a number of Spanish Jews fled to Egypt, including the Jewish philosopher Moses Maimonides. In Israel a small community survived the Crusades and was later supplemented by Jewish pilgrims who migrated to the Holy Land. In Babylonia Jewry continued after the death of the last important gaon (Hai bar Sherira) in 1038. Nevertheless the Mongol conquests in the middle of the thirteenth century had devastating repercussions for the region. In western North Africa Jewish communities were free to follow their religious traditions when the Almohades were removed, and many Jews prospered. At this time a number of North African Jewish merchants took part in the Saharan gold trade, maintaining links with the Spanish kingdom of Aragon.

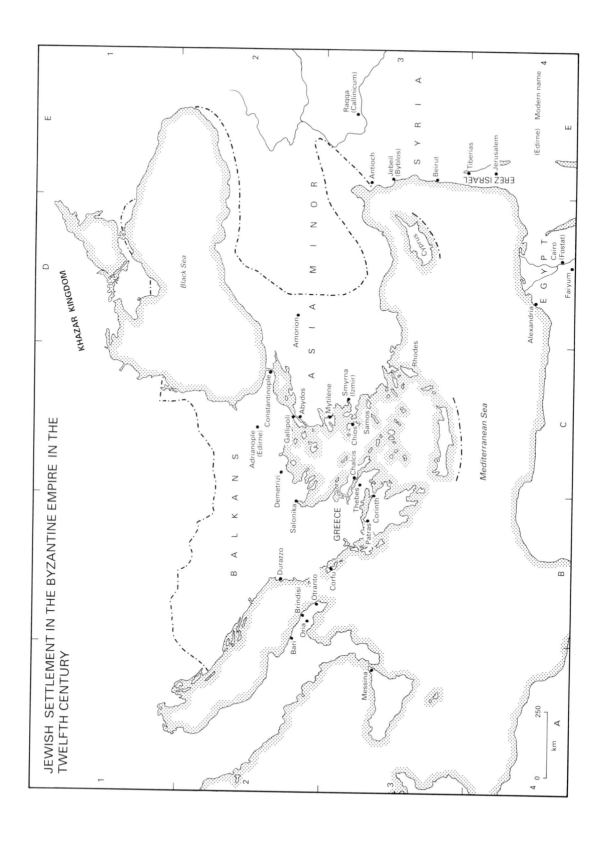

JEWISH SETTLEMENT IN THE BYZANTINE EMPIRE IN THE
TWELFTH CENTURY

KHAZAR KINGDOM

Black Sea

BALKANS

ASIA MINOR

SYRIA

Raqqa
(Callinicum)

Antioch

Jebeil
(Byblos)

Beirut

Tiberias

Jerusalem

EREZ ISRAEL

EGYPT

Cairo
(Fostat)

Faiyum

Alexandria

Constantinople

Adrianople
(Edirne)

Abydos

Gallipoli

Mytilene

Smyrna
(Izmir)

Chios

Samos

Rhodes

Cyprus

Mediterranean Sea

Demetrizi

Salonika

Chalcis

Thebes

Corinth

GREECE

Patras

Corfu

Durazzo

Otranto

Oria

Brindisi

Bari

Messina

Amorion

(Edirne) Modern name

km 0   250

A

7 JEWS IN MEDIEVAL CHRISTIAN EUROPE

Western European Jewry under Christian rule

Not all of the Byzantine empire was conquered by the Muslims in the seventh century, nor did Muslim forces subdue France and Italy. Instead the Jewish communities of these countries remained under Christian rule. Jews living in the Byzantine empire (Asia Minor, Greece and southern Italy) enjoyed considerable stability, although occasionally they were beset by persecution and forced conversion. However, even in secure periods Byzantine Jewry did not produce scholars and theologians of equal importance to those in other parts of the medieval world.

In southern Italy and Sicily, Jews living in such cities as Bari, Taranto, Oria, Venosa and Brindisi maintained close economic contact with Arab lands, thereby facilitating the transplantation of Jewish learning to Christian Europe. From the ninth century Hebrew treatises were written in southern Italy, rabbinic scholarship flourished, and Jews were active in scientific and philosophical circles. During this period Rome also became a centre of rabbinical learning. In Italy only a small number of Jews lived in the northern part of the country, but in southern France (in the area known as Provence, including Languedoc and northern Catalonia), old Jewish settlements prospered after the decline of Muslim Spain.

In the Middle Ages provincial liturgical rites and dialects were found in various parts of this region. The best known of these sectional groupings were the Sephardim in Spain, the Provençal Jews in southern France, the Italyani of Italy, the Romaniyots in Greece, the Musta´rabim in North Africa and the Middle East, the Judaeo-Persians in Persia and Judaeo-Tat in the eastern Caucasus.

North of the Alps a new branch of Jewish civilization (Ashkenazi) was emerging from the late eighth century. After the German onslaught that devastated the western Roman empire, city life disintegrated and central government became virtually impossible, which led to the devolution of political power into the hands of local lords. This political situation was interrupted by the rise of a powerful monarchy brought about by the early Carolingian rulers of France. Charlemagne (742–814) in particular took on the imperial Roman title in the West and expanded his empire into central Europe. After his death, however, the Carolingian realm divided into three kingdoms which later fragmented. As a result, early Ashkenazi Jews lived in an agrarian and largely feudal culture.

In the Carolingian period Jewish merchants in northern France and the Rhineland were generally well treated because of their economic connections with Mediterranean lands and the East. Jewish merchant groups (the Radanites), for example, travelled from France through eastern Europe to India and China. One of these traders – Isaac the Jew – was sent by Charlemagne with a deputation to the Abbasid caliph, returning with an elephant as a gift. Later Charlemagne's son, Louis the Pious (778–840), gave royal protection to the economic activity as well as the property of Jewish traders (despite the criticism of

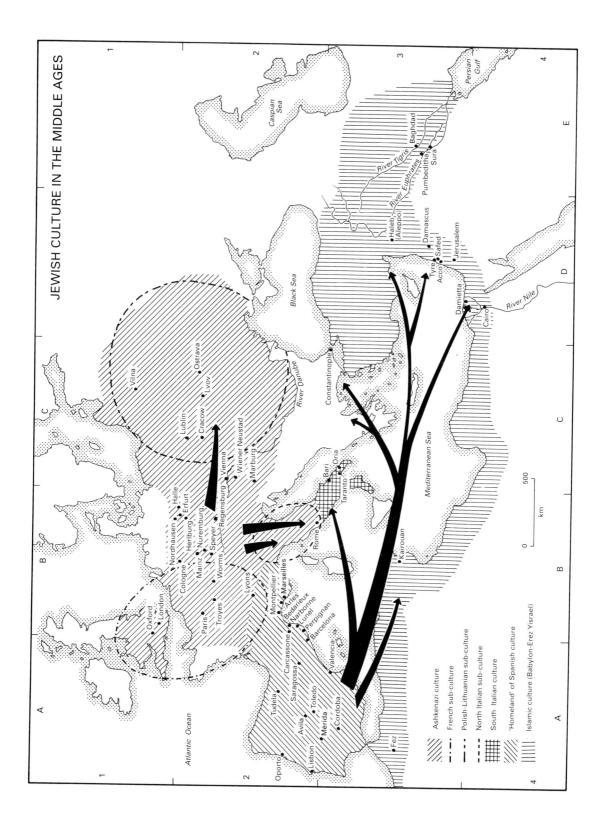

JEWISH CULTURE IN THE MIDDLE AGES

Ashkenazi culture

French sub-culture

Polish-Lithuanian sub-culture

North Italian sub-culture

South Italian culture

'Homeland' of Spanish culture

Islamic culture (Babylon-Erez Yisrael)

Atlantic Ocean

Oporto
Lisbon
Fez
Merida
Cordoba
Avila
Toledo
Valencia
Tudela
Saragossa
Barcelona
Perpignan
Carcassone
Lunel
Narbonne
Bedarieux
Arles
Montpellier
Marseilles
Lyons
Troyes
Paris
London
Oxford

Cologne
Nordhausen
Halle
Erfurt
Herlburg
Mainz
Nuremberg
Speyer
Regensburg
Worms
Wiener Neustad
Vienna
Marburg

Vilna
Lublin
Cracow
Lvov
Ostrava

Rome
Taranto
Bari
Oria

Kairouan

Cairo
Damietta
River Nile

Mediterranean Sea

Black Sea

Caspian Sea

Constantinople

River Danube

Acco
Tyre
Safed
Jerusalem
Damascus
Haleb
(Aleppo)

River Tigris
River Euphrates
Baghdad
Pumbeditha
Sura
Persian Gulf

0   500
km

Agobard, Bishop of Lyons). Subsequently in the tenth and eleventh centuries Jewish merchants established links with kings and barons in northern France and Germany. Although such Ashkenazi trade decreased towards the end of this period, these Jews were active in such urban centres as the county of Campagne and along the Rhine (at Mainz, Worms, Speyer and Cologne).

Ashkenazi Jewry

In lands where Ashkenazi Jews settled, their numbers were relatively small since the majority of Jewish craftsmen and artisans did not emigrate to northern Europe. None the less wherever they resided, the Jewish community in each respective town constituted an independent, self-governing body (*kahal*). Unlike Jewry in Muslim countries, these Ashkenazi communities had no professional bureaucracy or communal head such as the exilarch. Rather each *kahal* established its own spiritual regulations (*takkanot*). In addition, the judicial court in each *kahal* enforced its rulings with the threat of excommunication (*herem*): such a decree was used to censure individuals and deprive them of social relations with other Jews.

In such a setting biblical and talmudic studies flourished in the tenth century in the Rhineland cities of Mainz and Worms and later in northern France at Troyes and Sens. Initially rabbinic learning consisted largely of oral discussion – among the most distinguished scholars of this period was Rabbenu Gershom of Worms, who issued numerous *takkanot* and legal opinions which gained widespread acceptance. Another major figure of Ashkenazi Jewry was Solomon ben Isaac of Troyes (1040–1105) – known as Rashi – who produced commentaries on the Bible and the Talmud. These exhaustive works were based on midrashic literature and stress the plain meaning of the text. In the generation after Rashi, the analysis of talmudic law reached great heights, and scholars in northern France and Germany (including some of Rashi's family) evolved new methods of talmudic argumentation. These individuals, the tosafists, greatly expanded traditional teaching. Further, other Ashkenazi Jews composed religious poetry based on the liturgical poems (*piyyutim*) of fifth- and sixth-century Palestine.

Another important development of this period was the emergence of a mystical movement (*Hasidei Ashkenaz*) in the Rhineland. Among the leading figures of the twelfth century was Samuel ben Kalonymous of Speyer, his son Judah ben Samuel I of Regensberg, who wrote *The Book of the Pious*, and Eleazar ben Judah of Worms, who composed *The Secret of Secrets*. In their writings these mystics dwelt on the mystery of divine Unity. According to these sages God himself cannot be known by human reason; thus all anthropomorphic descriptions of God in the Bible should be interpreted as referring to his glory (*kavod*). This divine glory was revealed to the prophets and has been made manifest to mystics through the centuries. The aim of the *Hasidei Ashkenaz* was to gain a vision of God's *kavod* through the cultivation of pietism (*chasiduth*) – this involved devotion, saintliness and contemplation. The ultimate sacrifice for the mystics was selfless love resulting in martyrdom.

Within this framework the concept of the pious person (*hasid*) was of central importance. To be a *hasid* was a religious ideal, transcending all scholarly attainments. For the *Hasidei Ashkenazi*, the *hasid* must overcome all temptation; he should renounce worldly goods, mortify the flesh and make penance for transgression. Such asceticism, they believed, would lead the devotee to love and fear God. In its highest form such fear was viewed as identical with loving devotion, enabling joy to enter the *hasid*'s soul. Among these sages humility and self-abnegation were the hallmarks of authentic spirituality.

Another aspect of this movement was the espousal of prayer mysticism. As a result, pietistic literature focused on the techniques of mystical speculation based on the calculation of words in prayers and hymns. The number of words in a

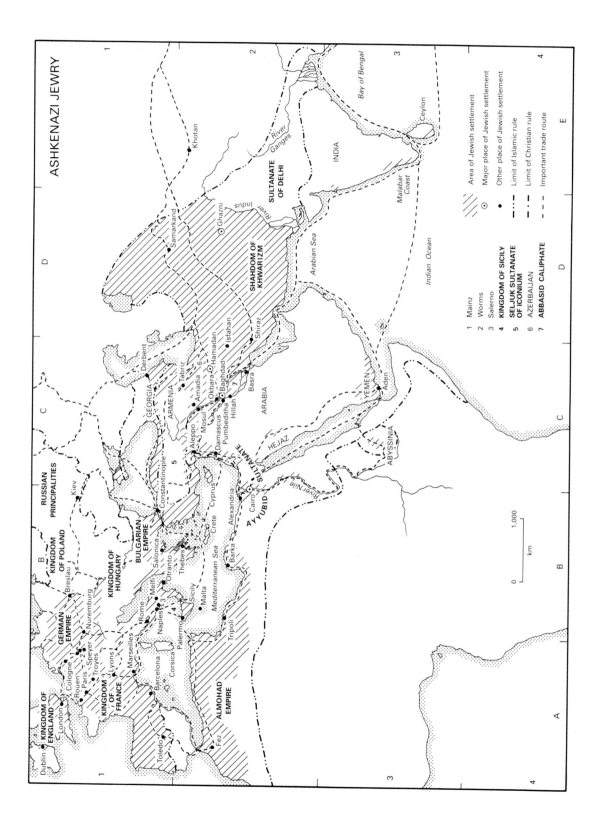

ASHKENAZI JEWRY

Legend:

- Area of Jewish settlement
- ⊙ Major place of Jewish settlement
- ● Other place of Jewish settlement
- —··— Limit of Islamic rule
- —·—·— Limit of Christian rule
- — — — Important trade route

1 Mainz
2 Worms
3 Salerno
4 **KINGDOM OF SICILY**
5 **SELJUK SULTANATE OF ICONIUM**
6 AZERBAIJAN
7 **ABBASID CALIPHATE**

Scale: 0 — 1,000 km

Labels on map: KINGDOM OF ENGLAND, Dublin, London, GERMAN EMPIRE, Cologne, Rouen, Nuremburg, Breslau, KINGDOM OF POLAND, KINGDOM OF HUNGARY, RUSSIAN PRINCIPALITIES, Kiev, KINGDOM OF FRANCE, Paris, Speyer, Troyes, Lyons, Marseilles, Barcelona, Toledo, Corsica, ALMOHAD EMPIRE, Fez, Tripoli, Sardinia, Rome, Naples, Palermo, Sicily, Malta, Melfi, Otranto, Thebes, Salonica, BULGARIAN EMPIRE, Constantinople, Crete, Cyprus, Mediterranean Sea, Barka, Alexandria, Cairo, AYYUBID SULTANATE, River Nile, HEJAZ, ARABIA, YEMEN, Aden, ABYSSINIA, Aleppo, Damascus, Pumbeditha, Hillah, Basra, Baghdad, Okbara, Mosul, Amadia, Hamadan, Isfahan, Shiraz, Tabriz, Armenia, ARMENIA, GEORGIA, Derbent, Samarkand, Ghazni, SHAHDOM OF KHWARIZM, River Indus, SULTANATE OF DELHI, INDIA, Malabar Coast, Ceylon, Khotan, River Ganges, Bay of Bengal, Arabian Sea, Indian Ocean

prayer and its numerical value were linked to scriptural passages of equal numerical value as well as with designations of God and the angels. In such calculations the mystical techniques of *gematria* (the calculation of the numerical value of Hebrew words) and *notarikon* (the interpretation of the letters of a word as abbreviations of sentences) were frequently employed. For these pious individuals prayer was viewed like Jacob's ladder leading to heaven, a process of mystical ascent.

The First Crusade and aftermath

During the medieval period Ashkenazi Jewry suffered a series of massacres. When Pope Urban II proclaimed the First Crusade in 1095 at Clermont in south-eastern France, groups of Crusaders set out for the Rhineland, where they devastated the local Jewish population. In some instances (such as at Speyer) local bishops aided the Jewish community; in other cities (Worms and Mainz), however, Jewry was less fortunate. Faced with this Christian onslaught many Jews died as martyrs for the sake of the Divine Name. None the less, this massacre did not bring about an alteration in the status of medieval Jewry — Jews who had been forcefully converted were allowed to return to the faith of their ancestors. In 1103 the emperor extended to Jews the protection afforded to clergy; any pogrom against them was accountable to the emperor himself.

In the following two centuries Ashkenazi Jews of Germany, northern France and England were forced out of trade by Christian guilds and began to engage in moneylending. In this activity they stood outside the legal jurisdiction and control of the Church, and there was considerable competition for loans from Jews. Any Church effort to abolish usury was inapplicable to Jews as long as they were supported by the aristocracy and royalty. The secular authorities thereby became partners in the business of moneylending, extracting their share of profits through taxation. Despite such connivance, this practice exacerbated Christian hostility toward Jews, particularly among those who were unable to repay their debts.

In the later Middle Ages religious anti-Semitism served to inflame Christian Judaeophobia. For many Christians the persistence of Jews and Judaism was perceived as posing a serious threat to society. As a result Jews were frequently accused of demonic activities. In Norwich, England in 1144, for example, Jews were charged with killing Christian children to use their blood for making unleavened bread (*matzah*) for Passover. Other blood libels appeared in Blois in 1171 and Lincoln in 1255. Another common medieval accusation was the claim that Jews profaned the Host; they allegedly attacked the wafer to torture the body of Jesus. In the light of such Christian contempt, Pope Innocent III adopted a critical attitude toward Jewish moneylending. In a letter to the King of France in 1205 he wrote:

> The Lord made Cain a wanderer and a fugitive over the earth, but set a mark upon him ... Thus the Jews, against whom the blood of Jesus Christ calls out, although they ought not to be killed ... yet as wanderers ought they to remain upon the earth, until their countenance be filled with shame and they seek the name of Jesus Christ, the Lord. That is why blasphemers of the Christian name ought not to be aided by Christian princes to oppress the servants of the Lord, but ought rather be forced into the servitude of which they made themselves deserving when they raised sacrilegious hands against Him Who had come to confer true liberty upon them, thus calling down His blood upon themselves and upon their children.
>
> (Solomon Grayzel, *The Church and the Jews in the Thirteenth Century* (New York: Herman Press, 1966), p. 127)

In 1215 the First Lateran Council, convened by

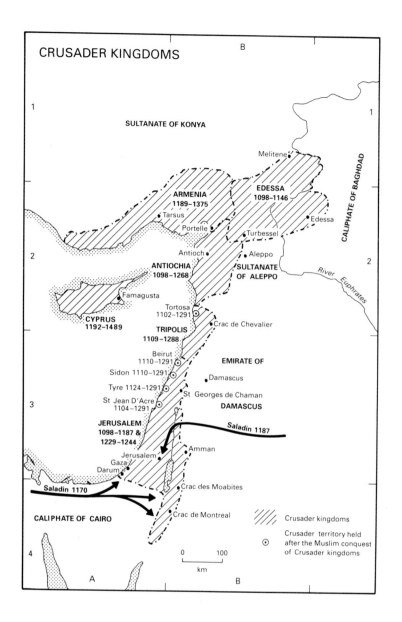

CRUSADER KINGDOMS

SULTANATE OF KONYA

Melitene

ARMENIA
1189–1375

EDESSA
1098–1146

Edessa

Tarsus

Portelle

Turbessel

Antioch

Aleppo

ANTIOCHIA
1098–1268

SULTANATE
OF ALEPPO

CALIPHATE OF BAGHDAD

River Euphrates

Famagusta

CYPRUS
1192–1489

Tortosa
1102–1291

Crac de Chevalier

TRIPOLIS
1109–1288

EMIRATE OF

Beirut
1110–1291

Damascus

Sidon 1110–1291

Tyre 1124–1291

St Georges de Chaman

St Jean D'Acre
1104–1291

DAMASCUS

JERUSALEM
1098–1187 &
1229–1244

Saladin 1187

Jerusalem

Amman

Gaza

Darum

Crac des Moabites

Saladin 1170

Crac de Montreal

CALIPHATE OF CAIRO

0   100
km

/// Crusader kingdoms

⊙ Crusader territory held
   after the Muslim conquest
   of Crusader kingdoms

Innocent III, attempted to regulate Jewish affairs by reaffirming the previous Christian regulations against the Jews. In addition, in the same century the Dominicans took an active role in anti-Jewish polemic. In 1240 they participated in a public debate with Jews in Paris – this resulted in the decision to burn the Talmud since it was viewed as slandering the Christian religion. Subsequently another disputation was held in Barcelona, where Jews sought to demonstrate that rabbinic teaching supported the Christian conception of the Messiah.

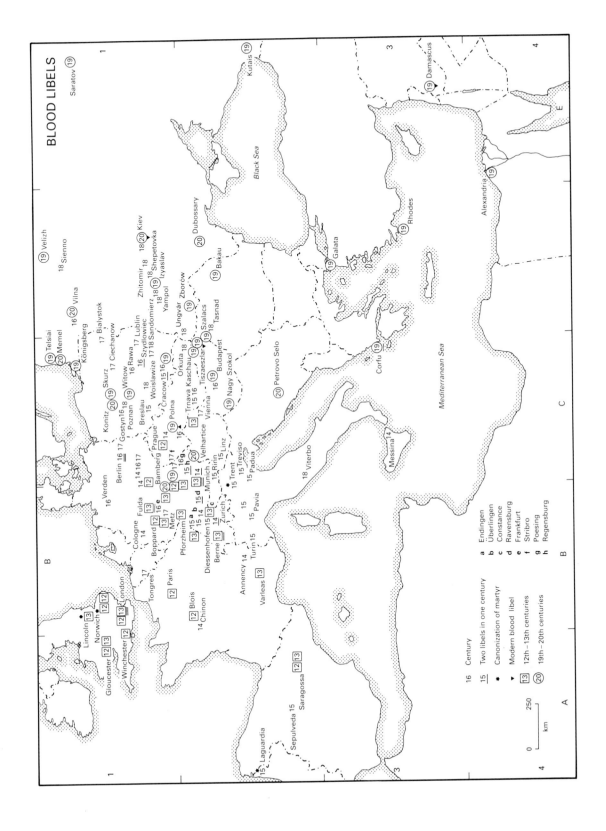

BLOOD LIBELS

Saratov ⑲

Velizh ⑲
Sienno 18

Kutais ⑲

Damascus ⑲
⑲▸

Kiev 18
Zhitomir 18
Shepetovka 18
Izyaslav 18⑲
Yampol 18

Alexandria ⑲

Rhodes ⑲

Dubossary ⑳

Galata ⑲

Bakau ⑲

Black Sea

Telsiai ⑲
Memel ⑳
Vilna ⑳ 16
Bialystok 17
Königsberg

Szalacs ⑲
Tasnad 18
Ungvár ⑲
Zborów ⑲
Orkuta 18
Tiszaeszlár ⑲▸
Budapest ⑲ 18
Nagy Szokol 16
Vienna ⑲
Petrovo Selo ⑳

Corfu ⑲

Mediterranean Sea

Skurz 17 Ciechanow
Konitz ⑳⑲
Gostyn 16 18
Poznan ⑲
Witow
Rawa 17 Lublin
Szydlowiec 16
Woislawize 17 18 Sandomierz
Cracow 15 16 ⑲
Polna ⑲
Trnava Kaschau ⑲
Velhartice 17
15 16
Rinn
Linz
Treviso
Padua 15
Pavia 15

Verden

Berlin 16 17
Breslau 18
Prague 15
Bamberg 14
Fulda 14
Boppard 12 16
Metz 13 17
Pforzheim 13
Diessenhofen 15 13
Berne 14
Turin 15
Varleas 13
Annency 14

Cologne 14
16

Viterbo 18

Messina 14

Tongres 17
Paris
Blois 12
Chinon 14

Lincoln 13
Norwich 12
Gloucester 12 13
Winchester 12
London 12 13

Sepulveda 15
Saragossa 12 13

Laguardia 15

Munich 13 14
Zurich
Trent 15
15 d
15 e
15 a
15 b
c
f
g
h
15

16	Century
15	Two libels in one century
*	Canonization of martyr
▸	Modern blood libel
13	12th–13th centuries
20	19th–20th centuries

a	Endingen
b	Überlingen
c	Constance
d	Ravensburg
e	Frankfurt
f	Stribro
g	Poesing
h	Regensburg

km 0 250

A   B   C

1   2   3   4

Figure 10 *The profanation of the Host,* a series of six panels, Paolo Uccello (Galleria Nazionale delle Marche, Soprintendenza per i Beni Artistici e Storici delle March, Urbino)

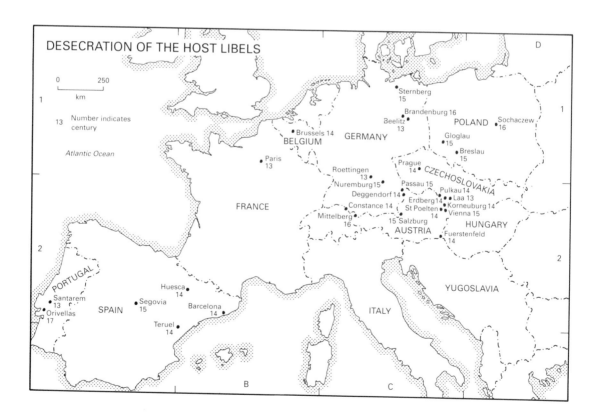

Figure 11 Six panels illustrating a legend about the theft by a Jew of a picture of the Virgin Mary (Biblioteca de el Escorial, Madrid)

Expulsion and devastation

In 1182 Jews were expelled from the French royal domains; their property was confiscated and all Christian debts were cancelled. Twelve years later, however, Jewry was recalled, and an additional tax was added to its burdens. In thirteenth-century England the kings similarly increased Jewish taxation. But when Italian banking firms began to supply the monarch with funds, Jews were no longer needed: in 1290 they were expelled, and their dwellings and capital transferred to the king. During this period the French king Louis IX instituted a campaign against usury, thereby freeing his subjects from part of their debts to Jewish creditors. Later Philip IV encouraged hostility toward the Jewish population by supporting a ritual murder trial at Troyes in 1288, and another trial in Paris in 1290 concerning the profanation of the Host. In 1306 an edict of expulsion was promulgated, and the French treasury took over all debts owed to Jews.

In Germany Jews founded new communities and became an important source of revenue for the crown. In other lands (Bohemia, Austria, Hungary and parts of eastern central Europe) they received charters which protected their lives and property. None the less at the end of the thirteenth century Jewry was subject to persecution and violence – in Germany mobs destroyed 140 Jewish communities. Three decades later a series of massacres took place, and during the Black Plague (1348–9) it was widely assumed that the Jews were responsible for this plague by poisoning wells. In consequence the slaughter of Jewry spread from southern France in September 1348 to Switzerland and western Germany, and later to Belgium, northern Germany and Bavaria.

This onslaught was in part instigated by flagellants who travelled from place to place condemning the Jews. As a chronicler, Jean d'Outremouse, recorded:

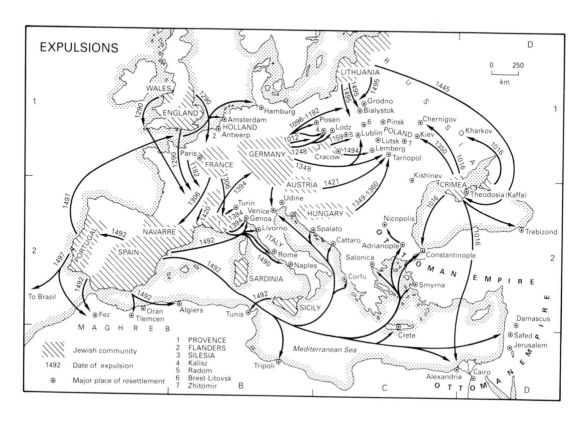

EXPULSIONS

1 PROVENCE
2 FLANDERS
3 SILESIA
4 Kalisz
5 Radom
6 Brest-Litovsk
7 Zhitomir

Jewish community

1492 Date of expulsion

⊙ Major place of resettlement

The good cities were full of these flagellants, and the streets as well … in the time when these flagellants went among the countries … it was commonly said and certainly believed that this epidemic came from the Jews, and that the Jews had cast great poisons in the wells and springs throughout the world, in order to sow the plague and poison Christendom.

In Germany Jews who survived this devastation were not expelled since there was no central authority able to issue such a decree. Yet in the following centuries many German localities expelled the Jews only to recall them, confining Jewish residents to special quarters. Legally they were serfs of the royal exchequer (property of the emperor or the agency which regulated their affairs).

The expulsions and massacres of these centuries traumatized the Jewish population throughout Europe. Some of their reactions were incorporated into the Jewish liturgy; others served as the basis of religious chants. In various chronicles of this period Jewish animosity was expressed in the most vehement terms. The chronicler Solomon bar Simeon, for example, declared:

O God of vengeance, O Lord God of vengeance, appear: It is from thee that we have let ourselves be slaughtered every day. Return sevenfold the wrongs of neighbours so that they may curse you! Before our very eyes let the nations be punished for the blood of their servants that they have shed.

Those who died in the Christian onslaught and remained faithful to their ancestral faith were regarded as hallowing God's Name. In their heroism and faithfulness these victims cried out to God for revenge. Hatred and devotion were thus mixed together in the blood and tears of those who perished in these terrible centuries of suffering.

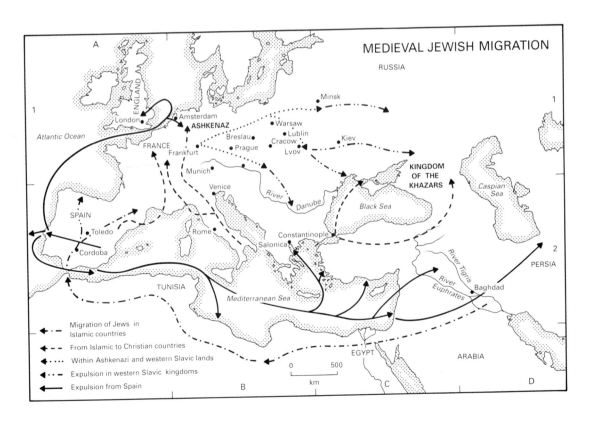

MEDIEVAL JEWISH MIGRATION

◄─·─ Migration of Jews in Islamic countries
◄─ ─ From Islamic to Christian countries
◄····· Within Ashkenazi and western Slavic lands
◄─··· Expulsion in western Slavic kingdoms
◄─── Expulsion from Spain

Jews in Christian Spain

After the conquest of the Iberian peninsula, the Christian kingdoms of Castile, Aragon and Portugal contained both Jews and Muslims – for two centuries these three monotheistic faiths lived together in relative harmony. In these lands Jews engaged in a wide range of activities: they worked as shopkeepers, artisans, physicians and money-lenders. During this period Spanish Jews were more numerous than the Ashkenazi Jews of any single country and contained a broader range of social classes. In addition, in the thirteenth century nearly all Spanish kings had Jewish royal advisers. The legal status of the Spanish Jewry resembled the *kehillot* in northern Europe: these communities were granted charters which guaranteed economic rights as well as the freedom to follow Jewish law. These Sephardic communities (*aljamas*) had more members than northern *kahals*; they were essentially Spanish Jewish cities within Christian cities. Each Jewish locality regulated its bureaucratic structure, social services, educational institutions and judicial procedures.

As in Muslim Spain, a number of Spanish Jews were exposed to secular learning, making contributions to geography, astronomy and medicine. In addition, the thirteenth century witnessed an efflorescence of mystical activity, resulting in the emergence of the mystical tradition known as kabbalah. In the field of legal inquiry, such rabbis as Moses ben Nahman and Solomon ibn Adret of Barcelona made major contributions to the development of *halakhah* (Jewish law). In the same century Jacob ben Asher compiled a major code of Jewish law, the *Arbaah Turim*, which summarized Jewish law in the diaspora.

Despite such cultural and religious activity, Jews in the north were subject to continual persecution. In the 1360s Henry of Trastamara

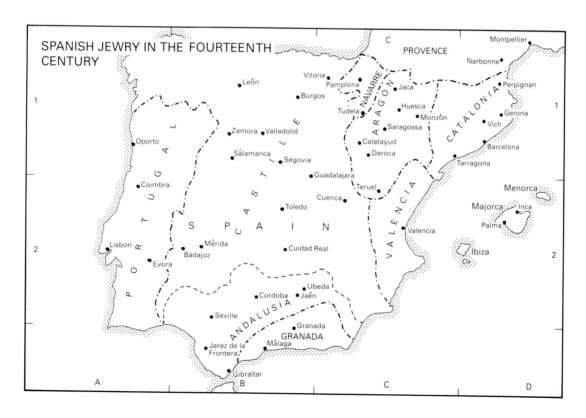

SPANISH JEWRY IN THE FOURTEENTH CENTURY

93

encouraged Jew-hatred, which set the stage for widespread violence. In 1391 mobs massacred Jewish communities throughout Castile and Aragon. In the same year thousands of Jews converted to Christianity to protect themselves from such danger. None the less Spanish rulers introduced legislation which sought to isolate the Jewish community from Christians. This new policy was intensified by the initiation of a public disputation in 1413–14 in Tortosa, where Jewish representatives were compelled to defend their doctrine of the Messiah. The prosecution was conducted by a converted Jew, and the proceedings were blessed by the Pope. As a consequence of this debate, further pressure was applied to the Jewish community to convert. Eventually the number of Jewish converts (*conversos*) was equal to the number of those who had refused to abandon their ancestral faith.

Initially the *conversos* discovered that their position in society had dramatically improved – they were able to enter into Spanish communal life. Many obtained positions in city government, state administration and the Church. Even the Spanish nobility and the royal family of Aragon married the offspring of rich *conversos*. Faced with such widespread apostasy, those Jews who had not converted attempted to rebuild their communities and strengthen the Jewish tradition. In some locations *aljamas* were resurrected, and new Jewish settlements were established in northern Castile.

In the fifteenth century a new wave of anti-Jewish sentiment affected Spanish society. Antagonistic to *conversos* who engaged in tax collection, anti-*converso* riots took place in Toledo in 1449 and later in other cities. This onslaught was rationalized by the conviction that these new Christians secretly engaged in Jewish religious practices. The term *marrano* ('swine') was used to designate these backsliders. By 1480 the Spanish Inquisition was established by King Ferdinand and Queen Isabella to investigate such allegations. Thousands of offenders were forced to make penance and their property was confiscated; those who refused to confess were burned at the stake. By the end of the century (1492) an edict was issued which expelled the Jews from Spain: many fled to Portugal; others went to north Africa, Italy and Ottoman Turkey.

8 MEDIEVAL JEWISH THOUGHT

Saadiah Gaon

Saadiah ben Joseph was the earliest philosopher of the medieval period. Born in Pithom in the Fayim district of Egypt, he settled in Babylonia in 921. In 928 he became gaon of Sura and wrote studies on various subjects including Hebrew philology, Jewish liturgy and *halakhah*. In addition he produced the first theological treatise of the Middle Ages, *The Book of Beliefs and Opinions*. In this work Saadiah countered the religious beliefs of Christians, Muslims and Zoroastrians. Basing his arguments on the *kalam* (teachings of the Muslim schools), he insisted that there are four sources of knowledge: sense experience, intuition of self-evident truths, logical inference and reliable tradition. The last source (derived from the first three) is the basis of civilization. Of divine origin, it provides guidance and protection against uncertainty.

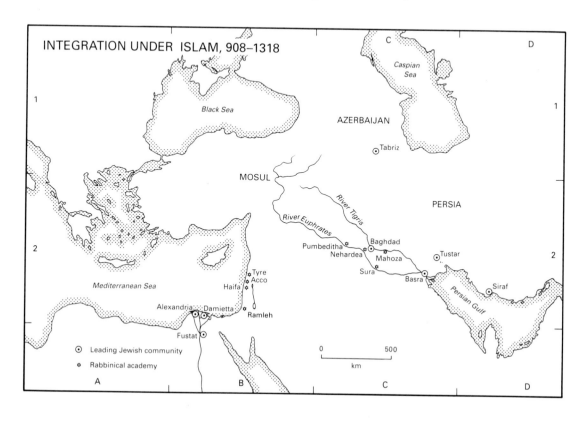

INTEGRATION UNDER ISLAM, 908–1318

⊙ Leading Jewish community
✿ Rabbinical academy

Applying the teachings of the Mutazilites (a school of Muslim thought), Saadiah maintained that faith and reason are compatible. On the basis of this assumption he attempted to prove that God exists since the universe must have had a beginning. According to Saadiah, time is only rational if it has a beginning since it is impossible to pass from an infinite past to the present. The Creator, he argued, is a single, incorporeal Being who formed the universe *ex nihilo*. Like the Mutazalite philosophers, Saadiah believed that if God has a plurality of attributes he must be composite in nature. Hence such terms as 'life', 'omnipotence' and 'omniscience' should be interpreted as implications of the concept of God as Creator rather than as divine attributes. We are forced to describe God in this way, he believed, because of the limitations of human language. But such terms do not denote plurality in God. In this light Saadiah stressed that the anthropomorphic expressions in the Bible should not be understood literally. Thus when we read in Scripture that God has a head, eye, ear, mouth, face or hand, these descriptions should be understood figuratively. Likewise when human activity is ascribed to God or when he appears in a theophany, such depictions should be interpreted in a figurative sense.

Regarding human nature Saadiah believed that individuals possess souls which are substances created by God at the time when bodies come into being. The soul is not pre-existent, nor does it enter the body externally; instead it uses the body as an instrument. When connected to a corporeal frame, the soul has three main faculties: reason, spirit and desire. None the less it is incapable of activity if it is separated from the body. As for the sufferings which the soul endures because of such a bodily connection, some are due to its negligence, whereas others are inflicted for the soul's good so that it can subsequently be rewarded.

So as to lead a fulfilled life, humans have been given commandments. These are of two types. The first consists of those acts which reason recognizes as good or bad through a feeling of approval or disapproval. For example humans perceive that murder is wrong because it would lead to the destruction of humanity and also frustrate God's purposes. The second type embraces those acts which are neither right nor wrong intrinsically but are made so through God's decree. Such laws are imposed on human beings so that they will be rewarded for obeying them. They are not arbitrary, however, since they have beneficial consequences. Laws of purity, for example, teach humility and make prayer more precious for those who have been prevented from praying because of ritual uncleanliness. Because these traditional laws are not inherently rational, divine revelation is required to supplement the human rational capacity. Further, divine legislation is needed to clarify the moral principles which are recognized by reason.

Jewish philosophy in Muslim Spain

From the eleventh century the Mutazilite *kalam* ceased to play an important role in Jewish philosophy. The Mutazalites were replaced by the more orthodox Asharyites, who attempted to offer a rational basis for unquestioning traditionalism. According to these Muslim thinkers, everything that occurs is the result of God's will. Moreover, they insisted that all existing objects are composed of elements of space and time which were directly created by God. Such views were less attractive to Jewish scholars than the systems of Neoplatonism and Aristotelianism as propounded by a number of Muslim philosophers.

The first Spanish Jewish Neoplatonic philosopher was Solomon ben Joseph ibn Gabirol (1020–57) from Malaga. In his *Fountain of Life*, published in the eleventh century, ibn Gabirol maintained that God and matter are not opposed as ultimate principles – rather matter is identified with God. It emanates from God's essence, forming the basis of all subsequent emanations.

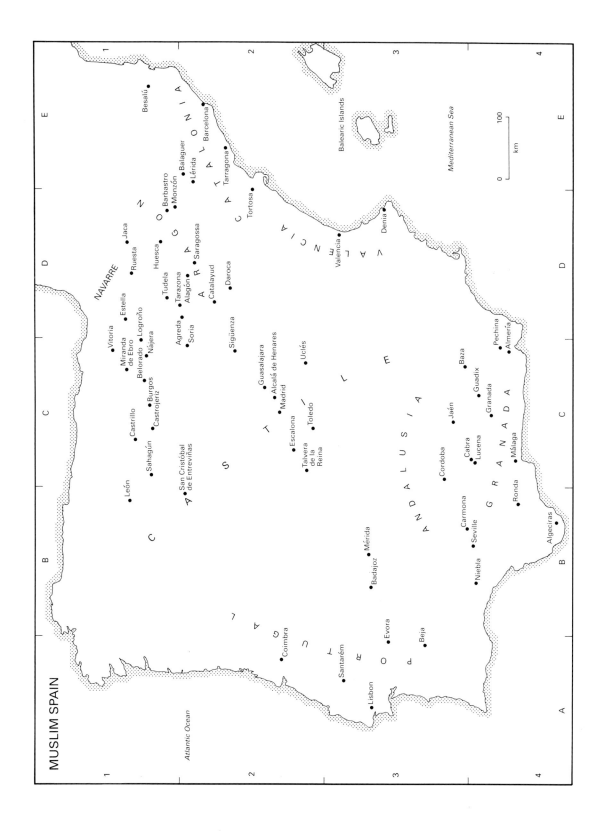

MUSLIM SPAIN

Atlantic Ocean

Mediterranean Sea

Balearic Islands

100

km

0

NAVARRE

Besalú

Barcelona
Balaguer
Lérida
Monzón
Barbastro
Tarragona
Tortosa

Jaca
Ruesta
Huesca
Saragossa
Tudela
Tarazona
Alagón
Catalayud
Daroca

VALENCIA

Denia

Valencia

Vitoria
Miranda
de Ebro
Estella
Logroño
Belorado
Nájera

Agreda
Soria

Sigüenza

Castrillo
Burgos
Castrojeriz

Sahagún

León

San Cristóbal
de Entreviñas

Guasalajara
Alcalá de Henares
Madrid

Uclés

Escalona
Toledo

Talvera
de la
Reina

Pechina
Almería

Baza
Guadix
Granada

Jaén

Cabra
Lucena

Cordoba

Málaga
Ronda

Carmona
Seville

Niebla

Mérida

Badajoz

Algeciras

ANDALUSIA

GRANADA

Coimbra

Santarém

Lisbon

Evora

Beja

PORTUGAL

CASTILE

NAVARRE

ARAGON

CATALONIA

The universe therefore consists of cosmic influences flowing out of the superabundant light and goodness of the Deity – creation is hence a reflection of God, though the Divine remains in himself and does not penetrate his creation with his essence. In his poem 'Kingly Crown' ibn Gabirol utilized Neoplatonic imagery to depict such activity: 'Thou art wise and from Thy wisdom didst cause to emanate a ready will, an agent and artist as it were, to draw existence out of non-existence, as light proceeds from the eye.'

Another Spanish philosopher of this period, Bahya ben Joseph ibn Pakuda (1050–1120) from Saragossa, also employed Neoplatonic conceptions in his ethical treatise, *Duties of the Heart*. The purpose of this work was to correct what ibn Pakuda perceived as an overemphasis on ritualism in rabbinic Judaism. For ibn Pakuda, there are two kinds of obligations. First, there are duties involving action such as ritual and ethical observances. Second, there are commands related to the inner life. Echoing the views of Islamic mystics, this study attempts to lead Jews through a number of ascending stages of the inner life toward spiritual perfection and communion with the Godhead. In accordance with Neoplatonism, ibn Pakuda stressed that the soul is celestial in origin and placed in the human body by God. However, through reason and revealed law the soul can overcome the evil inclination.

Another important thinker of this period was Abraham ben David Halevi ibn Daud (1110–80) from Cordoba. In his *The Exalted Faith*, he drew on Aristotelian categories to harmonize the Bible with rational thought. Following Islamic Aristotelianism, ibn Daud deduced God's unity from his necessary existence – this concept of absolute oneness precludes the possibility of ascribing any positive attributes to God. Concerning the afterlife, ibn Daud argued that the soul is able to survive death without the body because the activities of the intellect are not dependent on the existence of the body. Ibn Daud also argued that since human beings have free will God does not know beforehand the outcome of an individual's free choice.

In contrast to such rationalistic formulations of Jewish belief, Judah Halevi (1075–1141) from Toledo attempted to prove in his *The Book of the Khazars* that Judaism cannot be understood solely by the intellect. This treatise contains a dialogue between a king of the Khazars and a Jewish sage who defends Judaism against Aristotelian philosophy as well as Christianity and Islam. According to Halevi, it is divine revelation rather than philosophy which offers the true guide to the spiritual life. Aristotelianism, he insisted, is not scientific and its conclusions are inadequate. The God of the philosophers is not interested in human affairs, nor is he attentive to prayer. In contrast the God of the Bible is intimately involved in history and is near to those who call upon him.

Halevi was also critical of the Aristotelian contention that the highest human attainment is knowledge of the most elevated type. According to Halevi, the Torah declares that the highest human ideal is not an actualization of the intellect, but instead prophetic inspiration, which is a gift from God. It is bestowed on only a few individuals and can only occur in the land of Israel. Since most Jews live in the diaspora, no prophets have emerged since the biblical period; only when messianic redemption occurs will prophetic activity again take place. Regarding biblical law, Halevi emphasized its supra-rational qualities. For Halevi ritual observances transcend rational explanation. Yet despite these observations, Halevi believed that the Jewish faith does not conflict with the study of the natural world, nor does reason undermine the Torah.

Moses Maimonides

Born in Cordoba in the twelfth century, Moses Maimonides (1134–1204) was the greatest Jewish philosopher of the medieval period. When the Almohades came to power, he fled from Spain and settled in Cairo, where he produced numerous studies. In his *Guide for the Perplexed*, he relied on such Muslim expositors of Aristotle as Avicenna and Al-Farabi. According to Maimonides, faith and reason must be harmoniously related; in this work he criticized various features of Mutazalite and Asharyite philosophy, attempting to reconcile the Torah with the tenets of Aristotelianism.

In the introduction to the *Guide*, Maimonides explained that his book was intended for those whose study of logic, mathematics, natural science and metaphysics had led them into a state of perplexity about the apparent conflict between the Torah and reason. In the first part of this treatise, Maimonides discussed the anthropomorphic terms in Scripture. Like Saadiah, he argued that they must be interpreted figuratively rather than literally. In this connection he maintained, as did ibn Daud, that no positive attributes should be predicated of God since the Godhead is an absolute unity. The only true attributes are negative ones – they direct the faithful to a knowledge of God, since in negation no plurality is involved. These negative attributes exclude any imperfection from God's essence. For Maimonides, such negation draws one nearer to the true comprehension of the Deity.

Concerning prophecy, Maimonides noted that most people think that God chooses any person he wishes and inspires him with the prophetic spirit. Yet such a view is opposed by those philosophers who stress that prophecy is a human gift requiring prolonged study. Rejecting both positions, Maimonides declared that prophecy is an inspiration from God which passes through the mediation of the active intellect and then on to the faculty of imagination. Prophecy, he believed, requires perfection in theoretical wisdom and morality as well as the development of the imagination. On this basis, Maimonides

contended that human beings can be divided into three groups according to the development of their reasoning. First there are those whose rational faculties are developed and receive influences from the active intellect but whose imagination is defective. These are the wise men and philosophers. The second group is composed of those whose imagination is good, but the intellect lacking: these are statesmen, lawgivers and politicians. Finally there are the prophets, whose imagination is constitutionally perfect and whose active intellect is well developed. Maimonides stressed that God withholds prophetic inspiration

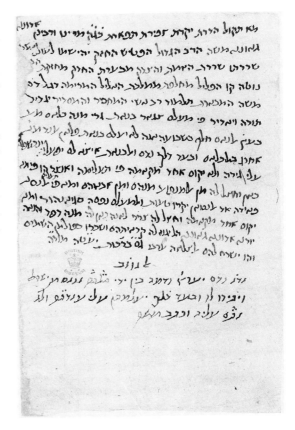

Figure 12 Autograph responsum of Maimonides (British Library)

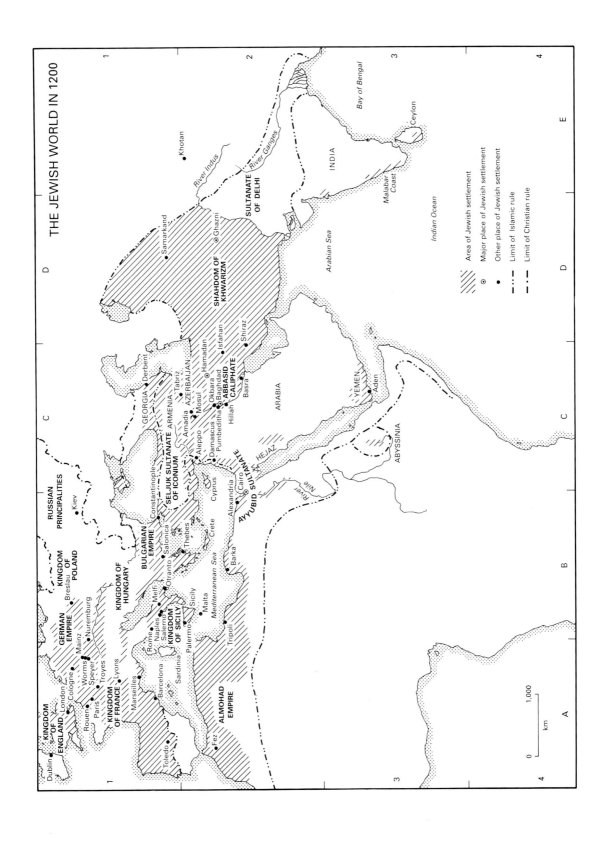

THE JEWISH WORLD IN 1200

Dublin

KINGDOM
OF
ENGLAND   London
                   Cologne
                   Mainz   Nuremburg
Rouen   Speyer
              Worms
Paris   Troyes   Lyons
KINGDOM OF FRANCE
Marseilles

Toledo   Barcelona
Fez   Sardinia
ALMOHAD
EMPIRE

RUSSIAN
PRINCIPALITIES

Kiev

KINGDOM
OF POLAND

Breslau

GERMAN
EMPIRE

KINGDOM OF HUNGARY

BULGARIAN
EMPIRE

Rome   Salernoo
Naples
Melfi
Otranto
KINGDOM
OF SICILY
Palermo   Sicily
Malta
Tripoli

Constantinople

Salonica
Thebes

Crete

Mediterranean Sea

Barka

Alexandria   Cairo
AYYUBID SULTANATE

Cyprus

SELJUK SULTANATE
OF ICONIUM

ARMENIA
Amadia
Aleppo
Damascus

GEORGIA   Derbent

Tabriz
AZERBAIJAN
Mosul   Hamadan
Okbara   Baghdad   Isfahan
Pumbeditha   ABBASID
Hillah   CALIPHATE
Basra   Shiraz

Samarkand

SHAHDOM OF
KHWARIZM

Ghazni

Khotan

River Indus

River Ganges

SULTANATE
OF DELHI

HEJAZ

River Nile

ABYSSINIA

ARABIA

YEMEN
Aden

Arabian Sea

INDIA

Malabar
Coast

Ceylon

Bay of Bengal

Indian Ocean

Area of Jewish settlement
Major place of Jewish settlement
Other place of Jewish settlement
Limit of Islamic rule
Limit of Christian rule

km
0   1,000

from certain individuals; but those he has chosen teach speculative truth and adherence to his law. Throughout Jewish history a number of individuals received such prophetic inspiration, but only Moses was capable of prophesying continually.

Another central philosophical issue of the *Guide* is the problem of evil. According to Maimonides, evil does not exist as an independent entity; instead it should be understood as a privation of good. Regarding divine providence, Maimonides believed that God's providential care is proportionate to the degree that a person has activated his intellect. The ideal of human perfection involves reason and ethical action. Only the person who has attained the highest level of intellectual attainment can be near the throne of God. Such philosophical attainment, however, is not sufficient – to reach perfection a person must reach an even higher state. Quoting Jeremiah, Maimonides proclaimed: 'Let not the wise man glory in his wisdom, let not the mighty man glory in his might, let not the rich man glory in his riches; but let him who glories glory in this, that he understands and knows me, that I am the Lord who practice steadfast love, justice and righteousness in the earth; for in these things I delight, says the Lord' (Jeremiah 9:23–4). As God is merciful, just and righteous, so the perfect individual should emulate his actions in his everyday life.

Jewish thought after Maimonides

In the twelfth century Jews living in southern France had translated many philosophical texts into Hebrew. Judah ibn Tibbon (1120–90), for example, who had emigrated from Muslim Spain to Provence, translated ibn Pakuda's *Duties of the Heart*, Judah Halevi's *Book of the Khazars* and Saadiah Gaon's *Book of Beliefs and Opinions*. Subsequently his son Samuel translated Moses Maimonides' *Guide for the Perplexed*. In addition, Aristotle and Plato as well as commentaries on Aristotle by Islamic scholars were translated into Hebrew. As a result Jews in Spain, Provence and Italy composed numerous philosophical and scientific treatises.

Although Maimonides was revered as a legal scholar, a number of Jewish writers were dismayed by his theological opinions. Believing his theology to be a threat to the Jewish faith, opponents attempted in 1230 to prevent the study of the *Guide* as well as the philosophical sections of his code. Although this conflict between Maimonideans and anti-Maimonideans subsided when Dominican inquisitors in France burned copies of Maimonides' writings, opposition to Maimonides' views continued throughout the century.

The most important Jewish thinker after Maimonides who was attracted to Aristotelianism was Levi ben Gerson (Gersonides) (1288–1344). Originally from Provence, he composed works dealing with a variety of topics including mathematics, astronomy, law and philosophy. In his *The Wars of the Lord*, he surveyed the main Aristotelian authorities on various subjects, and argued – in opposition to Maimonides – that God only knows human events if they are determined by the heavenly bodies. According to Gersonides such a limitation on divine knowledge is consonant with Scripture and coherent with the doctrine of the freedom of the will. Concerning providence, Gersonides' opinion was similar to that of Maimonides – the nearer a person is to the active intellect, the more he receives God's care. Regarding God's nature and attributes, Gersonides maintained that it is not necessary, as Maimonides believed, to confine knowledge of God to negative attributes. Positive attributes are legitimate because the qualities ascribed to God are analogous to those ascribed to human beings. According to Gersonides, if divine knowledge bears no relationship to human knowledge it would be impossible to attribute knowledge to God; indeed we would have no idea what the term 'knowledge' means when applied to God.

Another feature of Gersonides' thought deals with God's relation to the world. God was

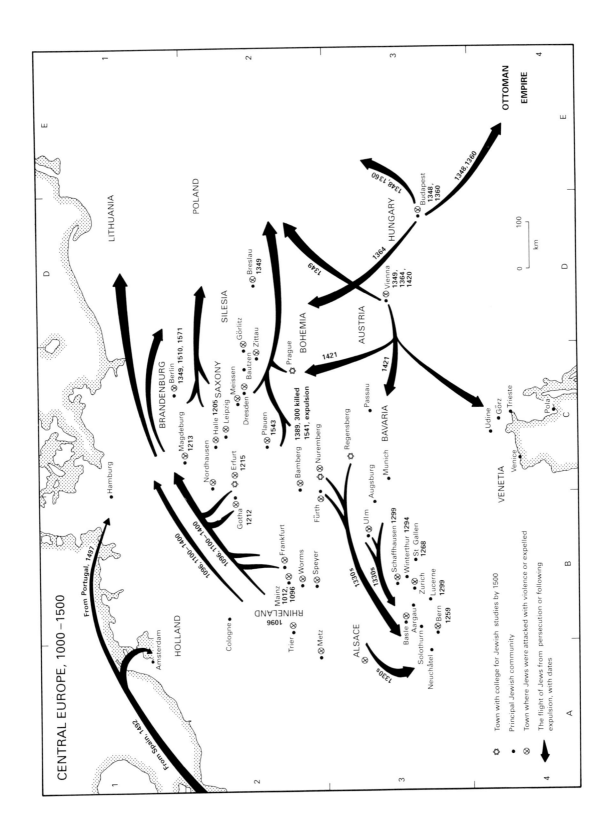

CENTRAL EUROPE, 1000–1500

From Spain, 1492

From Portugal, 1497

Amsterdam

HOLLAND

Hamburg

LITHUANIA

POLAND

BRANDENBURG

Berlin
1349, 1510, 1571

Magdeburg
1213

Nordhausen

Halle **1205** SAXONY

Leipzig

Meissen

Erfurt
1215

Dresden

Gotha
1212

Görlitz

Bautzen

Zittau

Breslau
1349

SILESIA

Plauen
1543

Prague

BOHEMIA

Cologne

RHINELAND
1096

1096, 1100–1400

1096, 1100–1400

Frankfurt

Mainz
1012, 1096

Worms

Trier

Speyer

Metz

Nuremberg

Bamberg **1389, 300 killed**
1541, expulsion

Fürth

Regensberg

Passau

BAVARIA

Munich

Augsburg

Ulm

Schaffhausen **1299**

Winterthur **1294**

St Gallen
1268

Zurich

Lucerne
1299

Aargau

Basle

Solothurn

Bern
1259

Neuchâtel

ALSACE

1330s

1330s

1330s

AUSTRIA

Vienna
1349,
1364,
1420

1421

1421

1349

1364

HUNGARY

Budapest
1348,
1360

1348, 1360

1348, 1360

OTTOMAN
EMPIRE

Udine

Görz

Trieste

Venice

Pola

VENETIA

C

0   100
└────┴────┘
km

⬡ Town with college for Jewish studies by 1500

• Principal Jewish community

⊗ Town where Jews were attacked with violence or expelled

➤ The flight of Jews from persecution or following
    expulsion, with dates

understood by Gersonides as remote from human life. Pure intelligences, he asserted, control the heavenly spheres and the lowest sphere – the active intelligence dominates earthly existence. In this light miracles should be understood as part of the natural order rather than as divine interventions. As far as creation is concerned Gersonides argued that the biblical concept of creation should be understood as the imposition of forms of being on eternal matter rather than *creatio ex nihilo*.

The last major thinker of Spanish Jewry was Hasdai Crescas (1340–1412) from Barcelona. After the Barcelona riots of 1391, Crescas settled in Saragossa. There he composed his treatise *The Light of the Lord*, which was intended to offer an account of the central beliefs of Judaism in contrast to Maimonides' thirteen principles. In Crescas' view there are several categories of belief in relation to Scripture. First, there are the logical presuppositions of the law: belief in the existence and nature of God. Added to these are the fundamental principles of the Torah. The third category consists of the logical consequences of belief in the Torah. In this work Crescas was anxious to refute Aristotelianism by criticizing a number of doctrines found in both Aristotle and Maimonides.

By the fifteenth century the philosophical approach to religious faith lost its appeal for most Spanish Jewish thinkers. Although some writers were still attracted to Maimonides, Aristotelianism ceased to be the dominant philosophy in the Jewish world. Instead of philosophizing about religious belief, subsequent Jewish thinkers directed their attention to defining the basic doctrines of the faith. Thus such Spanish theologians as Simon ben Zemah Duran (1361–1444), Joseph Albo (1380–1445) and Isaac Arama (1420–94) formulated critiques of Maimonides' presentation of the thirteen principles of the Jewish religion. Yet despite such criticism of Maimonides another Spanish Jewish philosopher, Isaac Abarbanel (1437–1508), attempted to defend Maimonides from his opponents. By the end of the fifteenth century the desire to interpret the Jewish tradition in philosophical terms had come to an end, and later generations of Jews turned to the mystical tradition as a source for speculation about God's nature and activity.

Kabbalah

Alongside the development of Jewish mysticism among the *Hasidei Ashkenaz*, Jewish mystics in southern France engaged in mystical speculation about God, the soul, the existence of evil and the religious life. In Provence in the twelfth century, the kabbalistic text the *Bahir* (*Brightness*) reinterpreted the notion of the *sefirot* (divine emanations) as depicted in the early mystical work, the *Sefer Yetsirah* (*Book of Creation*). In this treatise the *sefirot* are conceived as vessels, crowns or words that constitute the structure of the divine realm. On the basis of this anonymous work, various Jewish sages in Provence engaged in similar reflection. Thus Isaac the Blind (1160–1235) viewed the *sefirot* as emanations of a hidden dimension of the Godhead. Using Neoplatonic ideas, he maintained that out of the Infinite (*Ayn Sof*) came the remaining *sefirot*. In the world beneath, he believed, beings are materializations of the *sefirot* at lower degrees of reality. The aim of mystical activity is to unite with Divine Thought.

In Gerona kabbalists disseminated the teachings of Isaac the Blind. The most distinguished of these scholars was Moses ben Nahman (Nahmanides) (1194–1270), whose involvement in kabbalistic speculation persuaded many Jews that mysticism was compatible with rabbinic thought. In his commentary on the Torah, he often utilized kabbalistic concepts to explain the meaning of the text. In the discussion of sacrifice, for example, he stated: 'By means of the sacrifices blessing emanates to the higher powers.' In this passage sacrifice is understood as providing emanation to the *sefirot* – it raises human desire in order to draw it near and unite it with the desire of the higher powers; the higher desire and lower

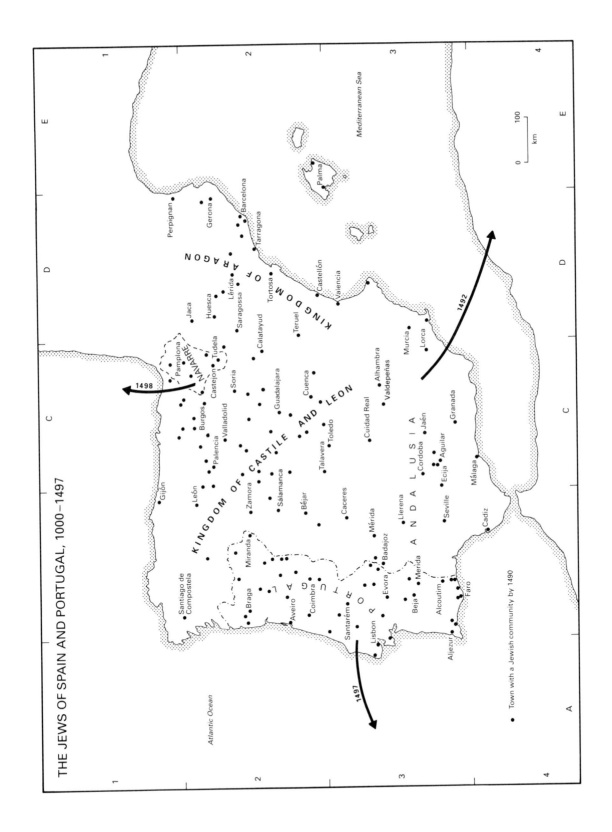

THE JEWS OF SPAIN AND PORTUGAL, 1000–1497

Atlantic Ocean

Mediterranean Sea

KINGDOM OF CASTILE AND LEON

KINGDOM OF ARAGON

NAVARRE

PORTUGAL

ANDALUSIA

Perpignan
Gerona
Barcelona
Tarragona
Castellón
Valencia
Tortosa
Teruel
Jaca
Huesca
Lérida
Saragossa
Calatayud
Tudela
Castejon
Pamplona
Soria
Cuenca
Guadalajara
Burgos
Palencia
Valladolid
León
Gijón
Santiago de Compostela
Zamora
Salamanca
Béjar
Talavera
Toledo
Cuidad Real
Alhambra
Valdepeñas
Murcia
Lorca
Jaén
Córdoba
Aguilar
Granada
Málaga
Ecija
Seville
Cádiz
Caceres
Mérida
Llerena
Badajoz
Evora
Mérida
Beja
Alcoutim
Faro
Aljezur
Lisbon
Santarém
Coimbra
Aveiro
Braga
Miranda

Palma

1492
1498
1497

• Town with a Jewish community by 1490

0   100
km

desire are then combined into one.

During this period different mystical schools of thought developed in other areas of Spain and elsewhere. Influenced by the *Hasidei Ashkenaz* as well as Islamic Sufism, Abrahm ben Samuel Abulafia from Saragossa (1240–71) composed texts concerning the technique of combining the letters of the alphabet as a means of realizing human aspirations toward prophecy. As a follower of Maimonides, he believed this system was a continuation of the teaching in the *Guide for the Perplexed.* Similarly another Spanish kabbalist, Isaac ibn Latif of Toledo, elaborated ideas found in the *Guide.* According to ibn Latif, the Primeval Will is the fountainhead of all emanations. Utilizing Neoplatonic conception he stressed that from the first created thing emanated all other stages which are referred to symbolically as light, fire, ether and water. Each of these elements is a branch of wisdom: mysticism, metaphysics, astronomy and physics. For ibn Latif, kabbalah is superior to philosophy: the highest intellectual comprehension reaches only the 'back' of the Divine, whereas the 'face' is revealed only in supra-intellectual ecstasy. According to ibn Latif, true prayer leads to communion with the active intellect, and then to union of the active intellect with the first created thing. Beyond this union is the union through thought – this is intended to reach the Prime Will and eventually to stand before God himself.

Other Spanish kabbalists were attracted to Gnostic ideas. Isaac ha-Kohen, for example, developed the concept of a demonic emanation whose ten spheres are counterparts of the *sefirot.* In time the combination of such Gnostic teaching with the kabbalah of Gerona resulted in the composition of the major mystic work of Spanish

Figure 13 Title page of *Portae Lucis*, a Latin translation by Paulus Ricius of J. Gikatilla, Sha'arei Orah (Jewish National and University Library, Jerusalem)

Jewry, the *Zohar.* Written by Moses ben Shem Tov de Leon (1250–1305) in Guadalajara, this work was attributed to the second-century sage Simeon bar Yochai. Written in Aramaic, this work is largely a midrash in which the Torah is given a mystical and ethical interpretation.

9 WESTERN EUROPEAN JEWRY IN THE EARLY MODERN PERIOD

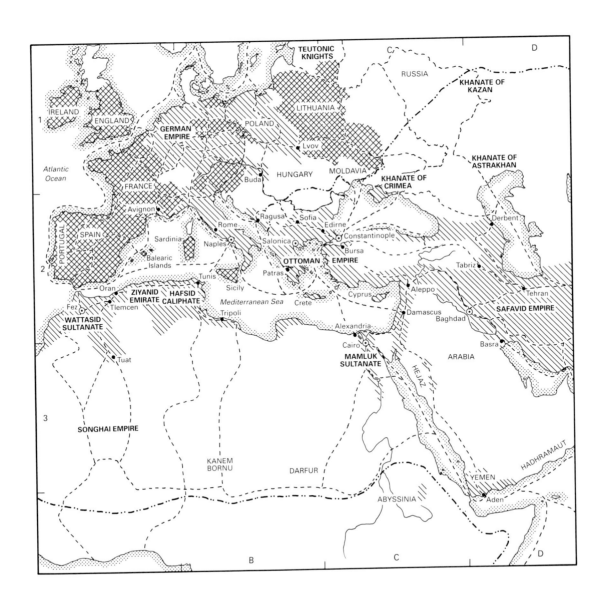

Jews in the Ottoman empire

Once the Ottoman Turks became a world power, many Ashkenazi Jews settled in Ottoman lands. During the first century these communities were supplemented by large numbers of Jewish *marranos* who fled from the Spanish and Portuguese Inquisitions. This Jewish population was further increased when Spanish Jewry was expelled in 1492. In the Balkans, Greece, Cairo, Damascus and Constantinople Jewish communities prospered into the sixteenth century. Some individuals such as Dona Gracia (1510–69) became part of the royal court. Her nephew Joseph Nasi (1524–79) also became an important figure in court circles and sponsored the foundation of a Jewish settlement in Tiberias. This project was inspired by messianic longing and paved the way for later spiritual activity in the Holy Land. As a result of this influx of Jews into the Ottoman empire, Jewish religious life underwent a major transformation, and rabbinic

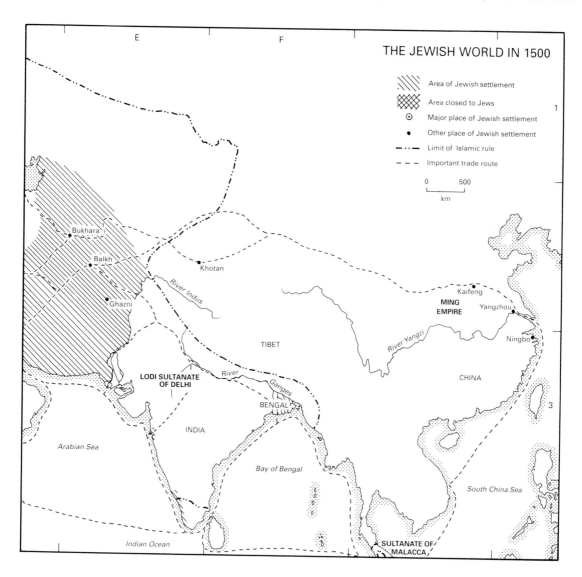

THE JEWISH WORLD IN 1500

- ⦸ Area of Jewish settlement
- ⊠ Area closed to Jews
- ⊙ Major place of Jewish settlement
- ● Other place of Jewish settlement
- –·–·– Limit of Islamic rule
- – – – Important trade route

0   500
km

Bukhara
Balkh
Khotan
Ghazni
Kaifeng
MING EMPIRE
Yangzhou
Ningbo
LODI SULTANATE OF DELHI
River Indus
TIBET
River Ganges
BENGAL
INDIA
CHINA
Arabian Sea
Bay of Bengal
River Yangzi
South China Sea
Indian Ocean
SULTANATE OF MALACCA

academies were established in Cairo, Constantinople and Salonica.

Among the rabbinic scholars of this period was Joseph ben Ephraim Caro (1488–1575), who emigrated from Spain to the Balkans. In the 1520s he produced a vast compendium of Jewish law, *The House of Joseph*; this was based on previous codes by Maimonides, Isaac ben Jacob Alfasi of Lucena (1013–1103), Asher ben Yechiel (1250–1327), and Jacob ben Asher (1270–1340). Relying on these previous codifications of law, Caro regarded as binding the majority decisions of the early scholars he regarded as most authoritative: Alfasi, Maimonides and Asher ben Yechiel. Although *The House of Joseph* was viewed as a monumental contribution to Jewish scholarship, Caro composed a shorter code, the *Shulchan Arukh*, which listed the binding rulings of the *halakhah*. Appearing in 1564, this compendium (together with notes by Moses Isserles (1525–72) specifying where Ashkenazi practices differ from Sephardic customs) became the authoritative legal code for the Jewish world.

Following the pattern of Jacob ben Asher's code (*Sefer Ha-Turim*), the *Shulchan Arukh* begins with laws concerning Jewish behaviour in the home and synagogue. In the next part objects which are forbidden and permitted are elaborated and discussed. In the following part of the *Shulchan Arukh* marriage and family matters are explained in detail. The final part of Caro's code deals with various aspects of civil law.

While he was working on the *Shulchan Arukh* Caro emigrated to Safed in Israel, which had become a major spiritual centre. In the sixteenth century this community had grown in size to a population of over 10,000 Jews and become a base for textile manufacturing. Talmudic academies were founded, and small groups of pious mystics engaged in the study of kabbalistic literature as they awaited the coming of the Messiah. Such messianic expectation was intensified by the expulsion of Jews from Spain and Portugal, and longing for messianic redemption became a prevalent theme of the religious poetry composed in Safed during this period. Thus the hymn 'Come My Beloved', composed by Solomon ha-Levy Alkabetz, depicts the Holy City as an abode for the Sabbath bride and the Davidic King:

Come, my beloved, to meet the bride:
Let us welcome the presence of the Sabbath.
Come, let us go to meet the Sabbath, for it is a
 well-spring of blessing;
From the beginning from of old it was
 ordained,
Last in production, first in thought.
O sanctuary of our King, O regal city, arise, go
 forth from thy overthrow;
Long enough hast thou dwelt in the valley of
 weeping;
Verily He will have compassion upon thee.
Shake thyself from the dust, arise;
Put on the garments of thy glory, O my
 people!
Through the son of Jesse, the Bethlehemite
 (David).
Draw Thou nigh unto my soul, redeem it.
Come in peace, thou crown of thy husband,
With rejoicing and with cheerfulness,
In the midst of the faithful of the chosen
 people.

In this centre mystics participated in various ascetic practices such as fasting, public confessions of sins, wearing sackcloth and ashes and praying at the graves of venerable scholars.

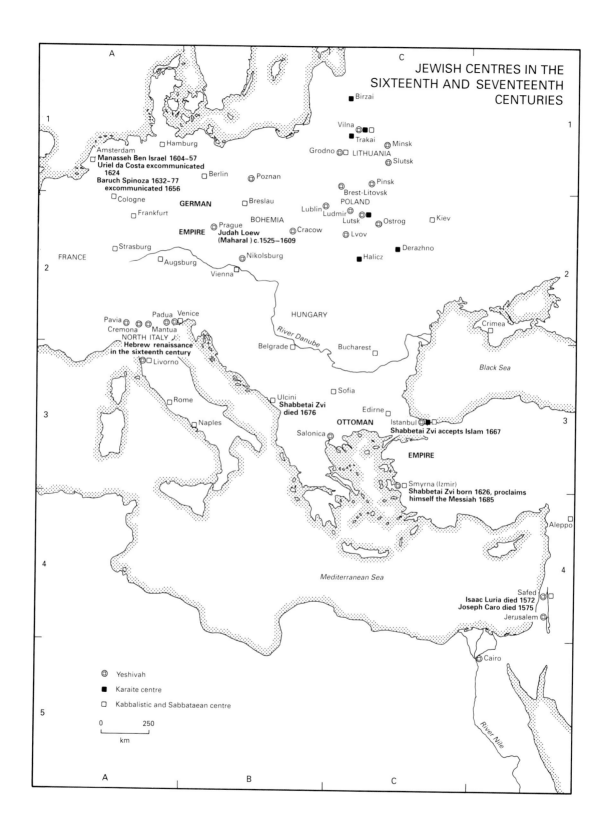

JEWISH CENTRES IN THE
SIXTEENTH AND SEVENTEENTH
CENTURIES

Birzai

Vilna
Trakai
Minsk
Grodno   LITHUANIA
Slutsk

Hamburg
Amsterdam
**Manasseh Ben Israel 1604–57
Uriel da Costa excommunicated
1624
Baruch Spinoza 1632–77
excommunicated 1656**

Berlin   Poznan

Pinsk
Brest-Litovsk

Cologne

GERMAN   Breslau   POLAND
Lublin
Ludmir
Frankfurt   Lutsk   Ostrog   Kiev

BOHEMIA
Prague
EMPIRE   **Judah Loew   Cracow   Lvov
(Maharal) c.1525–1609**

Derazhno

Strasburg

Halicz

Augsburg
Nikolsburg

FRANCE   Vienna

HUNGARY

Pavia   Padua   Venice
Cremona   Mantua
NORTH ITALY
**Hebrew renaissance
in the sixteenth century**

River Danube

Crimea

Belgrade   Bucharest

Black Sea

Livorno

Rome

Sofia

Ulcini
**Shabbetai Zvi
died 1676**

Edirne
OTTOMAN   Istanbul
Shabbetai Zvi accepts Islam 1667

Naples

Salonica

EMPIRE

Smyrna (Izmir)
**Shabbetai Zvi born 1626, proclaims
himself the Messiah 1685**

Aleppo

Mediterranean Sea

Safed
**Isaac Luria died 1572
Joseph Caro died 1575**
Jerusalem

Cairo

⊚   Yeshivah

■   Karaite centre

☐   Kabbalistic and Sabbataean centre

0   250
|————|————|
km

River Nile

Lurianic kabbalah

In Safed one of the greatest mystics of the period, Moses Cordovero (1522–70), gathered together the teachings of earlier mystical authors. His work comprises a systematic summary of kabbalistic thought up to his time. In his most important work, *Pardes*, he outlined the Zoharic concepts of the Godhead, the *sefirot*, the celestial powers and the earthly processes. According to Cordovero, the *sefirot* are vessels containing the light of the Infinite (*Ayn Sof*). In another treatise, *The Palm Tree of Deborah*, he argued that in order to achieve the highest level of spiritual existence one should not only observe the commandments but also intimate divine processes.

In the same century kabbalistic speculation was transformed by Isaac Luria (1534–72), the

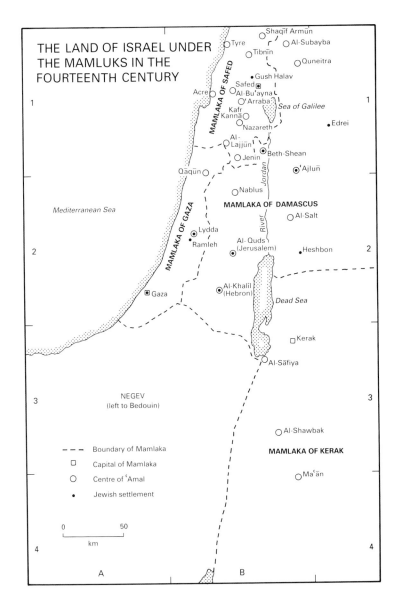

THE LAND OF ISRAEL UNDER THE MAMLUKS IN THE FOURTEENTH CENTURY

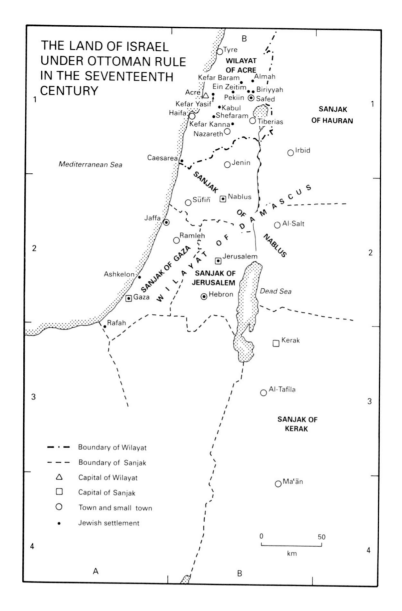

THE LAND OF ISRAEL
UNDER OTTOMAN RULE
IN THE SEVENTEENTH
CENTURY

WILAYAT OF ACRE

B

Tyre
Kefar Baram • Almah
Ein Zeitim
Acre △ • Biriyyah
Kefar Yasif • Pekiin ⊙ Safed
Haifa ○ • Kabul
Kefar Kanna • Shefaram
Nazareth ○ ○ Tiberias

SANJAK OF HAURAN

Mediterranean Sea

Caesarea

○ Jenin

○ Irbid

SANJAK OF DAMASCUS

○ Sūfīn ▣ Nablus

Jaffa ◉

○ Al-Salt

○ Ramleh

WILAYAT OF NABLUS

▣ Jerusalem

SANJAK OF GAZA

SANJAK OF JERUSALEM

Ashkelon •

Dead Sea

▣ Gaza

◉ Hebron

• Rafah

□ Kerak

○ Al-Tafila

SANJAK OF KERAK

— · — Boundary of Wilayat
— — — Boundary of Sanjak
△ Capital of Wilayat
□ Capital of Sanjak
○ Town and small town
• Jewish settlement

○ Ma'ān

0   50
km

A   B

greatest mystic of Safed. Brought up in Egypt, where he studied the Talmud, Luria settled on an island in the Nile, where he meditated on the *Zohar* for seven years. Eventually he arrived in Safed in 1569, where he passed on his teaching to a small group of disciples. Of central importance in Lurianic kabbalah is the mystery of creation. According to the early kabbalists, creation is a positive act: the will to create was awakened in the Godhead, resulting in a long process of emanation. Yet for Luria creation is a negative

event. The *Ayn Sof* had to form an empty space in which the creative process could take place, since divine light was omnipresent, leaving no room for creation to occur. This act was accomplished by a contraction of the Godhead into itself (*tzimtzum*). By withdrawing in this way God went into exile.

After this was accomplished, a line of light flowed from the Godhead into the empty space and took on the shape of the *sefirot* in the form of Primal Adam (*Adam Kadmon*). In this process divine lights created the vessels (the external

111

shapes of the *sefirot*) which give specific characteristics to each divine emanation. These vessels, however, were not strong enough to contain such pure light, and they shattered – this breaking of the vessels brought about disaster and upheaval to the emerging emanations. The lower vessels broke and fell; the three highest emanations were damaged; and the empty space divided into two parts.

After the shattering of the vessels occurred, the cosmos was separated into two: the kingdom of evil in the lower part and the realm of divine light in the upper part. According to Luria, evil is opposed to existence; thus it was not able to exist by its own power. Rather it had to derive spiritual force from the divine light. This was accomplished by capturing the sparks of the divine light that fell with the vessels when they were broken. This subsequently gave sustenance to the evil domain. Divine attempts to unify all existence now had to focus on the struggle to overcome the evil forces. Humanity was intended to serve as the battleground for this conflict between good and evil.

In this connection Adam symbolized the dualism in the cosmos – he possessed a sacred soul while his body represented evil. God's aim was that Adam defeat the evil within himself and thereby bring about Satan's downfall. But when this failed to occur, a catastrophe took place parallel to the breaking of the vessels: many new divine lights fell and evil became stronger. God then chose the people of Israel to vanquish evil and raise up the sparks that had been captured. This allotted task was symbolized by the giving of the Torah. When the ancient Israelites undertook to keep the Covenant, redemption seemed imminent. But when the people of Israel formed the golden calf, more divine sparks fell and the forces of evil were renewed. For Luria Jewish history is a record of attempts by the powers of good to rescue these captive sparks and unite the divine and earthly realms. Luria and his followers believed they were living in the final stages of this last attempt to overcome evil. According to Luria, if the Jews keep the ethical and religious law these sparks will be redeemed and lifted up: when this process is complete evil will be eliminated, and what was broken during the shattering of the vessels will be repaired.

Jewry in Italy

In the early Middle Ages Jews in southern Italy and Rome served as a cultural bridge between the Middle East and Ashkenazi Jewry. In addition contacts with Spain resulted in the transmission of philosophical learning to Italy. In the fourteenth century, Jewish communities in the South were subject to persecution and forced conversions; none the less a number of Jews were encouraged to settle in northern Italy to serve as moneylenders. In time Jews from southern France, Germany, Spain and Portugal emigrated to Italy as well. Eventually in the sixteenth century *marranos* fled to Italy, where they returned to their ancestral faith. In this century flourishing Jewish communities were founded in Ferrara, Mantua, Venice, Padua, Florence and Rome.

During the Renaissance the Italian Jewish community adopted the Italian language and absorbed Italian culture. Jewish bankers expressed an interest in art and literature, and a number of scholars came into close contact with Italian humanists. Through such contact the Florentine Christian philosopher Pico della Mirandola was able to engage in kabbalistic study, making use of the concept of the *sefirot* in his compositions. He and other Church humanists believed that the *Zohar* contained doctrines which support the Christian faith. In this milieu Judah Abravanel composed a Neoplatonic work which had an important impact on Italian humanism. Jews were also influenced by this cultural exchange; frequently Jewish preachers cited quotations from Greek and Latin literature in their sermons and Jewish biblical exegetes utilized the principles of classical rhetoric in their

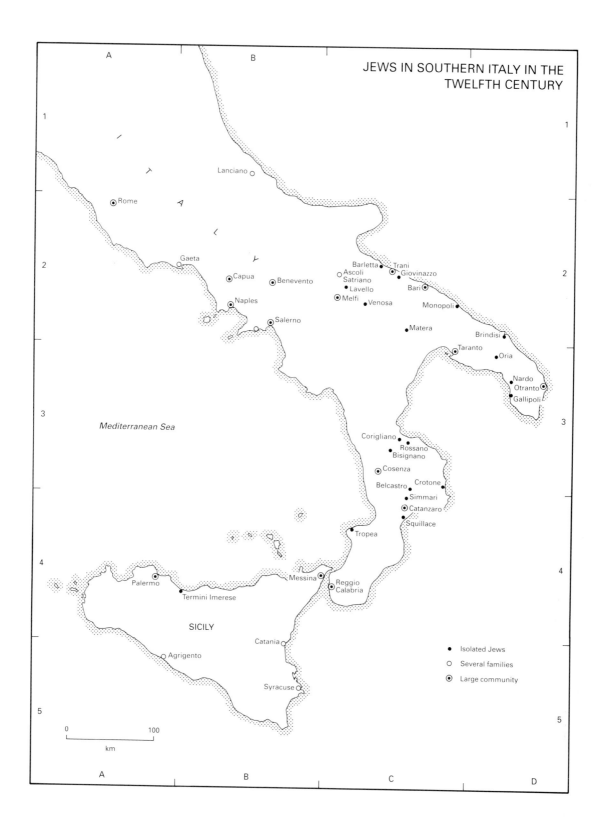

JEWS IN SOUTHERN ITALY IN THE
TWELFTH CENTURY

Lanciano

Rome

Gaeta

Barletta Trani
Ascoli Giovinazzo
Satriano
Capua Benevento Lavello Bari
Melfi Venosa Monopoli
Naples
Salerno Matera Brindisi
Taranto Oria

Nardo
Otranto
Gallipoli

Mediterranean Sea

Corigliano
Rossano
Bisignano
Cosenza
Crotone
Belcastro
Simmari
Catanzaro
Squillace
Tropea

Palermo
Messina
Reggio
Termini Imerese Calabria

SICILY

Catania

Agrigento

Syracuse

● Isolated Jews
○ Several families
◉ Large community

0   100
km

113

commentaries. Moreover, such composers as Solomone Rossi of Mantua wrote synagogue music in the Renaissance style, and Leone de' Sommo founded a Jewish theatre that produced Hebrew drama. In 1564 it was even suggested that a Jewish college be established in Mantua that would combine traditional Jewish study with secular learning.

Although such initiatives did not lead to a Jewish renaissance, certain writers became increasingly interested in historiography. Azariah dei Rossi, for example, produced a work, *Light to the Eyes*, which contained the findings of his research into Jewish literature. Having uncovered Hellenistic Jewish writers such as Philo and Josephus, dei Rossi attempted to evaluate talmudic legends in the light of non-Jewish sources. In this work he referred to authors of ancient Greece and Rome, as well as the New Testament, Augustine, Aquinas, Dante and Petrarch and Christian writers of Roman times, the Middle Ages and the Renaissance. Not surprisingly this study provoked outrage among rabbis in Italy, central Europe and the Middle

East, and Jews were forbidden to read it without special permission.

Despite the positive contact between Christians and Jews, traditional Christian anti-Semitism persisted in the early modern period. Jews were frequently accused of using Christian blood for ritual purposes — a charge that led to numerous expulsions. Eventually the Counter-Reformation Church initiated an onslaught against the Jewish population. In 1553 the papacy sponsored burnings of the Talmud; this led to the imposition of Church censorship on Jewish literature. In 1555 Pope Paul IV issued a bill which reinforced the segregationist policies of the Fourth Lateran Council. Later he decreed that Roman Jews should live in a ghetto, excluding them from most economic occupations. In addition *marranos* who reverted to Judaism were burned at the stake in papal territories and all Jews were expelled from these areas (except for Rome, the port of Anoona, and the papal possessions around Avignon). Jews were also driven out from the areas of Italy ruled by Spain.

Jewry in Germany and Holland

The spread of Protestanism in Germany in the sixteenth and early seventeenth centuries did not result in the improvement of Jewish existence. Initially Martin Luther sought to convert Jews to the Christian faith; when he failed to achieve this goal he denounced both Judaism and the Jewish people. In his pamphlet *Against the Jews and their Lies*, he proposed a number of remedies for German Jewish society:

First, their synagogues should be set on fire, and whatever does not burn up should be covered or spread over with dirt so that no one may ever be able to see a cinder or stone of it. And this ought to be done for the honour of God and of Christianity in order that God may see that we are Christians, and that we have not wittingly tolerated or approved of such public lying, cursing and blaspheming of his

Son and his Christians ... Secondly, their homes should likewise be broken down and destroyed. For they perpetrate the same things there that they do in their synagogues ... Thirdly, they should be deprived of their prayerbooks and Talmuds, in which such idolatry, lies, cursing and blasphemy are taught.

(*Encyclopaedia Judaica* (Jerusalem: Keter Publishing House, 1971–), vol. 3, p. 106)

In the face of such anti-Jewish sentiment Yosel of Rosheim attempted to protect the rights of his co-religionists and interceded with the government. He was successful in blocking the expulsion of Jewry from Hungary and Bohemia and convened a rabbinical synod which adopted a code of commercial ethics. With regard to this policy, he declared: 'I shall cause this programme to be observed if the authorities do what is necessary to let us live in peace; to put an end to the expulsions, to permit us to move about, and to curtail their blood accusations.'

In the seventeenth century, German Jewish communities pursued a traditional way of life, yet during this period the court Jew came to play a crucial role in state affairs. Each royal or princely court had its own Jewish auxiliary. Throughout the country these court Jews administered finances, provisioned armies, raised money, provided textiles and precious stones to the court, began new industries, and initiated manufacturing enterprises. In return for these services, royalty and nobles maintained social contact with those who regulated their affairs.

Such court Jews stood at the pinnacle of the social scale, forming an elite class. None the less the majority of Jews continued to live simple lives and frequently endured considerable discrimination. During this period the invention of printing made it possible to popularize numerous works

on Judaism which denigrated Judaism and the Jewish nation. Throughout the century hundreds of texts were produced, including missionary tracts intended to convert the Jewish population, studies of Jewish customs and treatises dealing with the Jewish problem. In addition, numerous polemical works were published which echoed Christian anti-Semitic attitudes of the Middle Ages. During this century the Christian myth of the wandering Jew also became prevalent – in 1602 *The Brief Account and Description of a Jew Named Ahasuerus* was published and translated into various European languages. According to this work, the wandering Jew witnessed the crucifixion and was condemned by Jesus to wander until the time of the Last Judgement.

In Holland a number of Jews during this period played an important role in trade and finance. By the mid-seventeenth century *marranos* as well as Ashkenazi Jews emigrated to Amsterdam, where they established themselves in various spheres of economic activity. Nearly

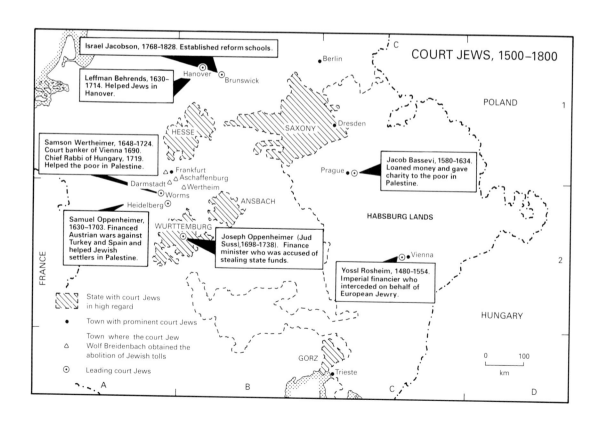

COURT JEWS, 1500–1800

Israel Jacobson, 1768–1828. Established reform schools.

Leffman Behrends, 1630–1714. Helped Jews in Hanover.

Samson Wertheimer, 1648–1724. Court banker of Vienna 1690. Chief Rabbi of Hungary, 1719. Helped the poor in Palestine.

Jacob Bassevi, 1580–1634. Loaned money and gave charity to the poor in Palestine.

Samuel Oppenheimer, 1630–1703. Financed Austrian wars against Turkey and Spain and helped Jewish settlers in Palestine.

Joseph Oppenheimer (Jud Suss),1698–1738). Finance minister who was accused of stealing state funds.

Yossl Rosheim, 1480–1554. Imperial financier who interceded on behalf of European Jewry.

State with court Jews in high regard

Town with prominent court Jews

Town where the court Jew Wolf Breidenbach obtained the abolition of Jewish tolls

Leading court Jews

Berlin, Hanover, Brunswick, POLAND, HESSE, SAXONY, Dresden, Frankfurt, Aschaffenburg, Darmstadt, Wertheim, Worms, Heidelberg, ANSBACH, Prague, HABSBURG LANDS, WURTTEMBURG, FRANCE, Vienna, HUNGARY, GORZ, Trieste

0   100
km

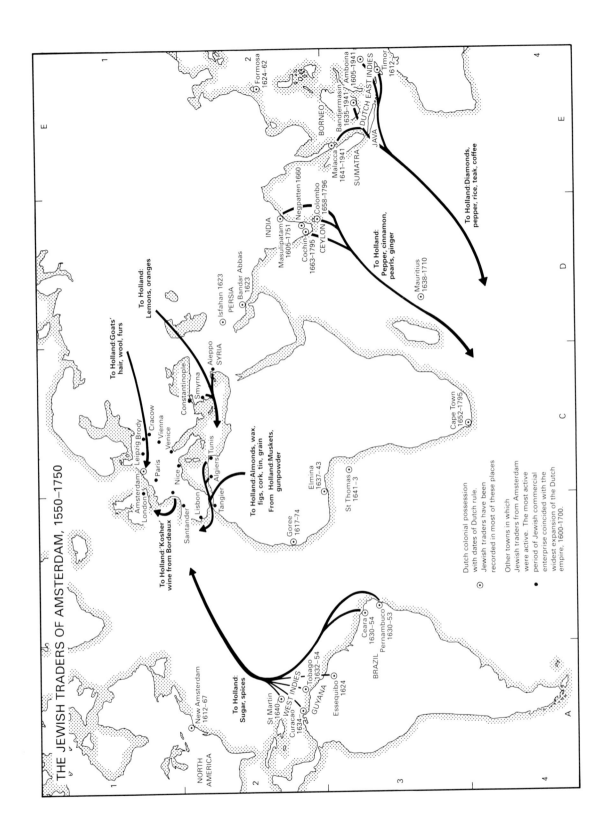

THE JEWISH TRADERS OF AMSTERDAM, 1550–1750

To Holland: Goats' hair, wool, furs

To Holland: Lemons, oranges

To Holland: 'Kosher' wine from Bordeaux

To Holland: Almonds, wax, figs, cork, tin, grain
From Holland: Muskets, gunpowder

To Holland: Sugar, spices

To Holland: Pepper, cinnamon, pearls, ginger

To Holland: Diamonds, pepper, rice, teak, coffee

NORTH AMERICA

New Amsterdam 1612–67

St Martin 1640
Curacao 1634
Tobago 1632–54
WEST INDIES
Essequibo 1624
GUYANA
Ceara 1630–54
Pernambuco 1630–53
BRAZIL

Amsterdam
London
Paris
Leipzig Brody
Cracow
Vienna
Venice
Nice
Tangier
Santander
Lisbon
Algiers
Tunis
Constantinople
Smyrna
Aleppo
SYRIA

Goree 1617–74
St Thomas 1641–3
Elmina 1637–43

Cape Town 1652–1795

Isfahan 1623
PERSIA
Bandar Abbas 1623

INDIA
Masulipatam 1605–1751
Cochin 1663–1795
Negpatten 1660
Colombo 1658–1796
CEYLON

Mauritius 1638–1710

Formosa 1624–62

BORNEO
Bandjermasin 1635–1941
Amboina 1605–1941
DUTCH EAST INDIES
Malacca 1641–1941
SUMATRA
JAVA
Timor 1612–

⊙ Dutch colonial possession
with dates of Dutch rule.

• Other towns in which
Jewish traders from Amsterdam
were active. The most active
period of Jewish commercial
enterprise coincided with the
widest expansion of the Dutch
empire, 1600–1700.

Jewish traders have been
recorded in most of these places

Figure 14   *Rosh Ha-Shanah in the Synagogue,* Bernard Picart (Collection Haags Gemeentemuseum – The Hague)

10,000 Jews lived in the city by the end of the century: there they were employed in the stock exchange, in the sugar, tobacco and diamond trade and in insurance, manufacturing, printing and banking. In this milieu Jewish cultural life flourished, and writers produced works of drama, theology and mystical lore. Although these Jews were not granted full citizenship rights, they enjoyed considerable freedom, personal protection and economic opportunities.

The Shabbatean movement

Among Sephardic Jewry Lurianic kabbalah made an important impression, and messianic expectations became a central feature of Jewish life. In this milieu a self-proclaimed messianic king, Shabbatai Zevi (1626–76), was widely perceived as the long-awaited Messiah. Born in Smyrna, he received a traditional Jewish education and subsequently engaged in the study of the *Zohar*. In the 1650s he left Smyrna and travelled to various cities in Greece as well as Constantinople and Jerusalem. In time he became part of a kabbalistic circle in Cairo. Eventually he went to Gaza, where he met Nathan Benjamin Levi (1644–80), who announced that Shabbatai was the Messiah.

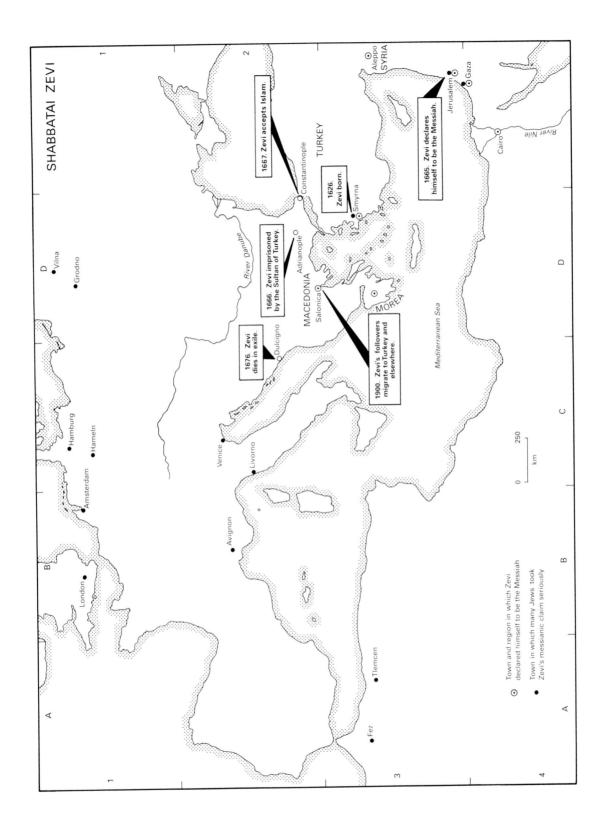

SHABBATAI ZEVI

1667. Zevi accepts Islam.

1626. Zevi born.

1667. Zevi accepts Islam.

1665. Zevi declares himself to be the Messiah.

1666. Zevi imprisoned by the Sultan of Turkey.

1900. Zevi's followers migrate to Turkey and elsewhere.

1676. Zevi dies in exile.

TURKEY

SYRIA

MACEDONIA

MOREA

Mediterranean Sea

River Danube

River Nile

Aleppo

Gaza

Jerusalem

Cairo

Constantinople

Smyrna

Adrianople

Salonica

Dulcigno

Venice

Livorno

Avignon

Fez

Tlemcen

Vilna

Grodno

Hamburg

Hameln

Amsterdam

London

⊙ Town and region in which Zevi declared himself to be the Messiah

● Town in which many Jews took Zevi's messianic claim seriously

0   250
└──────┘
km

Nathan then sent letters to Jews throughout the diaspora requesting that they repent and recognize Shabbatai Zevi as their deliverer. According to Nathan, Shabbatai would bring back the lost tribes and inaugurate the period of messianic redemption.

After a short period in Jerusalem, Shabbatai travelled to Smyrna, where he encountered fierce opposition from various local rabbis. In response he declared that he was the Anointed of the God of Jacob and criticized those who refused to accept him. This act provoked a hysterical response from his followers: a number fell into trances and had visions of him crowned on a royal throne as the King of Israel. In 1666 he went to Istanbul, where he was arrested and put into prison. After a brief time the prison quarters were transformed into a messianic court, and pilgrims from throughout the Jewish world travelled to Constantinople to join in messianic rituals and ascetic activities. Hymns were composed in Shabbatai's honour and new festivals introduced.

The same year Shabbatai met the Polish kabbalist Nehemiah ha-Kohen, who denounced him to the Turkish authorities. When Shabbatai was brought to the Turkish court, he was given the choice between conversion and death. Given this alternative, Shabbatai converted to Islam, taking the name Mehemet Effendi. This act of apostasy horrified his followers, yet he defended himself by explaining that he had become a Muslim in obedience to God. A number of his followers accepted his explanation and refused to abandon their belief in him as the Messiah. Some believed it was not Shabbatai who became a Muslim, but a phantom. Others cited biblical and rabbinic sources to justify this act. According to Nathan, the messianic role involved taking on the humiliation of being portrayed as a traitor to the Jewish people. Further, Nathan argued on the basis of Lurianic doctrine that there were two kinds of divine light – a creative light and another light opposed to the existence of anything other than the Infinite (*Ayn Sof*). Creative light formed

Figure 15 Engraving based on reports concerning Shabbatai Zevi (Israel Museum, Jerusalem)

structures of creation in the empty space; the other light became the power of evil. For Nathan the Messiah's soul had been struggling against the power of evil from the beginning – his aim was to allow divine light to penetrate this domain and thereby bring about cosmic repair (*tikkun*). To accomplish this task, the soul of the Messiah was free to descend into the abyss to liberate the sparks and thereby vanquish evil. In this light Shabbatai's conversion to Islam was explicable in mystical terms.

Once Shabbatai became a Muslim, Nathan visited him in the Balkans and later travelled to Rome, where he performed secret rites to end the papacy. Shabbatai, however, remained in Adria-nople and Constantinople, where he lived as both a Muslim and a Jew. In 1672 he was deported to Albania; there he disclosed his own kabbalistic teaching. When he died in 1676 Nathan proclaimed that Shabbatai had ascended to the supernal world. In time a number of groups continued in their belief that Shabbatai was the Messiah. One of these sects, the Dissidents (*Doenmeh*), professed Islam publicly while adhering to their own traditions. Eventually they evolved into antinomian sub-groups who transgressed Jewish sexual laws and declared that Shabbatai and their leader, Baruchiah Russo, were divine. In Italy other Shabbatean groups also emerged and propagated their views.

10 EASTERN EUROPEAN JEWRY IN THE EARLY MODERN PERIOD

The establishment of Polish Jewry

In the Middle Ages Ashkenazi Jewry in Poland was increased by an influx of Jews from the Crimea, the Russian steppes, the Middle East and Spain. In the middle of the thirteenth century Prince Kalisz issued a charter which granted the Jewish population legal protection. In the next century King Casimir III granted further decrees which expanded their charter to include the entire Polish kingdom. Eventually in 1388 the Grand Duke of Lithuania gave similar rights to the Jewish population which were renewed in the next century by Casimir IV Jagiello. Through these proclamations Polish and Lithuanian rulers supplied Polish Jewry with a secure basis for Jewish communal existence. In this milieu Polish Jews served as fiscal agents, tax collectors and managers of noblemen's estates. Other Jews leased lands and supervised agricultural activities such as farming, harvesting, manufacture and export. None the less Polish Jewry was subject to various forms of persecution: Jews were forced to wear distinguishing garments and were frequently victims of anti-Jewish outbursts.

At the beginning of the fifteenth century the Polish Jewish community numbered 10,000–15,000 Jews, increasing to over 150,000 in the next century. During this period Polish nobles who owned large estates in the Ukraine employed Jews on their estates to collect taxes, fees, tolls and produce from the serfs. Noblemen also founded private cities where they welcomed Jews as employees in their houses, where they conducted business activities. In this environment Polish Jewry was regulated along the lines of communal self-government. Each local community (*kehillah*) was controlled by a board of trustees that collected taxes for the government and supplied educational and other facilities for the Jewish population. In larger cities the *kehillot* were directed by paid officials who included rabbis employed generally for three-year periods to serve as experts in Jewish law as well as heads of talmudic academies.

Because of this efflorescence of Jewish life, Poland became a great centre for Jewish learning. In the rabbinical academies the method of *hilluk* (the differentiation and reconciliation of rabbinic opinions) fostered intense study of talmudic law. In addition, a number of scholars began to collect together the legal interpretations of previous scholars, and commentaries were written on the *Shulchan Arukh*. In order to regulate Jewish life in the country at large, regional federations were created which administered Jewish affairs. Further a Council of the Four Lands, composed of eminent rabbinical and lay leaders, met twice a year to allocate taxes to the synods of *kehillot*, select and finance Jewish representatives to the royal court, and issue ordinances concerning Jewish interests and activities.

Within the academies, rabbinic sources served as the core of the curriculum. According to a seventeenth-century chronicle:

Each community maintained young men and provided for them a weekly allowance of

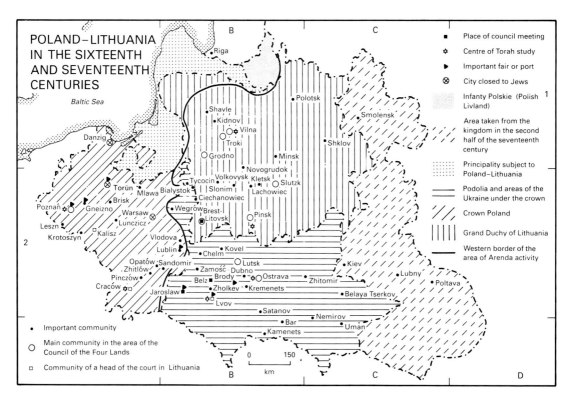

POLAND–LITHUANIA IN THE SIXTEENTH AND SEVENTEENTH CENTURIES

Baltic Sea

Legend:
- ■ Place of council meeting
- ✿ Centre of Torah study
- ▶ Important fair or port
- ⊗ City closed to Jews
- Infanty Polskie (Polish Livland) 1
- Area taken from the kingdom in the second half of the seventeenth century
- Principality subject to Poland–Lithuania
- Podolia and areas of the Ukraine under the crown
- Crown Poland
- Grand Duchy of Lithuania
- Western border of the area of Arenda activity

- • Important community
- ○ Main community in the area of the Council of the Four Lands
- ▫ Community of a head of the court in Lithuania

Riga, Shavle, Kidnov, Vilna, Troki, Grodno, Polotsk, Smolensk, Shklov, Minsk, Novogrudok, Volkovysk, Kletsk, Slutzk, Danzig, Torún, Mlawa, Bialystok, Tycocin, Slonim, Lachowiec, Ciechanowiec, Poznań, Gneizno, Brisk, Warsaw, Wegrów, Brest-Litovsk, Pinsk, Leszn, Lunczicz, Krotoszyn, Vlodova, Lublin, Chelm, Kovel, Kiev, Opatów, Sandomir, Zamość, Dubno, Lutsk, Lubny, Zhitlów, Belz, Brody, Ostrava, Zhitomir, Poltava, Pinczów, Cracov, Jaroslaw, Zholkev, Kremenets, Belaya Tserkov, Lvov, Satanov, Nemirov, Bar, Uman, Kamenets

0   150
km

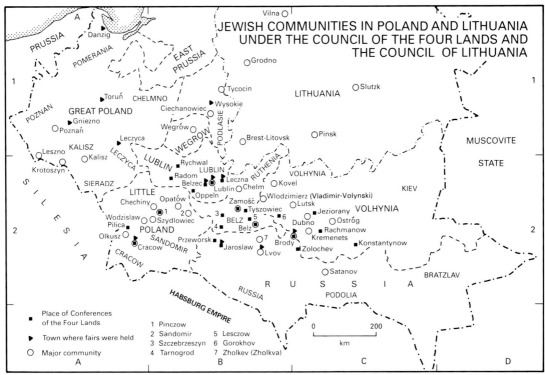

JEWISH COMMUNITIES IN POLAND AND LITHUANIA UNDER THE COUNCIL OF THE FOUR LANDS AND THE COUNCIL OF LITHUANIA

PRUSSIA, POMERANIA, EAST PRUSSIA, Danzig, Vilna, Grodno, Tycocin, LITHUANIA, Slutzk, Toruń, CHELMNO, Ciechanowiec, Wysokie, POZNAN, GREAT POLAND, Gniezno, Poznań, Wegrów, PODLASIE, Brest-Litovsk, Pinsk, MUSCOVITE STATE, Leszno, KALISZ, Leczyca, WEGRÓW, Kalisz, LECZYCA, LUBLIN, Krotoszyn, SIERADZ, Rychwal, RUTHENIA, VOLHYNIA, KIEV, LITTLE, Radom, LUBLIN, Leczna, Kovel, Chelm, Belzec, Lublin, Wlodzimierz (Vladimir-Volynski), Chechiny, Opatów, Oppeln, Zamość, Lutsk, VOLHYNIA, Jeziorany, Wodzislaw, Szydlowiec, Tyszowiec, Dubno, Ostróg, Pilica, BELZ, Rachmanow, Olkusz, POLAND, Belz, Kremenets, Konstantynow, SANDOMIR, Przeworsk, Brody, Zolochev, Cracow, Jaroslaw, Lvov, CRACOW, Satanov, BRATZLAV, RUSSIA, PODOLIA, HABSBURG EMPIRE

Legend:
- ■ Place of Conferences of the Four Lands
- ▶ Town where fairs were held
- ○ Major community

1 Pinczow
2 Sandomir
3 Szczebrzeszyn
4 Tarnogrod
5 Lesczow
6 Gorokhov
7 Zholkev (Zholkva)

0   200
km

money that they might study with the head of the academy. And for each young man they also maintained two boys to study under his guidance so that he would orally discuss the *Gemara*, the commentaries of Rashi, and the *Tosafot*, which he had learned, and thus would gain experience in the subtlety of talmudic argumentation.... The programme of study in the kingdom of Poland was as follows: The term of study consisted of the period which required the young men and the boys to study with the head of the academy. In the summer it extended from the first day of the month of *Iyar* till the fifteenth day of the month of *Av*, and in the winter from the first day of the month of *Heshvan* till the fifteenth day of the month of *Shevat*. After the fifteenth of *Shevat* or the fifteenth of *Av*, the young men and boys were to study wherever they preferred.

From the first day of *Heshvan* till Hanukkah all the students of the academy study Gemara, the commentaries of Rashi, and the *Tosafot*, with great diligence.... In each community great honour was accorded to the head of the academy. His words were heard by rich and poor alike. None questioned his authority. Without him no one raised his hand or foot, and as he commanded so it came to be. In this hand he carried a stick and a lash to smite and to flog, to punish and chastise transgressors, to instate ordinances, to establish safeguards, and to declare the forbidden.

(Nathan Hanover, *The Abyss of Despair*, trans. Abraham J. Mesch (New York: Bloch Publishing Co., 1950), pp. 111–15)

The Chmielnicki massacres and aftermath

In the seventeenth century in the midst of general prosperity Polish Jewry suffered a series of massacres. These were carried out by Cossacks of the Ukraine, Crimean Tartars, and Ukrainian peasants who rebelled against the Polish nobility. In 1648 Bogdan Chmielnicki became hetman of the Cossacks; thereupon he initiated an insurrection against the Polish gentry, who had previously oppressed the Cossack population. As administrators of estates owned by noblemen, Jews were devastated in this onslaught. As the Cossacks advanced manor houses were destroyed, victims flayed, burned alive and mutilated, infants killed and cast into wells, and women cut open and sewn up with live cats thrust into their wounds. According to one of the chronicles of the period:

These persons died cruel and bitter deaths. Some were skinned alive and their flesh was thrown to the dogs; some had their hands and limbs chopped off, and their bodies thrown on the highway only to be trampled by wagons and crushed by horses; some had wounds inflicted on them, and were thrown on the street to die a slow death; they writhed in their blood until they breathed their last; others were buried alive. The enemy slaughtered infants in the laps of their mothers. They were sliced alive into pieces like fish. They slashed the bellies of pregnant women, removed their infants and tossed them in their faces ... Some children were pierced by spears, roasted on the fire, and then brought to their mothers to be eaten. Many were taken by the Tartars into captivity. Women and virgins were ravished.... Similar atrocities were perpetrated in all the settlements through which they passed.

(Hanover, *The Abyss of Despair*, pp. 43–4)

As the Cossack mobs advanced, the Polish king died. He was succeeded by John Casimir, who negotiated with the attackers, who demanded their own state. After several years of battle, Chmielnicki appealed to the Russian allies, who penetrated into north-west Poland and the Ukraine. In 1655 the Swedes invaded western Poland, but by the following year they were driven back by a Polish partisan movement.

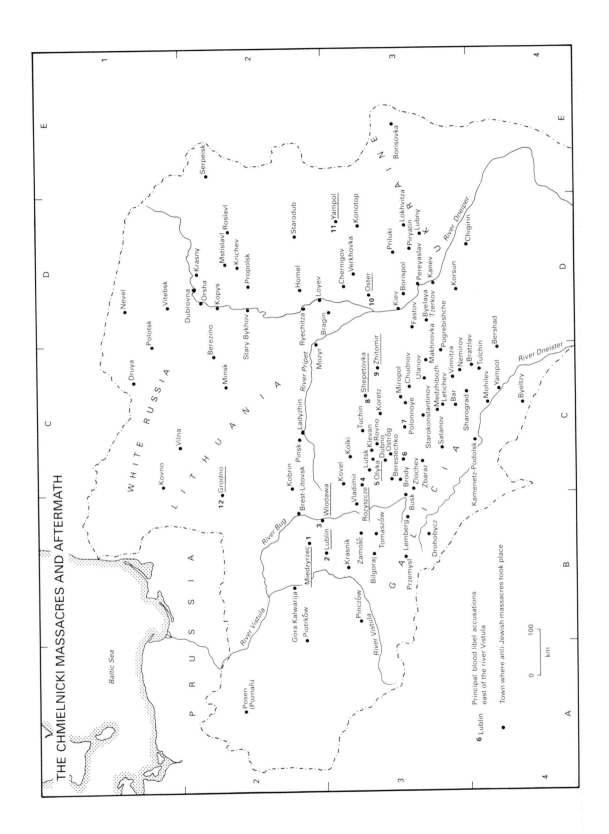

THE CHMIELNICKI MASSACRES AND AFTERMATH

Baltic Sea

PRUSSIA

WHITE RUSSIA

LITHUANIA

UKRAINE

GALICIA

River Vistula
River Bug
River Pripet
River Dnieper
River Dneister

Posen (Poznań)
Piotrków
Gora Kalwarija
Pinczów
Bilgoraj
Krasnik
Zamość
Przemysl
Lemberg
Tomaszów
Drohobycz
Kamenetz-Podolsk
Kovno
Vilna
Grodno **12**
Brest-Litovsk
Kobrin
Pinsk
Ladyzhin
Vladimir
Kovel
Kolki
Lutsk
Tuchin
Olyka
Rovno
Koretz
Shepetovka
Ostróg
Dubno
Berestechko
Brody
Zlochev
Zbaraz
Busk
Starokonstantinov
Satanov
Medzhibozh
Polonnoye
Ulanov
Makhnovka
Letichev
Bar
Vinnitza
Nemirov
Bratzlav
Pogrebishche
Sharograd
Mohilev
Tulchin
Yampol
Byeltzy
Bershad
Miropol
Chudnov
Zhitomir **9**
Byelaya
Tzerkov
Kanev
Korsun
Fastov
Borispol
Kiev
Oster **10**
Chernigov
Verkhovka
Konotop
Yampol **11**
Priluki
Lokhvitza
Piryatin
Lubny
Chigirin
Pereyaslav
Borisovka
Starodub
Homel
Loyev
Ryechitza
Bragin
Mozyr
Serpeisk
Mstislavl
Roslavl
Krichev
Propolsk
Krasny
Orsha
Kopys
Stary Bykhov
Berezino
Minsk
Dubrovna
Vitebsk
Polotsk
Nevel
Druya
Lublin **1**
Medzyrzec **1**
Rozyszcze **4**
Wlodawa **3**
Lublin **2**

6 Lublin — Principal blood libel accusations east of the river Vistula

• Town where anti-Jewish massacres took place

0   100
km

Eventually in 1667 Russia and Poland signed the Treaty of Adrusovo – this distributed the western Ukraine to Poland and the eastern Ukraine and the Smolensk region to Russia. Throughout these years of conflict, the Jewish population was decimated by the various opposing forces: the Cossacks and Ukrainian peasants viewed Jewry as representatives of the Polish aristocracy; the Russians prevented Jews from settling in their lands and joined the Cossacks in this massacre; and the Polish partisans viewed the Jews as allied with the Swedes. Eventually a quarter of the entire Jewish community died in this struggle, and thousands were ransomed from the Tartars in the Constantinople slave markets.

Later in the century Polish Jewish life became increasingly insecure because of political instability. None the less the Jewish community continued to increase in size. Nearly a third of all Polish Jews lived in the countryside in small groups, where they were subject to frequent accusations of blood libel. In the 1730s and 1740s the Cossacks known as Haidemaks invaded the Ukraine, robbing and killing the Jewish inhabitants. Finally they attacked the Jewish community of Uman in 1768. During this period the Polish *kehillot* were taxed heavily, and at times claims were made that the leaders of the Jewish population placed the heaviest tax burdens on the poor.

The Vilna Gaon and the rise of Hasidism

Despite the decline of eastern European Jewish life in the eighteenth century, Lithuanian Jewry underwent considerable renewal. Because of its proximity to Russia as well as its trade connections with Russia and the West, Jews in Vilna and other Lithuanian towns flourished during this century. Vilna in particular became a centre for Jewish scholarship. There traditional rabbinic learning reached great heights, and supporters of the Jewish Enlightenment and social radicalism engaged in fervent activity. The central figure of this period was Elijah ben Solomon Zalman (1720–97), known as the Vilna Gaon. Although he did not occupy an official position in the community, the Vilna Gaon was granted a stipend by the *kehillah* so that he could dedicate himself to rabbinic study. In addition he lectured on rabbinic topics to a circle of disciples who subsequently exerted an important influence on Lithuanian Judaism.

The appearance of the Vilna Gaon reflects the revitalization of sixteenth- and seventeenth-century rabbinic tradition. His writings embraced commentaries on the Bible, the Mishnah, the Babylonian and Jerusalem Talmuds, midrashic literature, the *Sefer Yetsirah*, the *Zohar* and the *Shulchan Arukh*. Despite such scholarly endea-

vours, the most important aspect of the Vilna Gaon's writing was his approach. Like a number of early Polish scholars, he rejected elaborate argumentation (as manifest in the technique of *hilluk*) in favour of an exact interpretation of the common-sense meaning of the text. Such an orientation led the Vilna Gaon at times to criticize sages of the talmudic period when he concluded that they had not adequately interpreted rabbinic law in the Mishnah. The Vilna Gaon also investigated various branches of secular study: algebra, geometry, geography, Hebrew grammar and chronology. Further he encouraged his followers to translate such works into Hebrew. Although critical of Maimonidean philosophy, he sought to harmonize kabbalistic doctrines with talmudic teaching. In Vilna the Gaon was viewed as a saint, and became a symbol of those who condemned the Hasidic movement, which sought to subordinate talmudic learning to religious experience.

This new mystical sect emerged in the latter half of the eighteenth century as the autonomous authority of the Jewish communal structure was weakened by social and political events. In 1764 the Polish government abolished the Council of the Four Lands as well as the Lithuanian Jewish

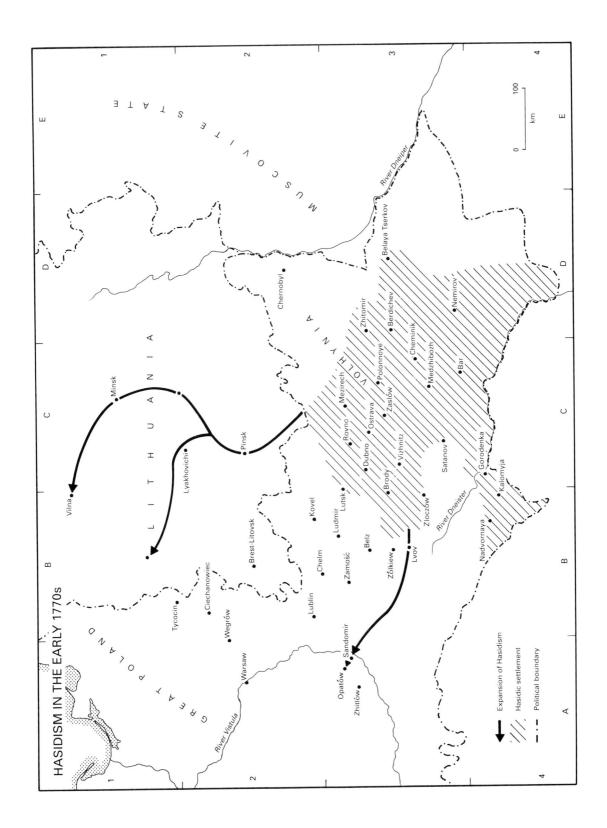

HASIDISM IN THE EARLY 1770s

E — MUSCOVITE STATE

UKRAINA

VOLHYNIA

Belaya Tserkov
Nemirov
Zhitomir
Berdichev
Chernobyl
Polonnoye
Cheminik
Bar
Zasłów
Medzhibozh
Mezirech
Ostrava
Rovno
Vizhnitz
Dubno
Satanov
Brody
Gorodenka
Zloczów
Kalomyja
Nadvornaya

River Dneiper
River Dneister

Minsk
Pinsk
Lyakhovichi
Vilna
Kovel
Lutsk
Ludmir
Brest-Litovsk
Chelm
Belz
Zamość
Żółkiew
Lvov
Lublin
Ciechanowiec
Tycocin
Wegrów
Sandomir
Opatów
Warsaw
Zhitlów

LITHUANIA

GREAT POLAND

River Vistula

100
km
0

Expansion of Hasidism
Hasidic settlement
Political boundary

Council. In the next decade Russia, Austria and Prussia agreed to annex large segments of Polish territory – this was the first partition of Poland. In 1793 a second partition took place; two years later a final partition resulted in the extinction of Poland. Although the *kehillah* system survived such partitions, its power was diminished and it was forced to contend with an internal rebellion in Jewish life: the development of Hasidism sought the allegiance of the Jewish population. This new pietism drew upon kabbalistic teaching to create an ideology which espoused the reinterpretation of the role of the rabbi. Hasidism first appeared in the villages of the Polish Ukraine, particularly in the province of Podolia, where the Shabbatean Frankists were widely known for their heretical views and licentious practices. In the first part of the eighteenth century Podolia also became the home of nonconformist Christian sects that had split off from the Orthodox Church.

Figure 16 Portrait of Elijah ben Solomon Zalman (Jewish National and University Library, Jerusalem)

The Baal Shem Tov

Israel ben Eleazer (1700–60), known as the Besht (Baal Shem Tov), was the founder of Hasidism. Through oral traditions handed down by his disciples as well as legendary tales about his life, it is possible to reconstruct the course of his activity. It is related that he was born in Okop in Podolia to poor and elderly parents. Orphaned as a child, he worked as an assistant in a Jewish school (*heder*), and later as a watchman in a synagogue. At Yazlovets, near Buchnach, he met Meir ben Zevi Hirsch Margolioth, who later became a talmudic scholar. According to Meir, Israel became a colleague and teacher. In his twenties Israel went with his second wife Hannah to the Carpathian Mountains, where he was a digger of clay. Subsequently he helped his wife in keeping an inn. In about 1730 he settled in Tluste, and had one son, Zevi, and a daughter, Adel.

Hasidic tradition relates that in the 1730s Israel revealed himself as a healer and leader. A circle of disciples were drawn to him, and reports of his miracles began to circulate widely. Some of the members of this Hasidic group were initially repelled by Israel's activity as a miracle healer. However, contemporaries who did not belong to his circle regarded such activity favourably, as indicated by their designation of him as 'the famous *baal shem tov*; may his light shine'. For many years Israel wished to go to Israel. Thus in 1751 he wrote to his brother-in-law: 'God knows that I do not despair of travelling to Erez Israel; however, the time is not right.'

During his ministry Israel undertook numerous journeys to effect cures, expel demons and evil spirits, and gain influence. In folktales, traditions of his pupils and in writings hostile to

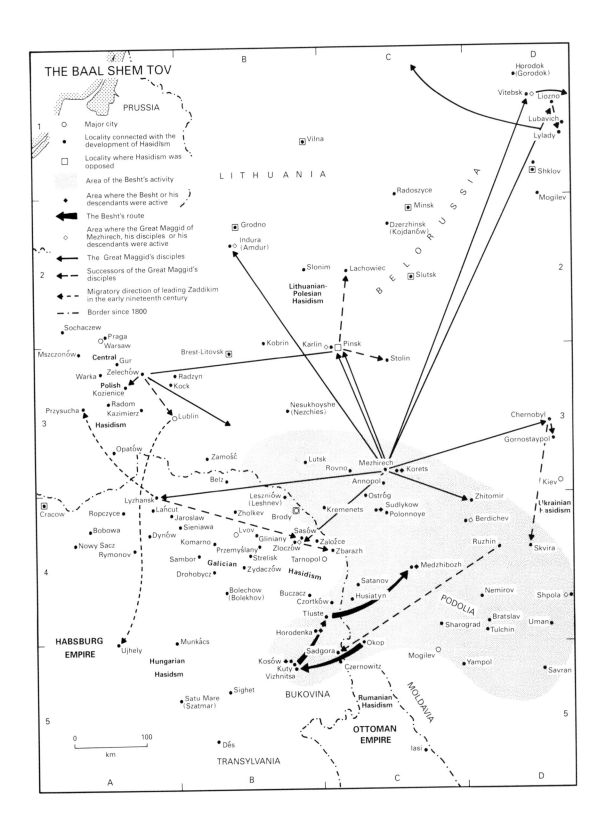

THE BAAL SHEM TOV

PRUSSIA

○ Major city

● Locality connected with the development of Hasidism

□ Locality where Hasidism was opposed

Area of the Besht's activity

◆ Area where the Besht or his descendants were active

◄ The Besht's route

◇ Area where the Great Maggid of Mezhirech, his disciples or his descendants were active

← The Great Maggid's disciples

◄-- Successors of the Great Maggid's disciples

◄·· Migratory direction of leading Zaddikim in the early nineteenth century

─·─ Border since 1800

LITHUANIA

BELORUSSIA

Horodok (Gorodok)
Vitebsk ◇ Liozno
Lubavich
Lylady
Shklov
Mogilev

Vilna

Radoszyce
Minsk
Dzerzhinsk (Kojdanów)
Slutsk

Grodno
Indura (Amdur)
Slonim
Lachowiec

Lithuanian-Polesian Hasidism

Sochaczew
Praga
Warsaw
Mszczonów
Central Gur
Warka Zelechów
Polish
Kozienice
Przysucha
Radom
Kazimierz
Hasidism
Opatów

Brest-Litovsk
Kobrin Karlin ◇ Pinsk
Stolin

Nesukhoyshe (Nezchies)

Lublin

Zamość
Lutsk
Rovno
Belz
Annopol
Kremenets

Mezhirech ◆◆ Korets

Chernobyl
Gornostaypol

Kiev ○

Ukrainian Hasidism

Lyzhansk
Cracow
Ropczyce
Lańcut
Jaroslav
Bobowa
Sieniawa
Nowy Sacz
Dynów
Komarno
Rymanov
Sambor
Galician
Drohobycz

Leszniów (Leshnev)
Zholkev
○ Lvov
Gliniany
Przemyślany
Strelisk
Zydaczów
Hasidism

Brody
Sasów
Zaloźce
Zloczów
Tarnopol ○
Zbarazh

Ostróg
Sudlykow
Polonnoye

Zhitomir
Berdichev
Ruzhin
Skvira
Shpola ◇

Medzhibozh
Satanov
Husiatyn
Czortków
Tluste
Horodenka
Sadgora
Okop
Kosów
Kuty
Vizhnitsa
Czernowitz

PODOLIA
Nemirov
Sharograd
Bratslav
Tulchin
Uman
Yampol
Savran

HABSBURG EMPIRE
Munkács
Ujhely
Hungarian
Hasidsm

Satu Mare (Szatmar)
Sighet

Dés

BUKOVINA

Buczacz

Mogilev ○

MOLDAVIA

Rumanian Hasidism

OTTOMAN EMPIRE
Iasi

TRANSYLVANIA

0   100
km

him his healing work and charismatic leadership are noted. (None the less later Hasidic tradition attempted to minimize the importance of these healing and magical practices.) For Israel prayer constituted the primary ecstatic and mystical approach to God – both intellectual study and learning occupied a secondary position. At certain times Israel was able to reach a state of mystical exaltation. Further in dreams future events and past personalities were revealed to him. The traditional depiction of the Besht – always with a pipe in his hand or mouth – stressed the importance of his edifying tales. Such teaching was devoid of talmudic scholarship, although Israel did utilize material drawn from the haggadah as well as moralistic and kabbalistic works. Israel himself was conscious of his mission as a leader of the Jewish people. His teaching emphasized the importance of charity, and he is portrayed as helping captives and prisoners. During his ministry he stressed that joy is the proper attitude of a Jew in every moment of his life, particularly in prayer.

From the eighteenth century to the present day the Besht's life served as an inspiration to thousands of followers. Although Israel did not commit his teachings to writing, twenty years after his death his disciple, Jacob Joseph, recorded hundreds of sermons and homilies which he had learned from the Besht. In addition, the first anthology of legends about the Besht was composed by Dov Baer ben Samuel of Linits, who served for some time as Israel's scribe. In the nineteenth century, several collections of legends about the Besht, his colleagues and disciples appeared which repeated stories in earlier sources.

Hasidism

After the death of the Besht in 1760 Dov Baer became the leader of Hasidism, and the movement spread to southern Poland, the Ukraine and Lithuania. Not surprisingly the growth of this sect evoked considerable animosity from rabbinic authorities. In Vilna the rabbinic leadership issued an edict of excommunication. Hasidim were charged with laxity in their study of the Torah, permissiveness in the observance of the divine commandments, excess in prayer, and preference for the Lurianic as opposed to the Ashkenazi prayerbook. Subsequently the Hasidim and their critics (*Mitnagdim*) denounced one another. Relations between these two groups further deteriorated when Jacob Joseph of Polonnoye wrote a book critical of the rabbinate – this work was banned in 1781, and the *Mitnagdim* decreed that all relations with members of the Hasidic movement should cease. At the end of the century the Vilna Jewish religious establishment denounced the Hasidim to Russian authorities – this act led to the imprisonment of a number of leaders. None the less the Hasidic movement was eventually officially recognized by both the Russian and the Austrian governments. As time passed the movement fragmented into a number of disparate groups under different leaders who passed on positions of authority to their descendants.

The Hasidic movement inaugurated a profound change in Jewish life. During the medieval period the *Hasidei Ashkenaz* sought to achieve perfection through mystical activities. Subsequently this tradition was carried on by Lurianic kabbalists, who participated in various types of self-mortification. Opposing such practices, the Besht and his disciples stressed the omnipresence of God, rather than the kabbalistic ideas of the shattering of the vessels and the imprisonment of divine sparks by the power of evil. According to Hasidim, God is everywhere; the doctrine of *tzimtzum* was viewed as only an apparent withdrawal of the divine presence. As the Besht explained, God is always present even in human suffering.

For some Hasidim the concept of *devekut* (cleaving to God) in prayer was understood as the annihilation of selfhood and the ascent of the soul

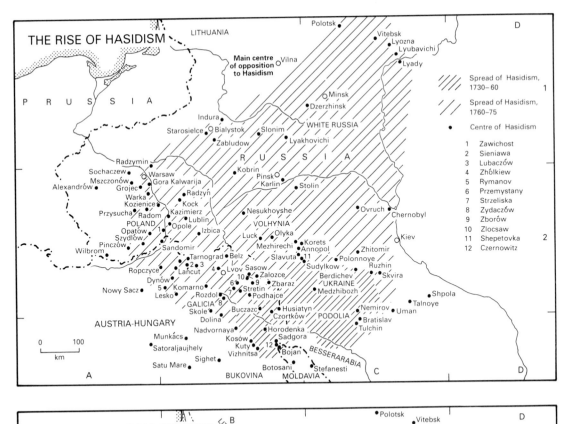

THE RISE OF HASIDISM

LITHUANIA

Main centre of opposition to Hasidism ○

○ Vilna

PRUSSIA

/// Spread of Hasidism, 1730–60

/// Spread of Hasidism, 1760–75

• Centre of Hasidism

Polotsk ○
Vitebsk •
Lyozna •
Lyubavichi •
Lyady •

Minsk ○
Dzerzhinsk •

Indura ○
Starosielce • Bialystok ○ Slonim •
Zabludow • Lyakhovichi •

WHITE RUSSIA

R U S S I A

Kobrin •
Pinsk ○
Karlin • Stolin •

Radzymin ○
Sochaczew • Warsaw ○
Mszczonów • Gora Kalwarija ○
Alexandrów • Grojec • Radzyń •
Warka • Kock •
Kozienice • Kazimierz •
Przysucha • Radom • Lublin •
POLAND Opole •
Opatów • Izbica •
Szydłów • Luck • Olyka •
Pinczów • Sandomir • Mezhirechi •
Wilbrom • Tarnograd • Belz • Slavuta •
Ropczyce • Lancut • Lvov ○ Sasow •
Dynów • 4 10 • Zalozce •
Nowy Sacz • 5 • Komarno • 6 • Stretin •
Lesko • Rozdol •
GALICIA 8 Podhajce •
Skole • Buczazc • Husiatyn •
Dolina • Czortków •
Nadvornaya • Horodenka •
Sadgora •

Nesukhoyshe •
VOLHYNIA

Ovruch •
Chernobyl •

Korets •
Annopol •
11 •
Polonnoye •
Zhitomir •
Berdichev •
Ruzhin •
Skvira •
UKRAINE
Medzhibozh •
Nemirov •
PODOLIA
Bratislav •
Tulchin •

Kiev ○

Shpola •
Talnoye •
Uman •

AUSTRIA-HUNGARY

Munkács •
Satoraljaujhely •
Satu Mare •

Kosów •
Kuty •
Vizhnitsa •
Sighet •
12 •
Bojan •

BESSERARABIA

Botosani •
Stefanesti •

BUKOVINA
MOLDAVIA

0   100
km

1 Zawichost
2 Sieniawa
3 Lubaczów
4 Zhólkiew
5 Rymanov
6 Przemystany
7 Strzeliska
8 Zydaczów
9 Zborów
10 Zlocsaw
11 Shepetovka
12 Czernowitz

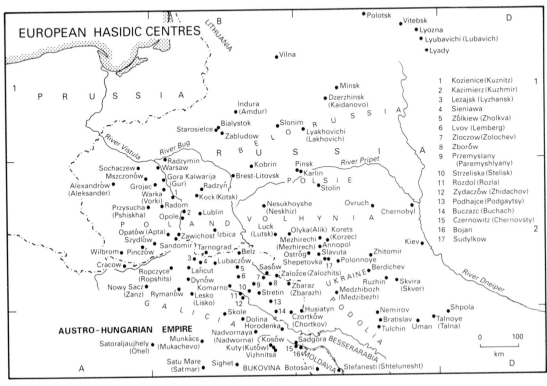

EUROPEAN HASIDIC CENTRES

LITHUANIA

PRUSSIA

River Vistula

River Bug

Polotsk •
Vitebsk •
Lyozna •
Lyubavichi (Lubavich) •
Lyady •

Vilna •

Minsk •

Indura (Amdur) •
Bialystok •
Starosielce • Slonim •
Zabludow • Lyakhovichi (Lakhovich) •

W H I T E   R U S S I A

Sochaczew • Radzymin •
Mszczonów • Warsaw •
Gora Kalwarija (Gur) •
Alexandrów (Aleksander) • Grojec •
Radzyń •
Warka (Vorki) •
Przysucha (Pshiskha) • Kock (Kotsk) •
Opole • Lublin •
POLAND
Opatów (Apta) •
Szydłów • Zawichost • Izbica •
Sandomir •
Wilbrom • Tarnograd • Belz •
Cracow • Lubaczów •
Ropczyce (Ropshits) • 3 • 4 •
Lancut • 5 •
Dynów • 6 •
Nowy Sacz (Zanz) • Komarno • 10 •
Rymanów • 11 •
Lesko (Lisko) • 12 • Stretin •
Skole •
G A L I C I A
Dolina •
Nadvornaya (Nadworna) •
Satoraljaujhely (Ohel) • Munkács (Mukachevo) •
Satu Mare (Satmar) •
Sighet •

Kobrin •
Brest-Litovsk •
Pinsk •
Karlin •
POLSIE
Stolin •
River Pripet

Nesukhoyshe (Neskhiz) •
VOLHYNIA
Luck (Lutsk) •
Olyka (Alik) • Korets •
Mezhirechi (Mezhirech) •
Ostróg • Annopol •
Shepetovka 17 • Slavuta •
Sasow • Polonnoye •
7 • Zalozce (Zalozhits) •
9 • 8 •
13 • Zbaraz (Zbarazh) •
14 • Husiatyn •
Czortków (Chortkov) •
Horodenka •
Kosów (Kutów) • Sadgora •
Kuty • 15 •
Vizhnitsa • 16 •
MOLDAVIA
Botosani •
BUKOVINA
Stefanesti (Shtelunesht) •

Ovruch •
Chernobyl •
Zhitomir •
Berdichev •
Ruzhin •
Skvira (Skver) •
UKRAINE
Medzhibozh (Medzibezh) •
PODOLIA
Nemirov •
Bratislav •
Tulchin •
Uman •
Talnoye (Talna) •
Shpola •

Kiev •

River Dneiper

AUSTRO-HUNGARIAN EMPIRE

1 Kozienice (Kuznitz)
2 Kazimierz (Kuzhmir)
3 Lezajsk (Lyzhansk)
4 Sieniawa
5 Zólkiew (Zholkva)
6 Lvov (Lemberg)
7 Zloczow (Zolochev)
8 Zborów
9 Przemyslany (Paremyshlyany)
10 Strzeliska (Stelisk)
11 Rozdol (Rozla)
12 Zydaczów (Zhidachov)
13 Podhajce (Podgaytsy)
14 Buczazc (Buchach)
15 Czernowitz (Chernovsty)
16 Bojan
17 Sudylkow

0   100
km

to the upper realms. In this context Hasidic worship embraced joy, humility, gratitude and spontaneity. The major obstacle to concentration in prayer is distracting thoughts. According to Hasidic teaching, such sinful intentions contain a divine spark which can be released. In this connection the kabbalistic stress on theoretical speculation was replaced by a concentration on mystical psychology in which inner bliss was viewed as the highest aim (rather than cosmic repair). For the followers of the Besht, it is possible to achieve *devekut* in everyday activities including eating, drinking, business affairs and sex. These ordinary acts become religious if in performing them one cleaves to God; *devekut* is thus obtainable by all Jews. In contrast with the earlier mystical tradition, Hasidism offered a means by which ordinary Jews could reach a state of mystical ecstasy.

Another important feature of the Hasidic movement was the institution of the *zaddik* (or *rebbe*). Rejecting the traditional position of the rabbinate, the Hasidim believed the *zaddikim* were spiritually superior individuals who had attained the highest level of *devekut*. Hasidic literature is filled with accounts of the spiritual and kabbalistic teaching of famous *zaddikim* as well as accounts of their miraculous deeds. Prominent among these figures were Zusya of Hanipol (eighteenth century), Shneur Zalman of Lyady (eighteenth–nineteenth century), Levi Yitzhak (eighteenth–nineteenth century), and Nahman of Bratislav (eighteenth–nineteenth century). These leaders developed their own doctrines, customs and musical traditions, and gathered around themselves disciples who travelled to their courts in the Ukraine and Polish Galicia.

11 JEWS IN EUROPE IN THE EIGHTEENTH AND NINETEENTH CENTURIES

Jewish status in Europe

European Jewish life in the eighteenth century was similar to that in medieval times. Although numerous changes had taken place in the early modern period, society and law were based on a hierarchy of privileges. Most monarchs ruled by divine right, and the nobility was exempt from

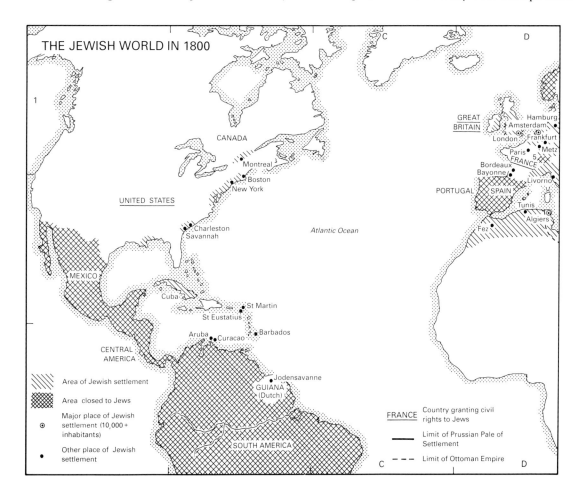

THE JEWISH WORLD IN 1800

Atlantic Ocean

CANADA

Montreal
Boston
New York

UNITED STATES

Charleston
Savannah

MEXICO

Cuba
St Martin
St Eustatius
Aruba   Barbados
Curacao

CENTRAL
AMERICA

Jodensavanne
GUIANA
(Dutch)

SOUTH AMERICA

GREAT
BRITAIN
London
Paris
FRANCE
Bordeaux
Bayonne
PORTUGAL   SPAIN
Fez

Hamburg
Amsterdam
Frankfurt
Metz
Livorno
Tunis
Algiers

///// Area of Jewish settlement

▨ Area closed to Jews

⊙ Major place of Jewish settlement (10,000 + inhabitants)

• Other place of Jewish settlement

FRANCE   Country granting civil rights to Jews

——— Limit of Prussian Pale of Settlement

- - - Limit of Ottoman Empire

direct taxation and enjoyed special rights for high office. In addition, the established Church was granted opportunities denied to other faiths, and guilds were frequently closed to outsiders. In many countries the peasantry owed the landowning nobility feudal dues and fees. Within this milieu Jews were denied numerous freedoms.

By 1770 there were approximately 2.25 million Jews world-wide, of whom 1.75 million lived in Christian Europe. In England and Holland the Jewish community was less burdened by economic restrictions – the Dutch and English governments did not interfere in their private or religious affairs. As a result Jews in these countries were restricted solely in those matters that affected all those not in communion with the established Church (such as owning real estate, becoming naturalized citizens and holding office). In Poland

Jews also had considerable freedom and were able to engage in a wide range of economic activities (including the export trade, many crafts, leasing of noble estates, and innkeeping). As in England and Holland, Polish Jewry was left to supervise its own communal affairs.

In contrast Jewish communities in central Europe were subject to numerous laws which limited their activities. Absolute monarchs sought to enhance the prestige of their countries, strengthen the civil administration and the army, and increase the wealth of society. As a result Jews were subject to regulation and supervision. According to these rulers, Jews should be prevented from having contact with Christians. Such a policy led to the creation of ghettos as well as special quotas which limited the number of Jewish families permitted to reside in a country.

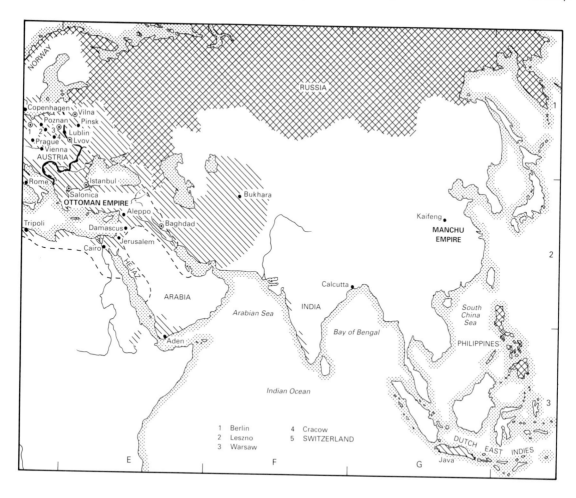

1	Berlin	4	Cracow
2	Leszno	5	SWITZERLAND
3	Warsaw		

These tolerated Jews were compelled to pay special protection taxes and marriage fees. Further, when Jewish travellers passed through a city or principality, they had to pay a body toll, and in court they had to swear a special oath (*more Judaico*). In addition, Jews were required to wear a distinctive sign on their clothing or hats of a special shape.

The treatment of Jews who were useful to the state can be seen in the charter issued in 1750 by Frederick II of Prussia. Jews were divided into four groups: (1) 'generally privileged' Jews, who were granted full residence and economic rights; (2) 'regularly protected' Jews, who were allowed to transmit the rights of domicile and occupation to their eldest son; (3) 'specially protected' Jews, who were favoured because of their pre-eminence; (4) 'tolerated' Jews, who were not allowed to marry and could live in Prussia only as long as they were employed by a licensed Jew. Business opportunities for all Jews were specifically defined. No Jew could engage in a manual trade if a Christian guild had a monopoly. Moreover, commodities that a Jewish merchant could buy were clearly delineated. Finally, the autonomy of the Jewish court was curtailed – rabbis were permitted to deal only with marriage, inheritance and other family affairs.

In the 1770s and 1780s defenders of Jewry argued that such restrictions should cease. The German historian and diplomat Wilhelm Christian Dohm, for example, published an essay in 1781 entitled 'Concerning the amelioration of the civil status of the Jews', in which he maintained that Jews would become patriotic citizens if they were granted various freedoms. According to Dohm, Jews were subject to oppressive conditions that caused them to be distrustful and concerned for their own economic interests. In conclusion he argued that a wise government would abolish those measures which prevented Jews from developing personal contact with Christians. All opportunities should be open to Jews to prepare them for taking an equal place in non-Jewish society.

Because of this shift in attitude the Holy Roman Emperor Joseph II (eighteenth century) instituted reform in the Habsburg territories of Austria, Hungary, Bohemia and Moravia. In 1780 he abolished the Jewish badge and body toll. The next year he issued an edict of toleration for Jews in Vienna and Austria which granted them access to trade and industry and eliminated ghettos. Jews were free to learn a craft or trade, employ Christian servants, and send their children to state schools.

French Jewry

In the 1770s and 1780s the improvement of French Jewish life became a topic of public concern. During this period French Jewry was divided into two distinct groups. The Sephardim living in Bordeaux and Bayonne were relatively prosperous – some of these Jews settled in Paris, where they constituted a semi-legal Jewish community. In addition Jews of the papal territory of Avignon benefited from the privileges granted to the Sephardic community. In Alsace and parts of Lorraine, however, Jewry was less advanced. Many engaged in trade and money-lending, retaining their autonomous communal structure and suffering from various disadvantages.

In 1789 the situation of French Jewry was transformed. Louis XVI summoned representatives of the clergy, the nobility and the rest of the population to Versailles to resolve the financial problems of the monarchy. This led to the creation of a National Assembly and popular uprisings throughout the country. In August 1789 the Assembly passed a Declaration of the Rights of Man and the Citizen which declared that 'all men are born, and remain, free and equal in rights'. Adopting principles of the French Enlightenment and the American Revolution, revolutionaries pressed for full equality. In July 1790 the Sephardim of south-west France and the Jews from papal Avignon were granted citizen-

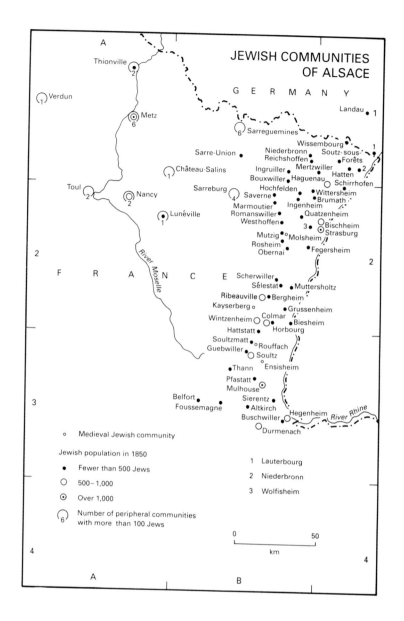

JEWISH COMMUNITIES
OF ALSACE

GERMANY

Thionville
Verdun
Metz
Sarreguemines
Landau
Wissembourg
Sarre-Union
Niederbronn
Reichshoffen
Soutz-sous-Forêts
Ingruiller
Mertzwiller
Hatten
Château-Salins
Bouxwiller
Haguenau
Schirrhofen
Toul
Sarreburg
Hochfelden
Wittersheim
Nancy
Saverne
Brumath
Marmoutier
Ingenheim
Lunéville
Romanswiller
Quatzenheim
Westhoffen
Bischheim
Strasburg
Mutzig
Molsheim
Rosheim
Fegersheim
Obernai

FRANCE

Scherwiller
Sélestat
Muttersholtz
Ribeauville
Bergheim
Kayserberg
Grussenheim
Wintzenheim
Colmar
Biesheim
Hattstatt
Horbourg
Soultzmatt
Rouffach
Guebwiller
Soultz
Thann
Ensisheim
Pfastatt
Mulhouse
Belfort
Sierentz
Foussemagne
Altkirch
Hegenheim
River Rhine
Buschwiller
Durmenach

River Moselle

o Medieval Jewish community

Jewish population in 1850

•   Fewer than 500 Jews
O   500–1,000
⊙   Over 1,000
(6) Number of peripheral communities
     with more than 100 Jews

1 Lauterbourg
2 Niederbronn
3 Wolfisheim

0   50
         km

ship rights, although the status of Ashkenazi Jewry was tabled. The next year the legal status of all Jews was debated. On 27–8 September the National Assembly decreed that the Jewish population should be liberated from previous restrictions.

The National Assembly, considering that the conditions requisite to be a French citizen, and to become an active citizen, are fixed by the constitution, and that every man who, being duly qualified, taxes the civic oath, and engages to fulfil all the duties prescribed by the constitution, has a right to all the advantages it insures – annuls all adjournments, restrictions, and exceptions, contained in the preceding decrees, affecting individuals of the Jewish persuasion, who shall take the civic oath, which shall be considered as a renunciation of all privileges granted in their favour.

During the 1790s French Jewry was affected by

the upheavals of society. In 1795 a revolution occurred in Holland with the assistance of the French army – Jews of the new Batavian republic were granted full citizenship rights on 9 September 1796. In the following year, when the French army conquered northern Italy, the ghettos of Padua and Rome were abolished. Similarly when the Rhineland was occupied, Jews were liberated from previous restrictions. In 1799 Napoleon became First Consul of France, later becoming emperor. Under Napoleon a new code of civil law was issued. In 1806 several German principalities were united in the French kingdom of Westphalia, where Jews were also granted citizenship rights.

The Napoleonic period thus made considerable progress toward the improvement of Jewish existence. None the less tensions existed between Jews and the peasantry in Alsace. In 1806 Napoleon suspended all debts owed Jews in eastern France, thereby siding with the peasantry against Jewish usury. In the same year he convened an Assembly of Jewish Notables from France and Italy who were presented with a number of questions about Jewish life, for example: Do Jewish marriage and divorce laws conflict with French legislation? Are Jews permitted to marry Christians? Do Jews consider Frenchmen their brothers and France their country? What are the Jewish views on usury?

In response the notables explained that Jewish religious law was compatible with French civil law. Further they stated that Jewish marriage and divorce were not valid unless preceded by a civil action, and that mixed marriages were binding according to civil law even though they could not be carried out by Jewish religious authorities. Moreover, they declared that French Jews regarded France as their fatherland and Frenchmen as their brothers. In 1807 Napoleon called a Grand Sanhedrin of rabbis and laymen to confirm the views of the notables. In response the Sanhedrin pledged its loyalty to the emperor and declared that any aspect of the Jewish faith that conflicted with the requirements of citizenship were no longer binding. In 1808 Napoleon

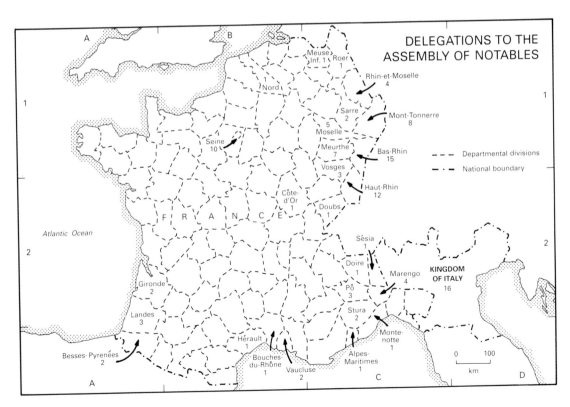

proclaimed two edicts: the first established a system of district consistories to supervise Jewish activities under a central Parisian consistory. These bodies were authorized to enforce conscription laws, encourage changes in Jewish occupations and act as Jewish policemen. The second edict reduced or postponed debts owed to Jews, restricted and regulated residence rights, and prevented Jewish conscripts from hiring substitutes.

Jewish emancipation in central Europe

Napoleon was defeated at the battle of Leipzig in October 1813, forced to abdicate in April 1814, and finally conquered at Waterloo in June 1815. From September 1814 to June 1815 the Congress of Vienna attempted to stabilize power in Europe: France was returned to the Bourbon dynasty, German states were drawn into the Germanic Confederation and the map of Europe was redrawn. At the Congress of Vienna Jewish delegates sought to ensure that their rights under French rule would be continued. Eventually the Congress instructed the Germanic Confederation to consider ameliorating the condition of Jewry. Despite such an agreement, German governments discarded the equality bestowed on Jews by the French and revitalized earlier discriminatory practices.

In pre-1815 Europe, rulers overturned the progressive attitudes fostered by France. In place of the stress on equal rights, Europe witnessed a revival of nationalism and racism. In Germany academics maintained that Jews were 'Asiatic aliens' unable to participate fully in German–Christian culture. As a result of such sentiments, riots (known as Hep Hep riots) took place in 1819 in a number of German cities. However, after 1830 political liberation began to affect central European society. Such literary figures as Ludwig Boerne and Heinrich Heine (who had both converted to Christianity) pressed for greater toleration, and the Jew Gabriel Riesser in a series of articles and pamphlets defended Jewry from persecution. According to Riesser, the Jews do not constitute a separate nation, nor does the Jewish tradition prevent Jews from being loyal to the countries where they live.

The spirit of emancipation was further intensi-fied by the French Revolution of 1848, which exerted a powerful influence on European society. Rebellions occurred in Prussia, Austria, Hungary, Italy and Bohemia. As a consequence European monarchs granted constitutions which guaranteed various liberties. In Germany a National Assembly was summoned to produce a constitution for the country; in December it issued a bill of rights. The following year, however, the Prussian king rejected the crown of a United Germany from the Assembly, thereby undermining the development of political liberalism in central Europe. Nevertheless in the 1850s and 1860s German liberals continued to struggle for the civil equality of all citizens. In the early 1860s the southern German states granted Jewry full rights, and in 1869 the North German Confederation decreed full emancipation to all its constituent states. Eventually when all Germany outside Austria was brought into the German Reich under the Hohenzollern dynasty, Jewish emancipation was complete.

In other parts of Europe Jewish civil liberties gained increasing acceptance. During the Austrian Revolution of 1848 the new constitution included freedom of religious conscience. In Hungary opposition to the Jews was expressed by the rebels in 1848, but when Jewish support was required their rights were confirmed. Later after the Hungarian uprising was suppressed, Franz Joseph adopted a favourable attitude to the Jews. In 1867, when the Habsburg realm was reorganized as Austria–Hungary, the constitutions of both parts incorporated equal rights for the Jewish population. In the same year Jewish equality was also extended to the Austrian province of Galicia. During the same period the

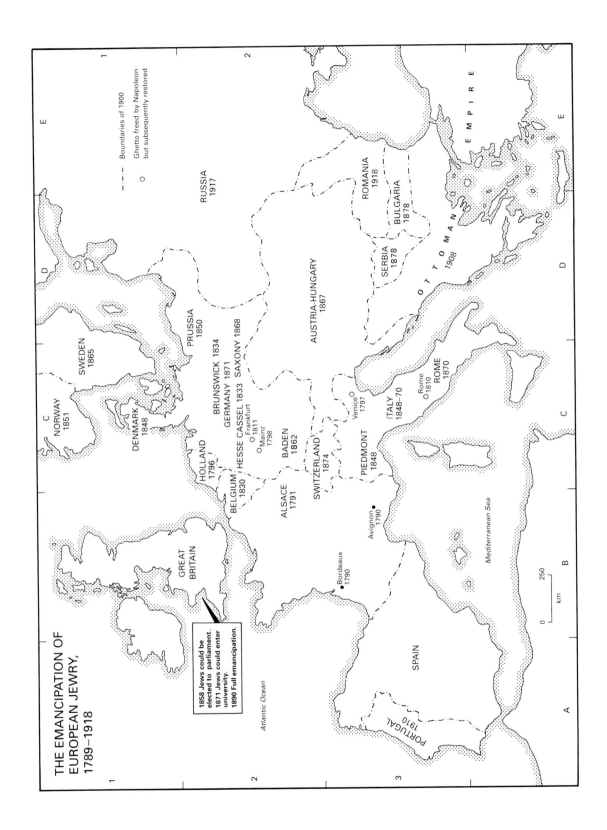

THE EMANCIPATION OF
EUROPEAN JEWRY,
1789–1918

——·—— Boundaries of 1900

○ Ghetto freed by Napoleon
but subsequently restored

1858 Jews could be
elected to parliament.
1871 Jews could enter
university.
1890 **Full emancipation.**

GREAT
BRITAIN

NORWAY
1851

SWEDEN
1865

DENMARK
1848

PRUSSIA
1850

RUSSIA
1917

HOLLAND
1796

BELGIUM
1830

BRUNSWICK 1834
GERMANY 1871
HESSE CASSEL 1833 SAXONY 1868
○ Frankfurt
1811
○ Mainz
1798

BADEN
1862

ALSACE
1791

SWITZERLAND
1874

PIEDMONT
1848

AUSTRIA-HUNGARY
1867

Venice ○
1797

Rome ○
1810

ITALY
1848–70

ROME
1870

SERBIA
1878

ROMANIA
1918

BULGARIA
1878

O T T O M A N

E M P I R E

1908

SPAIN

PORTUGAL
1910

Avignon
1790

Bordeaux
1790

Atlantic Ocean

Mediterranean Sea

0   250

km

elimination of restrictive laws against Jewry was enforced in Italy and later in Switzerland. These steps toward Jewish emancipation in Europe heralded a new stage in Jewish history in which Jews ceased to be subject to intolerance and discrimination.

Russian Jewry

In eastern Europe conditions were less favourable to Jewish emancipation. After the partitions of Poland in the latter half of the eighteenth century and the decision of the Congress of Vienna to place the Duchy of Warsaw under Alexander I, the majority of Polish Jews lived under Russian rule. At the beginning of the nineteenth century social classes in Russia were legally separated, the aristocracy retained its privileges, the peasantry lived as serfs and the Church was under state supervision. Throughout the century Jews were in the minority and worked in a wide range of occupations. In the countryside they were leasers of estates, mills, forests, distilleries and inns. None the less many of these individuals migrated to urban centres, where they laboured as members of the working class.

At first Catherine the Great was tolerant of her Jewish subjects, but in 1791 Jewish merchants were forbidden from living in central Russia. The only exception to this policy was in the southern Ukraine, where Jews were permitted to settle. Several years later this was followed by the granting of permission for Jews to reside in other areas, such as Kiev. At the beginning of the nineteenth century Alexander I designated territory in west Russia as an area where Jewish people would be allowed to reside – the Pale of Settlement. After several attempts to expel Jews from the countryside, in 1817 the Tsar attempted to integrate the Jewish community into the population by founding a society of Israelite Christians which extended various concessions to baptized Jews. Some time later Jews began to be deported from villages; in 1824 Alexander I died and was succeeded by Nicholas I, who adopted a restrictive policy toward the Jews. In 1827 he initiated a programme which inducted Jewish boys into the Russian army for a service of twenty-five years. In addition he deported Jews from villages in various areas.

In 1831 the Russian government promulgated a revised code of laws in order to regulate Jewish settlement on the eastern border. So as to reduce Jewish isolation, Nicholas I sought to reform Jewish education. In 1841 a Jewish educator, Max Lilienthal, was asked to found a number of Jewish schools in the Pale of Settlement which combined western educational methods with a secular curriculum. At first Lilienthal sought to persuade Jewish leaders that if this proposal were endorsed, Jewish life would be improved. However, when he found that the intention of the Tsar was to undermine traditional Jewish life, he left the country. In 1844 new schools were established, but they attracted small numbers. As a result the Russian government abandoned its plans to reform Jewish educational practices.

In 1844 the Tsar also abolished the *kehillot* and placed the Jewish population under the authority of the police as well as local government. Despite this initiative, the Russian administration found it was unable to carry out the functions of the *kehillot*. It soon became clear that a Jewish body was required to recruit students for state military schools and collect taxes. Later the government attempted to forbid Jewish dress, men's sidecurls, and the ritual of shaving women's hair. In 1851 an attempt was made to categorize Jews according to economic criteria: those considered to be useful included craftsmen, farmers and wealthy merchants, while the majority of Jews were subject to numerous restrictions. Several years later Alexander II emancipated the serfs, modernized the judiciary, and created a system of local self-government. Further, he permitted various groups – including wealthy merchants, university graduates, certified artisans,

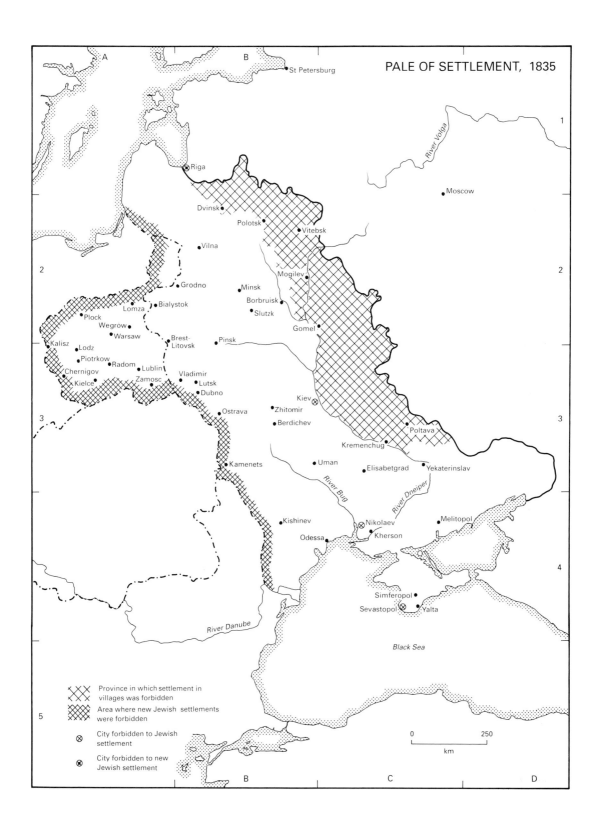

PALE OF SETTLEMENT, 1835

St Petersburg

River Volga

Moscow

Riga

Dvinsk
Polotsk
Vitebsk
Vilna
Mogilev
Grodno
Minsk
Lomza • Bialystok
Borbruisk
Plock
Slutzk
Wegrów
Warsaw
Gomel
Kalisz
Brest-Litovsk
Pinsk
Lodz
Piotrkow
Radom • Lublin
Chernigov
Vladimir
Kielce • Zamosc
Lutsk
Dubno
Kiev
Ostrava
Zhitomir
Berdichev
Poltava
Kremenchug
Kamenets
Uman
Elisabetgrad
Yekaterinslav

River Bug

River Dnieper

Kishinev
Nikolaev
Melitopol
Odessa
Kherson

River Danube

Simferopol
Sevastopol • Yalta

Black Sea

XXX Province in which settlement in
villages was forbidden

Area where new Jewish settlements
were forbidden

⊗ City forbidden to Jewish
settlement

⊗ City forbidden to new
Jewish settlement

0   250
km

140

discharged soldiers and holders of diplomas – to live outside the Pale of Settlement. In addition, a limited number of Jews were allowed to enter the legal profession and serve on district councils. During this period government-sponsored schools attracted increasingly large numbers of students, and in the 1860s and 1870s many Russian Jews began to take an active role in the professions and economic life.

The emancipation of Jewry

With the abolition of social disabilities throughout Europe, Jews were freed from previous social and economic restrictions. The dissolution of monopolistic patterns of employment opened up a wide range of economic opportunities. Jews were free to innovate in the production and distribution of goods as well as accumulate capital. In addition, a number of descendants of German court Jews became prominent merchant bankers in such financial centres as Frankfurt, Hamburg, London, Paris, Berlin, Vienna and St Petersburg. The most famous of these bankers were the Rothschilds, who founded banks in Vienna, Paris and London which floated governmental loans. Other Jewish bankers participated in railway construction. In Russia Jewish capitalists engaged in sugar refining, textile and tobacco manufacture, timber and grain export, railway construction and shipping. In Germany and Austria a number of Jews became active in journalism as publishers and reporters.

These changes in socio-economic life reversed the previous pattern of Jewish migration. Whereas in former times Jews moved from developed to less developed areas, Jewry in the nineteenth century left impoverished districts and villages to live in localities where the economy was more favourable. In Germany they moved from former Polish territory in the East to the Rhineland as well as to such cities as Leipzig, Cologne, Frankfurt and Berlin; in France they left Alsace for Paris; in Austria they migrated from Moravia and Galicia to Vienna; in Hungary they went to Budapest; in Russia from White Russia to cities in the Ukraine such as Odessa; and in Poland to Warsaw. The economic expansion and opportunities of the nineteenth century greatly improved the condition of western and central European Jewry, making them a middle-class group. However, for the mass of Russian Jews the situation deteriorated. Once the serfs were emancipated, Jews were squeezed out of their traditional roles in villages and towns. In the Russian Pale of Settlement most Jews worked in workshops and as domestic servants.

This alteration in Jewish life profoundly affected traditional Jewish institutions. The old corporate status of Jewry was eliminated, the *kehillot* no longer served any political function, and the community was unable to enforce religious discipline. Jewish identity thereby became a private concern instead of a legal status. Despite this transition, most Jews remained loyal to Judaism. Some, however, abandoned the Jewish faith and converted to Christianity. Among the descendants of Moses Mendelssohn, the father of the Jewish Enlightenment, his youngest son converted to Protestantism, and Abraham (the father of the composer Felix Mendelssohn) had his children converted. His brother-in-law, Bartholdy, was convinced this was the right course of action.

Do you think you have done something wrong in giving our children that religion which you think the better for them? It is a real tribute which you and we all are paying to your father's efforts for true enlightenment in general, and he would have acted like you have done for your children.... One can remain faithful to an oppressed, persecuted religion; one can force it on one's children in expectation of a life-long martyrdom – so long as one

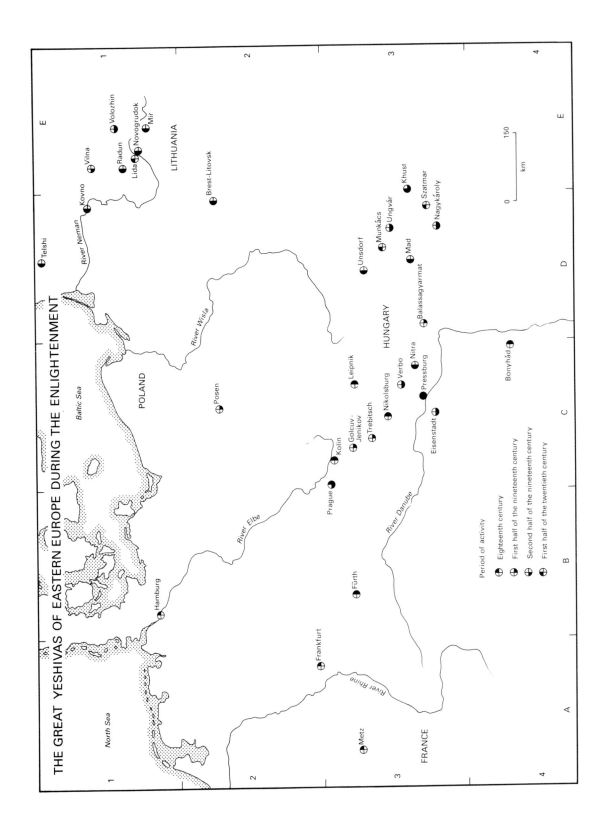

THE GREAT YESHIVAS OF EASTERN EUROPE DURING THE ENLIGHTENMENT

North Sea

Baltic Sea

Hamburg

River Elbe

River Wisla

POLAND

Posen

Prague

Kolin

Golcuv-
Jenikov

Trebitsch

Leipnik

Nikolsburg

Verbo

Nitra

Pressburg

Eisenstadt

Bonyhád

HUNGARY

Balassagyarmat

Mad

Ungvár

Munkács

Unsdorf

Szatmar

Khust

Nagykároly

River Danube

Fürth

Frankfurt

River Rhine

Metz

FRANCE

Telshi

River Neman

Kovno

Vilna

Radun

Lida

Novogrudok

Mir

Volozhin

Brest-Litovsk

LITHUANIA

0   150
km

Period of activity

Eighteenth century

First half of the nineteenth century

Second half of the nineteenth century

First half of the twentieth century

Figure 17 Portrait of David Friedländer
(Jewish National and University Library, Jerusalem)

believes it to be the only religion that can save you. But if one no longer believes this; then it is barbarous.

(Dan Cohn-Sherbok, *The Crucified Jew: Twenty Centuries of Christian Anti-Semitism* (London: Harper Collins, 1992), pp. 136–7)

During this period other Jews sought to transcend their Jewishness through conversion, yet unlike ordinary Christian converts they wished to form a new Judaeo-Christian sect. Under the leadership of David Friedländer, a group of the heads of enlightened Jewish families in Berlin declared their willingness to submit to baptism as long as they were not obliged to accept traditional Christian dogma. This request was addressed to Pastor Wilhelm Teller of the Lutheran consistory, who responded that he would grant baptism, but only if certain conditions were fulfilled: 'To be Christian', he stated, 'you must at least accept the sacraments of baptism and communion and acknowledge the historical truth that Christ is the founder of the most sublime moral religion.' Once this Jewish appeal was made public, numerous Christian objections were raised. Thus, though the ideals of the Enlightenment animated many Christians to seek the improvement of Jewish existence, undercurrents of Christian antipathy flowed just beneath the surface of public life.

12 THE DEVELOPMENT OF REFORM JUDAISM

The emergence of Jewish thought in the Enlightenment

The development of Jewish thought during the Enlightenment stemmed from seventeenth-century Holland. There various Jewish thinkers attempted to interpret the Jewish tradition in the light of scientific advances. In the seventeenth century Uriel Acosta maintained that the Torah was not of divine origin because it contained features contrary to natural law. In the same century Baruch Spinoza published a treatise (*Tractatus Theologico Politicus*) in which he argued that the prophets possessed moral insight rather than theoretical truth. Rejecting the Maimonidean conviction that Scripture contained a hidden meaning, Spinoza argued that the Bible was intended for the masses. According to Spinoza, God is depicted in Scripture as a lawgiver in order to appeal to the multitude. He believed that the Torah was not composed in its entirety by Moses; instead the historical books were compilations assembled by many generations.

For Spinoza the function of religion is to serve as a basis for ethical action; philosophy, however, is concerned with truth. In his writings Spinoza propounded a metaphysical system based on a pantheistic conception of nature. Beginning with the belief in an infinite, unlimited, self-caused Substance (which he conceived of as God or nature), Spinoza argued that Substance possesses a theoretical infinity of attributes. Only two of these – extension and thought – can be apprehended by human beings. In addition, God or

nature can be seen as a whole made up of finite individual entities. Given this view God exists in all things as their universal essence, and they exist in God as modifications. According to Spinoza, God is the sum of all natural laws. Further, he stressed that God is not incorporeal; rather he is the totality of all bodies in the universe. On this view, creation is ruled out, and the whole is free only in so far as it is self-caused.

Such reflection provided the background to the philosophical investigations of Moses Mendelssohn (1729–86). Born in Dessau, Mendelssohn went to Berlin, where he pursued secular and religious studies and became a friend of Gotthold Ephraim Lessing (1729–81), a leading figure of the German Enlightenment. When challenged by a Christian apologist to explain his dedication to Judaism, Mendelssohn published *Jerusalem, or on Religious Power and Judaism* in 1783. In this work he argued that no religious institution should attempt to coerce belief. Addressing the question whether the Mosaic law sanctions such coercion, Mendelssohn insisted that Judaism does not coerce the mind through dogma. Yet although Jewish law does not empower authorities to persecute individuals for holding false opinions, Jews should not absolve themselves from following Jewish law. 'Adopt the modes and constitution of the country in which you find yourself', he declared, 'but be steadfast in upholding the religion of the fathers too.'

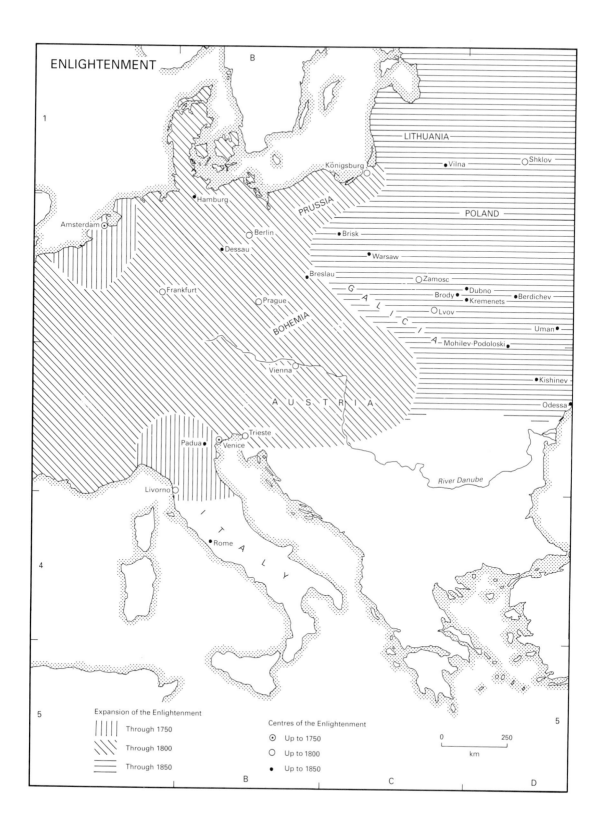

ENLIGHTENMENT

LITHUANIA

• Vilna   ○ Shklov

Königsburg ⊙

PRUSSIA

POLAND

• Hamburg

Amsterdam ⊙

• Berlin   • Brisk

• Dessau   • Warsaw

Breslau ○ ○ Zamosc
          • Dubno
○ Frankfurt   G   • Brody • Kremenets • Berdichev
                A
                L ○ Lvov
○ Prague   C   • Uman
                /
BOHEMIA   A — Mohilev-Podoloski •

Vienna ○

A U S T R I A   • Kishinev

                                  Odessa •

Trieste
Padua • ⊙ Venice

                    River Danube

Livorno ○

I
T
A
L   • Rome
Y

Expansion of the Enlightenment

| | Through 1750 |
| |||| Through 1800 |
| — Through 1850 |

Centres of the Enlightenment

⊙ Up to 1750

○ Up to 1800

• Up to 1850

0   250
          km

145

Figure 19 Moses Mendelssohn, on the left, playing chess with the Lutheran theologian J.C. Lavater (Jewish National and University Library, Jerusalem)

Figure 18 Portrait of Baruch Spinoza (The Mansell Collection, London)

Despite such a traditional orientation, Mendelssohn encouraged his fellow Jews to enter the mainstream of western European culture. To bring about such a modernization of Jewish life, Mendelssohn translated the Pentateuch into German so that Jews would be able to learn the language of the country in which they resided. In addition, he spearheaded a commentary on Scripture which combined Jewish scholarship with secular learning. Following this example, a number of followers (*maskilim*) fostered a Jewish Enlightenment – the Haskalah – which encouraged Jews to transcend the constrictions of ghetto life. To accomplish this end, they attempted to reform Jewish education by widening the curriculum to include secular subjects, wrote text-

books, and founded Jewish schools. In addition, they also produced the first Jewish literary magazine, *The Gatherer*, in 1783. Those who contributed to this publication wrote poems and fables in the classical style of biblical Hebrew and contributed studies of biblical exegesis, Hebrew linguistics and Jewish history.

In the 1820s the centre of this movement shifted to the Austrian empire. In Vienna a new journal, *First Fruits of the Times*, was published between 1821 and 1832; this was followed by a Hebrew journal, *Vineyard of Delight*, published between 1833 and 1856. In the 1840s the Haskalah spread to Russia; there writers made contributions to Hebrew literature and translated textbooks as well as European fiction into Hebrew. During the reign of Alexander II Hebrew weeklies appeared, and in 1863 the Society for the Promotion of Culture among the Jews was founded. During the next two decades *maskilim* also published works of social and literary criticism.

The beginnings of Reform Judaism

The first steps toward the reform of Judaism were initiated by the Jewish communal leader Israel Jacobson. At the beginning of the nineteenth century he established a school for boys at Seesen in Westphalia. Subsequently he founded other schools throughout the kingdom where general subjects were taught by Christians while a Jewish instructor gave lessons about the Jewish faith. In addition the consistory under Jacobson's leadership introduced external reforms to the Jewish liturgy including hymns and addresses, prayers in German and choral singing. In 1810 Jacobson founded the first Reform temple near the school; it was dedicated in the presence of Christian clergy and local dignitaries. After the defeat of Napoleon, Jacobson settled in Berlin, where he continued to put these reforms into practice.

During this period a Reform temple was opened in Hamburg, where similar alterations were made to the service of worship. In defence of these changes, the Hamburg reformers cited the Talmud for support. In 1819 the community published its own prayerbook, which omitted repetitions of prayers as well as medieval poems; it also changed some of the traditional prayers dealing with Jewish nationalism and messianic redemption. Such scholars as Aaron Chorin declared that it was obligatory to free the liturgy from its adhesions, to hold the service in a language understandable to the congregation, and to accompany it with organ and song. Not surprisingly such innovations provoked traditionalists to condemn the Hamburg Reform community.

The intention of these early reformers was to adapt Jewish worship to modern times. For these innovators the informality of the traditional service was undignified and unaesthetic. They therefore insisted on greater decorum, unison in prayer, a choir, hymns, musical responses and a shorter service. The quest for reform also generated a new intellectual development within post-Enlightenment Jewry, the creation of a Society for the Culture and Academic Study of Judaism. This body encouraged the scientific study of

history in order to gain a true understanding of the origins of the Jewish tradition in the history of western civilization. In 1824, however, the society collapsed, and several of its members converted to Christianity to advance their careers.

In opposition to these developments, some Orthodox Jews argued that any change to the tradition was a violation of the Jewish heritage. According to these traditionalists both the Written and Oral Torah comprise an infallible chain of divinely revealed truth. The most important of these scholars was Samson Raphael Hirsch, who received a secular education at the German gymnasium and the University of Bonn. In 1836 he published the *Nineteen Letters on Judaism*, a defence of Orthodoxy in the form of essays by a young rabbi to a friend who questioned the importance of remaining a Jew. The work began with a critique of Judaism of this period: 'While the best of mankind climbed to the summit of culture, prosperity, and wealth, the Jewish people remained poor in everything that makes human beings great and noble and that beautifies and dignifies our lives.'

In response Hirsch maintained that the purpose of human life is not to attain personal happiness and perfection. Instead human beings should strive to serve God by doing his will. As an example of such devotion, the Jewish people was formed so that through its way of life all nations would come to know that true happiness lies in obeying God. Thus, Hirsch maintained, the people of Israel were given the Promised Land so that they would be able to keep the Covenant. When the nation was exiled, they fulfilled this mission by remaining loyal to God and the Torah despite continual persecution and suffering. According to Hirsch, the purpose of the divine commandments is not to repress physical gratification of material prosperity; rather the goal of following God's law is to lead a religious life and thereby bear witness to the messianic ideal of universal brotherhood. Given this vision of God's plan, Reform Judaism was denounced for abandoning this sacred duty. For Hirsch citizenship rights are of little importance, since Jews are united by a bond of obedience to God's laws until the time when the 'Almighty shall see fit in his inscrutable wisdom to unite again his scattered servants in one land, and the Torah shall be the guiding principle of a state, a model of the meaning of Divine revelation and the mission of humanity' (*Nineteen Letters on Judaism*).

THE JEWS IN THE RUSSIAN EMPIRE IN THE LATE NINETEENTH CENTURY

- ● Large city with at least 40,000 Jews
- ⊙ Community of 30,000–40,000 Jews
- ○ Community of 20,000–30,000 Jews
- • Community of 10,000–20,000 Jews
- ⊗ City barred to Jewish residence (by order of Nicholas I)
- ——— Pale of Settlement
- – – – Regional boundary
- - - - Provincial boundary
- 58,000 Jewish population of province

The growth of Reform

Despite the criticisms of traditionalists, a number of German rabbis began to re-evaluate the Jewish tradition. In this milieu such scholars as Leopold Zunz made a profound impact. As this new movement increased in strength, Orthodox rabbis increasingly attacked its ideas and leadership. In 1838, for example, the Chief Rabbi of Breslau, Solomon Tiktin, denounced Abraham Geiger as a radical. In 1842 Tiktin published a tract in which he insisted on the validity of the Jewish tradition. In response Geiger's supporters issued *Rabbinic Responses on the Compatibility of Free Investigation with the Exercise of Rabbinic Functions*. These religious exchanges between reformers and traditionalists resulted in bitter animosity.

During this period Reform Judaism spread to other European cities. In 1842, for example, the Society of the Friends of Reform was founded in Frankfurt. In a declaration of its principles, the society stated that it recognized the possibility of unlimited progress in the Jewish faith and rejected the authority of the legal code and the doctrine of the Messiah. In addition, members of the society viewed circumcision as a barbaric rite. Incensed by such opinions, the Chief Rabbi of Prague, Solomon Rapoport, cautioned against associating with reformers: 'We must strictly insist and warn our coreligionists not to have any social contacts with the members of this Reform association, and especially not to enter into matrimonial union with them.'

In Berlin a similar association was founded in 1844 under the leadership of Samuel Holdheim. This association published a prayerbook in German which contained little Hebrew and abolished such customs as praying with covered heads and the blowing of the shofar. In its proclamation the Berlin group declared:

We can no longer recognize a code as an unchangeable law-book which maintains with unbending insistence that Judaism's task is expressed by forms which originated in a time which is forever past and which will never return ... we are stirred by the trumpet sound of our own time. It calls us to be of the last of a great inheritance in this old form, and at the same time, the first who, with unswerving courage are bound together as brothers in word and deed, shall lay the cornerstone of a new edifice.

The first Reform synod took place in Brunswick in 1844 in which participants argued for the formulation of a Jewish creed, the modification of Sabbath and dietary laws, and a reformulation of the traditional liturgy. The following year another consultation took place in Frankfurt which recommended that petitions for the return to Israel as well as the restoration of the Jewish state be eliminated from the prayerbook. At this conference one of the more conservative participants, Zacharias Frankel, expressed his unease with the synod's decision to regard the use of Hebrew in worship as advisable rather than necessary. After resigning from the Assembly, he became head of a Jewish theological seminary in Breslau based on free enquiry combined with a commitment to the Jewish tradition. A third synod was held in 1846 in Breslau which discussed Sabbath observance. Although these reformers upheld the rabbinic prescriptions against working on the Sabbath, they maintained that the talmudic injunctions regarding the boundary for walking on the Sabbath were no longer binding. In addition, they stipulated that second-day observances of festivals should be discarded.

The revolution of 1848 and its aftermath brought an end to these conferences – nearly a generation passed before reformers met together to formulate a common policy. In 1868 a group of twenty-four rabbis assembled in Kassel to lay the foundations for a conference of rabbis, scholars and communal leaders. The next year over eighty congregations were represented when this synod met in Leipzig under the leadership of Moritz Lazarus. Two years later another conference was held in Augsburg which dealt with theological issues and practical problems. In a statement

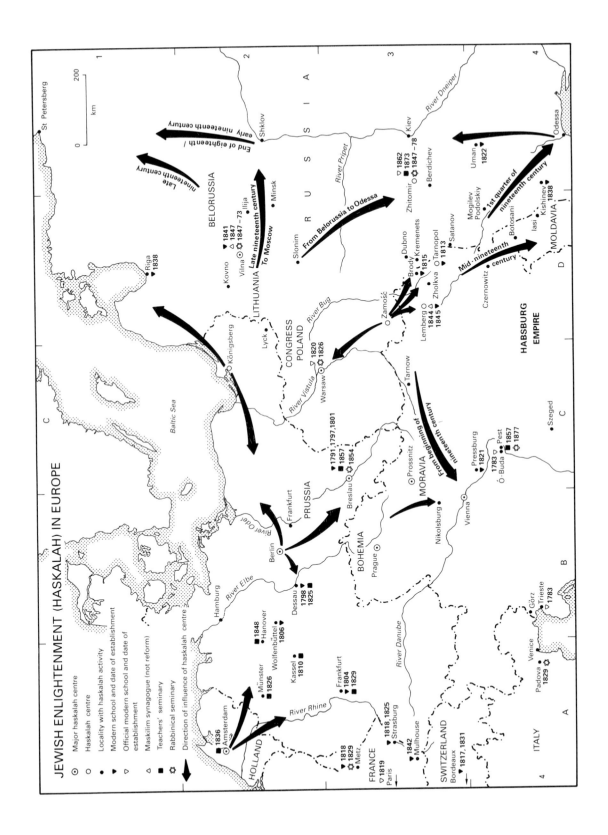

JEWISH ENLIGHTENMENT (HASKALAH) IN EUROPE

⊙ Major haskalah centre
○ Haskalah centre
● Locality with haskalah activity
▶ Modern school and date of establishment
▽ Official modern school and date of establishment
△ Maskilim synagogue (not reform)
■ Teachers' seminary
✡ Rabbinical seminary
→ Direction of influence of haskalah centre

St Petersberg

RUSSIA

BELORUSSIA

End of eighteenth / early nineteenth century

Late nineteenth century

To Moscow

Late nineteenth century

From Belorussia to Odessa

Shklov

Kiev

▽ 1862
▽ 1873
Zhitomir ✡ 1847–78
Berdichev

Uman ●
▪ 1822

Odessa

River Dnieper

River Pripet

Minsk

LITHUANIA

Kovno ●
Vilna ⊙ ▼ 1841
△ 1847
✡ 1847–73
Ilija

Slonim ●

1st quarter of nineteenth century

Mogilev Podolskiy ●

Satanov ●

Kremenets
Dubno
Brody ○
Tarnopol ○ 1813
Zholkva ○
Lemberg ○ 1815
1844 △
1845 ▶

Botosani ●

Czernowitz ●

Mid-nineteenth century

Iasi ●

Kishinev ▪ 1838

MOLDAVIA

Riga ▪ 1838

Baltic Sea

Königsberg

Lyck ●

CONGRESS POLAND

River Bug

Zamość ○

Warsaw ⊙ ▶ 1820
✡ 1826

River Vistula

Tarnow ●

HABSBURG EMPIRE

Hamburg

River Elbe

Münster ■ 1848
Hanover
Wolfenbüttel ■ 1826
1806

Frankfurt

PRUSSIA

Berlin ⊙

Dessau ▶ 1798
■ 1825

River Oder

Breslau ▶ 1791,1797,1801
■ 1857
✡ 1854

BOHEMIA

Prague ⊙

From beginning of nineteenth century

MORAVIA

Nikolsburg ●

Vienna ●

Pressburg ▶ 1821
Ó-Buda 1783 ▽
Pest ● ▪ 1857
✡ 1877

Prossnitz ●

Szeged ●

Kassel ● 1810

Frankfurt ▶ 1804
■ 1829

Amsterdam ■ 1836

HOLLAND

River Rhine

FRANCE
Paris ▽ 1819
Metz ▶ 1818
✡ 1829

Strasburg 1818, 1825

Mulhouse ▶ 1842

SWITZERLAND
Bordeaux 1817,1831

ITALY

Venice ●

Görz ●
Trieste ✡ 1783

Padova ✡ 1829

River Danube

km
0   200

issued by this synod, the participants enumerated the principles and tasks of Reform Judaism. According to these reformers, Judaism has always undergone change and development; in the light of this they argued that Reform marks a new and important beginning. Although the essence and mission of Judaism remain unchanged, numerous ceremonies should be regenerated and obsolete and antiquated elements of the tradition should be discarded. To complete this task of renewal, the synod viewed itself as the vehicle of change. Dedicated to the quest for truth, the participants declared 'It [the synod] intends to labour with clear purpose so that the reform of Judaism for which we have striven for several decades should be secured in the spirit of harmony.'

The development of Reform in the United States

By the beginning of the nineteenth century the Jewish population in the United States had undergone a substantial increase as immigrants from Europe sought refuge from persecution. With this influx of European Jews Reform Judaism began to flourish. In 1824 a small congregation in Charleston, South Carolina, introduced some of the reforms of Germany's Hamburg Temple into their liturgy. According to one of these reformers, Isaac Harby, the desire of the Reform community was 'to take away everything that might excite the disgust of the well-informed Israelite'. Following the revolution of 1848 a number of Reform Jews from Germany fled to the United States; many of these immigrants settled in New York. Among these German newcomers were several Reform rabbis who had taken an active part in the European Reform synods of previous years.

Prominent among these reformers were David Einhorn of Har Sinai congregation in Baltimore, and Samuel Adler and Gustave Gottheil of Temple Emanuel in New York. Yet it was not until Isaac Mayer Wise began to exercise his leadership and organizing skills that Reform Judaism took firm root on American soil. Born in Bohemia, Wise came to the United States in 1846 to accept a rabbinical post in Albany, New York. Initially his efforts provoked outrage. He was assaulted during a New Year service. 'At the conclusion of the song', he wrote, 'I stopped before the ark in order to take out the scrolls of the Law as usual, and to offer prayer. Spaniel [a member of the congregation] stepped in my way, and without saying a word, smote me with his fist so that my cap fell from my head. This was the signal for an uproar the like of which I have never experienced.' Subsequently Wise settled in Cincinnati, Ohio, where he published several Jewish newspapers as well as a new Reform prayerbook (*Minhag Amerika*). In addition, Wise was anxious to convene an American synod as well as bring the scattered Reform communities together under a single body. After several attempts at rabbinic union, the first conference of American Reform Rabbis met in Philadelphia in 1869; four years later the Union of American Hebrew Congregations was established, comprising both lay and rabbinical representatives. In 1875 Wise established the Hebrew Union College for the training of Reform rabbis.

In 1885 a gathering of Reform rabbis took place in Pittsburgh, Pennsylvania, to set out the principles of the movement. Under the chairmanship of Kaufmann Kohler, this body formulated its policy statement: the Pittsburgh Platform. In his address to this gathering, Kohler stated that their aim was to demonstrate that Judaism must be modernized in order to embrace the findings of scientific research, biblical criticism and comparative religion. The Platform itself commenced with the declaration that Judaism presents the highest conception of God. In this regard the conference declared that the Bible is the most potent instrument of religious and moral instruction. For these reformers, Scripture was

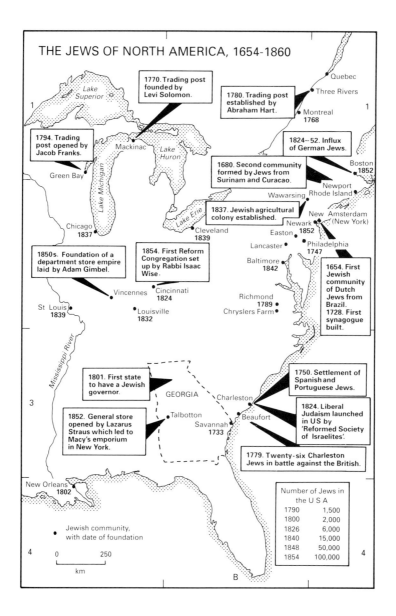

THE JEWS OF NORTH AMERICA, 1654-1860

1770. Trading post founded by Levi Solomon.

1780. Trading post established by Abraham Hart.

Quebec

Three Rivers

Montreal 1768

1794. Trading post opened by Jacob Franks.

Mackinac

1824–52. Influx of German Jews.

1680. Second community formed by Jews from Surinam and Curacao.

Boston 1852

Green Bay

Newport Rhode Island

Wawarsing

New Amsterdam (New York)

Chicago 1837

1837. Jewish agricultural colony established.

Cleveland 1839

Newark 1852

Easton

Philadelphia 1747

1850s. Foundation of a department store empire laid by Adam Gimbel.

1854. First Reform Congregation set up by Rabbi Isaac Wise.

Lancaster

Baltimore 1842

1654. First Jewish community of Dutch Jews from Brazil. 1728. First synagogue built.

Vincennes

Cincinnati 1824

Richmond 1789

Chryslers Farm

St Louis 1839

Louisville 1832

1801. First state to have a Jewish governor.

GEORGIA

Charleston

1750. Settlement of Spanish and Portuguese Jews.

1852. General store opened by Lazarus Straus which led to Macy's emporium in New York.

Talbotton

Savannah 1733

Beaufort

1824. Liberal Judaism launched in US by 'Reformed Society of Israelites'.

1779. Twenty-six Charleston Jews in battle against the British.

New Orleans 1802

Mississippi River

Lake Superior

Lake Huron

Lake Michigan

Lake Erie

• Jewish community, with date of foundation

0   250

km

Number of Jews in the U S A	
1790	1,500
1800	2,000
1826	6,000
1840	15,000
1848	50,000
1854	100,000

B

viewed as compatible with the findings of science: 'We hold that the modern discoveries of scientific researches in the domains of nature and history are not antagonistic to the doctrines of Judaism, the Bible reflecting the primitive ideas of its own age and at times clothing its conception of Divine providence and justice dealing with man in miraculous narratives.'

The participants also proclaimed that they recognized as binding only the moral commandments and those rituals which they viewed as spiritually meaningful. Ritual laws regulating diet, priestly purity and dress were eliminated as anachronistic. The belief in a personal Messiah was also rejected; in its place the conference endorsed the messianic hope for the establishment of a kingdom of justice and peace for humanity. For these reformers Judaism was conceived as a progressive religion 'ever striving to be in accord with the postulates of reason'. Concerning the afterlife, the doctrines of bodily resurrection and reward and punishment in the hereafter were replaced by a belief in the immortality of the soul: 'We reject as ideas not rooted in Judaism the belief both in bodily resurrection and in *Gehinnom* and Eden as abodes for everlasting punishment and reward.' In conclusion the delegates pledged their commitment to social action. This declaration of religious beliefs together with the rabbinical and congregational organizations of Reform Judaism provided a framework for the growth and development of Reform Judaism in the next century.

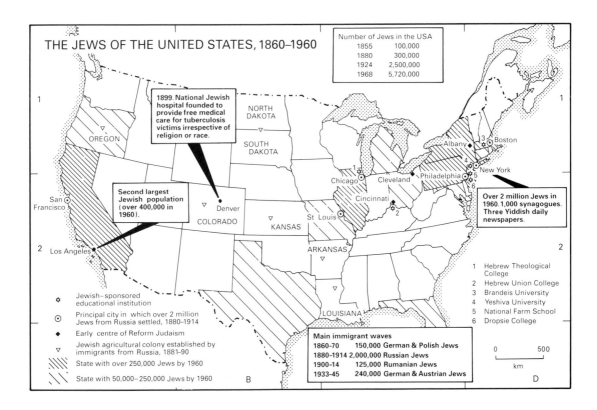

THE JEWS OF THE UNITED STATES, 1860–1960

Number of Jews in the USA	
1855	100,000
1880	300,000
1924	2,500,000
1968	5,720,000

1899. National Jewish hospital founded to provide free medical care for tuberculosis victims irrespective of religion or race.

Second largest Jewish population (over 400,000 in 1960).

Over 2 million Jews in 1960. 1,000 synagogues. Three Yiddish daily newspapers.

1 Hebrew Theological College
2 Hebrew Union College
3 Brandeis University
4 Yeshiva University
5 National Farm School
6 Dropsie College

✿ Jewish-sponsored educational institution
⊙ Principal city in which over 2 million Jews from Russia settled, 1880–1914
◆ Early centre of Reform Judaism
▽ Jewish agricultural colony established by immigrants from Russia, 1881–90
▨ State with over 250,000 Jews by 1960
▧ State with 50,000–250,000 Jews by 1960

Main immigrant waves	
1860-70	150,000 German & Polish Jews
1880-1914	2,000,000 Russian Jews
1900-14	125,000 Rumanian Jews
1933-45	240,000 German & Austrian Jews

0   500
km

Jewish thought in the age of Reform

During the nineteenth century a number of German Reform rabbis sought to investigate the course of Jewish history. Of particular prominence was Abraham Geiger. Born in Frankfurt, Geiger served as a rabbi in Wiesbaden, where he edited the *Scientific Journal for Jewish Theology*. In 1838 he was appointed rabbi in Breslau, where he published studies on various Jewish subjects as well as a book on the ancient text and translations of the Bible. Although Geiger did not produce a systematic Jewish theology, his approach was based on a programme to reformulate Judaism according to the scientific spirit of the age. For Geiger the evolution of history is divided into four stages: in the age of revelation the idea of Judaism was understood as a moral and spiritual concept capable of continual development. During the second stage – the age of tradition – the Bible was constantly reshaped and reinterpreted. The third stage – the age of legalism – formalized the tradition to ensure its continuance. Finally in the age of critical study, legalism was transcended through historical investigation. Even though Jewish law is not binding in this fourth stage, this does not imply that Judaism is severed from its past. Rather historical study can revitalize the faith.

Another major thinker of this period, Heinrich Graetz, was similarly concerned with the scientific study of Judaism. In the 1840s Graetz endorsed Zacharias Frankel's approach to the Jewish tradition. For Graetz the essence of Judaism resides not only in a theoretical conception of the Jewish faith but also in those aspects of the Jewish tradition that the reformers rejected. Following Hegel, Graetz argued that all aspects of Judaism are an unfolding of the faith as a religious system. According to Graetz this was not a logical but rather a historical process, and he attempted to demonstrate how Jewish beliefs and practices evolved through history. Judaism, he maintained, cannot be reduced to an abstract definition – instead the Jewish heritage is historically based and can be divided into three periods.

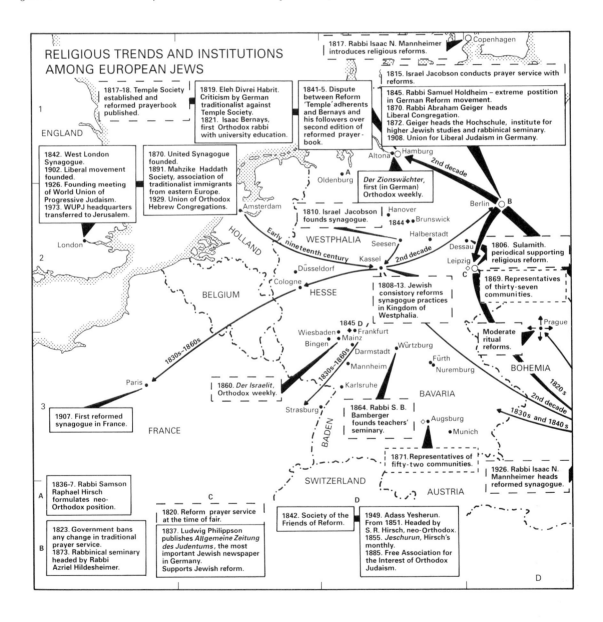

RELIGIOUS TRENDS AND INSTITUTIONS AMONG EUROPEAN JEWS

154

The first stage began with the conquest of the land and ended with the destruction of the Temple in 586 BC. The second stage occurred after the Babylonian exile and lasted until the destruction of the Temple in AD 70. For Graetz the third stage was the diaspora period, when Jews attempted to attain intellectual self-perfection and rationalize the faith.

Like Geiger and Graetz, other Jewish thinkers sought to integrate German philosophical ideas into their conceptions of Judaism. In 1841

Solomon Formstecher published *The Religion of the Spirit*. According to Formstecher, the ultimate reality is in the Divine World Soul, which manifests itself in nature and in spirit. Nature, Formstecher argued, is an organic hierarchy of events and forces which reaches self-consciousness in the realm of spirit. As the highest form of consciousness, spirit can be known through its manifestations, yet Formstecher was anxious to point out that such ideas are simply symbols incapable of describing God's essence. On the

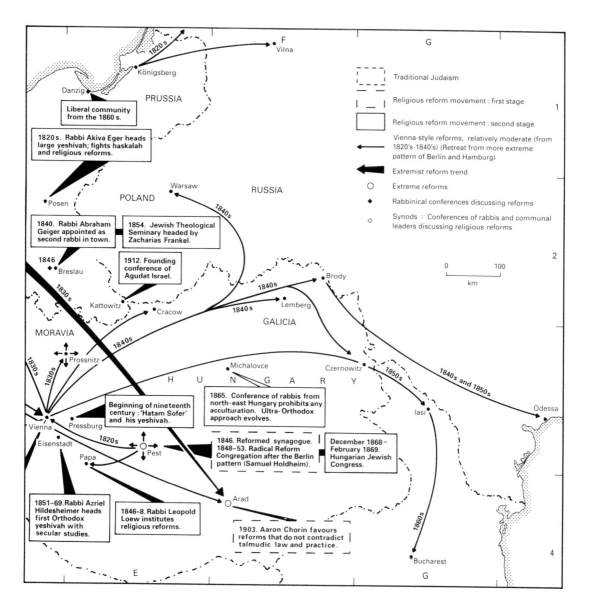

basis of this scheme, Formstecher distinguished between the religion of nature and the religion of spirit. The religion of nature, he argued, refers to paganism; the religion of spirit, on the other hand, identifies God not only with nature but also with the ethical good. In the history of religions, Judaism was the first religion of spirit, but has undergone development. In the early stages of Jewish history, truth was understood through statehood and later by a theocracy of religious law. After the emancipation of Jewry occurred, it became possible for Jews to accomplish the mission of establishing a universal ethical religion of spirit for all peoples.

Another Reform rabbi, Samuel Hirsch, utilized German idealism in the presentation of his conception of Jewish history. In 1842 Hirsch published *The Religious Philosophy of the Jews*, in which he adopted Hegel's view that human beings become free by viewing themselves as distinct persons. According to Hirsch sin is moral rather than intellectual in character; it can only be eliminated through moral action. Thus the central feature of religion is not the self-realization of God, but the actualization of moral freedom. In this light Hirsch understood religion as either passive or active. Within passive religions (such as paganism), believers are dominated by their sensual side, and nature is understood as divine. But in active religions the believers can attain self-chosen moral freedom. During the patriarchal period Judaism possessed the insight of active religion: miracles and prophecies were necessary to eliminate paganism. Yet the need for miraculous occurrences has ceased – the only miracle is the survival of the Jewish people. On this basis Hirsch argued that there is no evolution of truth in Judaism. The purpose of education is to encourage Jews to become moral and to act as God's suffering servants.

A fourth central figure of this period was Solomon Ludwig Steinheim, who published *Revelation and the Doctrine of the Synagogue* in the mid-nineteenth century. For Steinheim Judaism should not be confused with philosophical reflection. Unlike previous Jewish writers, Steinheim argued that the Bible contains beliefs contrary to ancient Greek philosophy as well as modern thought. Adopting Kant's notion of things-in-themselves (which cannot be known through human knowledge), Steinheim maintained that reason is limited in scope and must be supplemented by revelation. In advancing this view, Steinheim asserted that natural religion is based on the assumption that everything has a cause as well as the belief that nothing can come from nothing. Such concepts, however, are incompatible: the first implies that God is the First Cause, whereas the second rules out the need for God. The only way out of this difficulty is through the biblical view that the creation of the universe was due to the divine act. Such a belief qualifies determinism and supplies a basis for moral freedom.

13 JEWRY IN THE NINETEENTH AND EARLY TWENTIETH CENTURIES

The rise of anti-Semitism

By the latter part of the nineteenth century Jews in Europe were largely emancipated. None the less political conditions after 1870 caused considerable disruption. A number of independent nations emerged and fought against indigenous minority groups in their midst. Under such conditions Jews were viewed as unassimilable. Typical of such attitudes was the coinage of the term 'anti-Semitism' by Wilhelm Marr in the 1870s. Unlike previous anti-Jewish notions based on religious grounds, Marr focused on biological descent. Anti-Semitism was thus a racist policy directed against the Jewish population. According to Marr, the Jews have 'corrupted all standards, have banned all idealism from society, dominate commerce, push themselves ever more in state services, rule the theatre, form a social and political phalanx'.

Such antipathy intensified in the 1870s in Germany because of economic and cultural upheaval. In 1878 Adolf Stocker founded a Christian Social Party on the basis of such anti-Jewish policies. By accusing the press as well as financial institutions of being controlled by Jewish interests, he drew numerous artisans, shopkeepers, clerks and professionals to his political movement. German nationalists also supported such allegations, emphasizing that Jews needed to assimilate to German life before they could be accepted as full citizens. In 1881 Eugen Duhring maintained that the Jewish type constituted a biological threat to the German people. In the same year a petition of 225,000

signatures was presented to stop all Jewish immigration; this was followed in 1882 by an international anti-Semitic congress. In the next decade sixteen deputies from anti-Semitic parties were elected to the German Reichstag. Finally, at the end of the century Karl Lueger utilized anti-Semitism to establish the first political party in Europe which obtained power on the basis of anti-Jewish sentiment.

In France anti-Semitism was also fostered by the monarchy and clergy, who were dissatisfied with the liberal ideas propounded during the French Revolution. Such antipathy reached a climax with the Dreyfus affair: accused of treason, Alfred Dreyfus was expelled from the army and sentenced to life imprisonment in 1894. Later it was found that forged evidence was used to implicate Dreyfus: this discovery evoked a public scandal which divided public opinion. Many believed Dreyfus was part of a Jewish conspiracy to undermine the military and discredit France. His supporters however viewed the court martial of Dreyfus as a major injustice. Although Dreyfus was eventually pardoned, this episode illustrated that despite the forces of emancipation anti-Semitism was deeply rooted in European life.

In Russia anti-Semitism became a state policy. After the assassination of Alexander II in 1881, a series of pogroms against the Jewish population took place in the southern Ukraine. In 1882 the Minister of the Interior issued various laws which curtailed Jewish residence in the Pale of Settlement. By the later 1880s quotas were imposed on

Figure 20   Lithograph of Dreyfus' second trial before a court-martial at Rennes, 1899 (Leo Baeck Institute, New York)

the admission of Jews to Russian schools, universities and professions. In 1891–2 more than 20,000 Jews were expelled from Moscow, and at the beginning of the next century a violent pogrom was unleashed on the Jews of Kishinev. In 1904 Jews were accused of aiding the enemy in the war against Japan; as a consequence armed gangs attacked Jews throughout the country. Although such outbursts ceased in 1907, a right-wing political party (the Union of the Russian People) instigated a campaign of anti-Semitic propaganda. In the next decade Mendel Beilis –

a Jew from Kiev – was accused of ritual murder, but was exonerated in 1913.

These manifestations of hostility toward Jewry were based on the conviction that the Jewish people constitute a dangerous racial group. According to anti-Semitic propagandists, the Jewish mentality is egoistic, materialistic, economic-minded, cowardly and culturally degenerate. Pre-eminent among racist theorists was Houston Stewart Chamberlain, whose *The Foundations of the Nineteenth Century* was published at the turn of the century. In this work Chamberlain

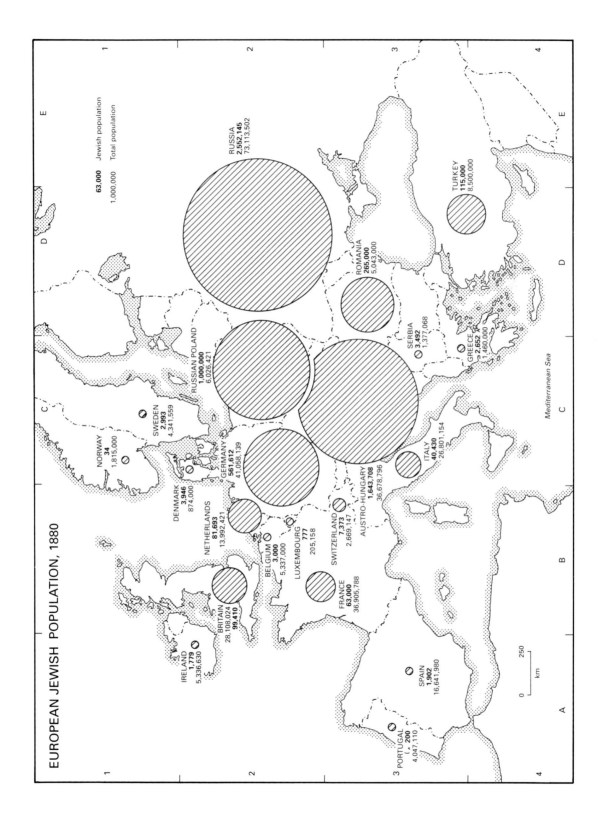

EUROPEAN JEWISH POPULATION, 1880

63,000 Jewish population
1,000,000 Total population

RUSSIA
2,552,145
73,113,502

TURKEY
115,000
8,500,000

ROMANIA
265,000
5,043,000

SERBIA
3,492
1,377,068

GREECE
2,652
1,460,000

RUSSIAN POLAND
1,000,000
6,026,421

SWEDEN
2,993
4,341,559

NORWAY
34
1,815,000

DENMARK
3,946
874,000

GERMANY
561,612
41,058,139

ITALY
40,430
26,801,154

NETHERLANDS
81,693
13,992,421

AUSTRO-HUNGARY
1,643,708
36,678,796

BELGIUM
3,000
5,337,000

LUXEMBOURG
777
205,158

SWITZERLAND
7,373
2,669,147

FRANCE
63,000
36,905,788

BRITAIN
28,108,024
99,410

IRELAND
1,779
5,336,630

SPAIN
1,902
16,641,980

PORTUGAL
200
4,047,110

Mediterranean Sea

0   250
km

argued that the antiquity and mobility of the Jewish nation illustrate that the confrontation between superior Aryans and parasitic Semites is the central theme of history. During this period the forgery *Protocols of the Elders of Zion* was believed to be the minutes of a clandestine world government. In this document the Jewish elders were described as attempting to increase their hold over the European economy, the press, the parties opposed to the Tsar, and other autocratic regimes.

Zionism

After the pogroms of 1881–2 many Jews emigrated from eastern Europe to the United States and elsewhere. In the Pale of Settlement nationalists formed Zionist groups (Lovers of Zion): these bodies collected money and organized courses in Hebrew and Jewish history. Subsequently thousands of Jews left for Palestine, where they worked as shopkeepers and artisans. Other Jews, known as Bilu, combined Marxist principles with Zionist ideals and worked as farmers and labourers. During this period Leon Pinsker published *Autoemancipation*, in which he insisted that the liberation of Jewry could only be secured by the creation of a Jewish homeland.

By the end of the century the idea of Jewish nationalism had spread to other European centres. Foremost among its advocates was Theodor Herzl. In 1887 the First Zionist Congress was convened in Basle; at this gathering Herzl argued that the emancipation of Jewry had been an illusion: Jews were inevitably the targets of discrimination and persecution. The only solution for Jewry, he believed, was to establish a Jewish homeland in Palestine. At this time the Zionist Organization was created, with branches in Europe and America. After these basic institutions of the Zionist movement were formed, Herzl met with Kaiser Wilhelm II, who promised he would take up the matter with the Sultan. When nothing came of this, Herzl arranged for the interview to take place in 1901. During this interview Herzl suggested that wealthy Jewish bankers might be willing to pay off the Jewish debt in exchange for a charter of Jewish settlement. The following year the Sultan agreed to approve a plan of Jewish settlement throughout the Ottoman empire, but not a corporate Jewish homeland in Palestine.

Undaunted, Herzl then met with Joseph Chamberlain, the British Secretary of State for Colonial Affairs. During their discussion Herzl suggested that El Arish in the Sinai Peninsula might be a possible solution. Although this plan was examined in detail, it never reached fruition. In a second talk with Chamberlain in 1903, the Secretary of State proposed an alternative area of settlement. 'On my travels', he stated, 'I saw a country for you: Uganda. On the coast it is hot, but in the interior the climate is excellent for Europeans. You can plant cotton and sugar. I thought to myself: That's just the country for Dr Herzl. But he must have Palestine and will move only in its vicinity' (Dan Cohn-Sherbok, *The Jewish Heritage* (Oxford: Basil Blackwell, 1988), p. 153). Deeply disturbed by the continuing persecution in Russia, Herzl was unsure whether to wait for Palestine and asked for time to consider this offer. After encountering poverty and deprivation on a trip to the Pale of Settlement, Herzl finally agreed to Chamberlain's proposal in August 1903. At the next Zionist congress in Basle this plan was considered. When the scheme was explained, it was stressed that Uganda was not meant to serve as a permanent solution: rather it was to be a temporary residence. When the resolution was passed by a small margin, the delegates from eastern Europe walked out of the auditorium. At the end of the congress, the Russian representatives reassembled at Kharkov to hold their own conference, where they committed themselves to the idea of Palestine. In England public opinion was against

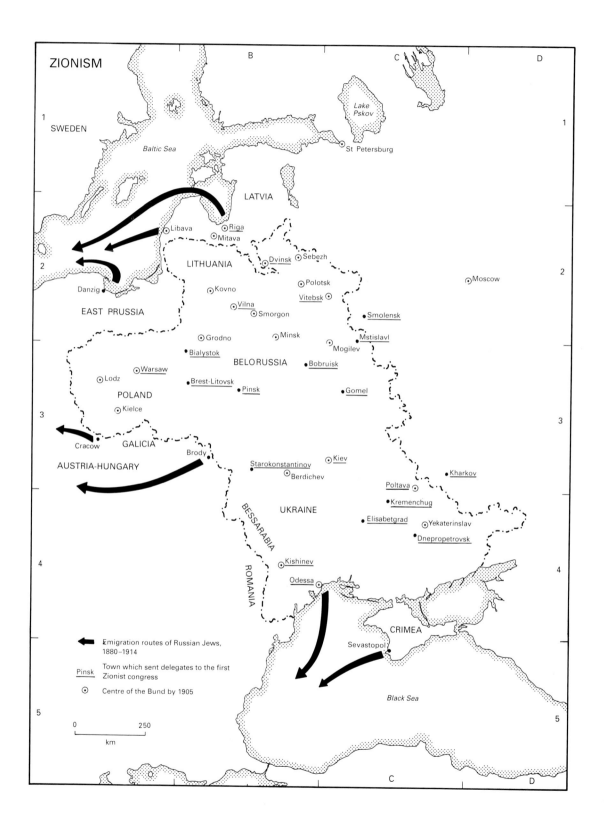

ZIONISM

SWEDEN

Baltic Sea

LATVIA

Lake Pskov

St Petersburg

⊙ Libava   ⊙ Riga
⊙ Mitava

Danzig •   LITHUANIA   ⊙ Dvinsk   ⊙ Sebezh

EAST PRUSSIA   ⊙ Kovno   ⊙ Polotsk   ⊙ Moscow

Vitebsk ⊙

⊙ Vilna   Smolensk
⊙ Smorgon

⊙ Grodno   ⊙ Minsk   Mstislavl

• Bialystok   BELORUSSIA   Mogilev

⊙ Warsaw   • Bobruisk

⊙ Lodz   • Brest-Litovsk   • Pinsk   • Gomel

POLAND
⊙ Kielce

Cracow •   GALICIA   Brody •

AUSTRIA-HUNGARY   Starokonstantinov   ⊙ Kiev   Kharkov

⊙ Berdichev

Poltava ⊙

UKRAINE   • Kremenchug

• Elisabetgrad   ⊙ Yekaterinslav

Dnepropetrovsk

⊙ Kishinev

Odessa ⊙   CRIMEA

Sevastopol •

Black Sea

Emigration routes of Russian Jews,
1880–1914

Pinsk   Town which sent delegates to the first
Zionist congress

⊙   Centre of the Bund by 1905

0   250
km

161

Figure 21 Herzl with his mother in Vienna, 1902 (Central Zionist Archives, Jerusalem)

Zionist Party. In 1907 the congress passed a resolution which pledged the movement to the quest for a charter, the settlement of Palestine, and the revival of Hebrew.

In the next decade the major developments in the Zionist movement occurred in Palestine. By the beginning of the twentieth century a considerable number of Jews had migrated to the Holy Land. Many of these pioneers lived in cities, but a minority worked on farm colonies under the auspices of the Palestine Jewish Colonization Association. In 1904 a second wave of Jewish immigrants were determined to work as farmers. Pre-eminent among these newcomers was Aaron David Gordon, who stated: 'Too long have the hands been the hands of Esau and the voice the voice of Jacob. It is time for Jacob to use his hands too' (Cohn-Sherbok, *The Jewish Heritage*, p. 154). In this milieu socialist ideas were espoused by such figures as Nachman Syrkin, who founded the Poale Zion Party, and Ber Borochov, the leader of the radical Hapoel Hatzair Party. Among those who were drawn to socialism was David Ben Gurion, the future Prime Minister, who wrote of his first night in Palestine: 'I did not sleep. I was among the rich shells of corn. Above were massed clusters of stars clear against the deep blue firmament.... My dreams had become a reality' (Cohn-Sherbok, *The Jewish Heritage*, p. 154). Those who joined this second wave organized trade unions, edited their own newspapers, established collective settlements and created a Hebraic culture for the country.

the transference of Uganda to the Jews, and in time the offer was withdrawn. In 1904 Herzl died, and his place was taken by David Wolffsohn, who attempted to heal the rifts between the various factions. Under his leadership, the Orthodox Jewish party (Mizrahi) joined the Zionist Organization, as did socialist Jews through the Labour

Emigration to the United States and the First World War

Between 1881 and 1914 approximately 3 million eastern European Jews emigrated: about 350,000 settled in continental Europe; 200,000 went to England; 40,000 emigrated to South Africa; 115,000 to Argentina; 100,000 to Canada, and nearly 2,000,000 to the United States. This enormous influx profoundly affected the composition of American Jewry. In previous centuries

Sephardic Jews dominated Jewish life in the coastal cities of the New World. Later Jews of German origin settled throughout the country and quickly assimilated into American life. At the end of the nineteenth century eastern European immigrants settled in the North-East. In the lower East Side of New York City settlers engaged in various manual trades. These newcomers were

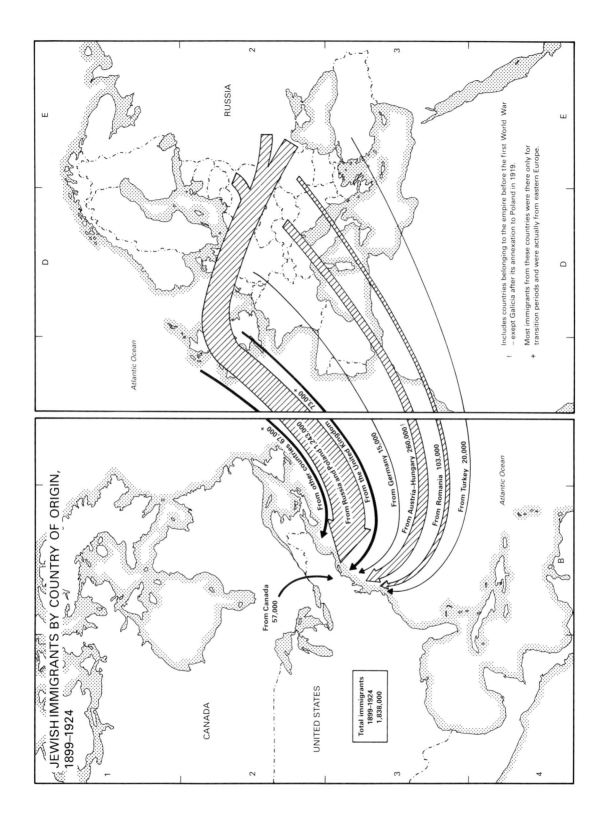

JEWISH IMMIGRANTS BY COUNTRY OF ORIGIN, 1899–1924

RUSSIA

Atlantic Ocean

CANADA

UNITED STATES

From Canada 57,000

Total immigrants 1899–1924 1,838,000

From other countries 67,000 +

From Russia and Poland 1,243,000

From the United Kingdom

From Germany 15,000

From Austria–Hungary 260,000 !

From Romania 103,000

From Turkey 20,000

73,000 +

Atlantic Ocean

! Includes countries belonging to the empire before the first World War
– exept Galicia after its annexation to Poland in 1919.

+ Most immigrants from these countries were there only for
transition periods and were actually from eastern Europe.

crowded together in tenements and worked in unhealthy conditions, but after 1900 trade unions brought about enormous improvements. In addition, these immigrants created an extensive network of societies to regulate religious and social life.

During this period the American Jewish population was divided between native-born Jews of German origin and eastern European settlers. Those German Jews who had already established themselves in American society were embarrassed by these foreigners. In consequence a number of assimilated German Jews attempted to advance the process of assimilation. In 1902 they revived the Jewish Theological Seminary in New York to train modern rabbis; in time this rabbinical seminary became the centre for Conservative Judaism. This movement appealed to many of these new immigrants who desired to combine loyalty to the Jewish tradition with an openness to new surroundings. German Jews also established settlements for immigrants and a number of Jewish charities. The German community was also instrumental in founding the Anti-Defamation League to counter anti-Semitism.

After the First World War Jewish immigration to the United States increased, but was curtailed by laws passed in 1921 and 1924. This policy was followed by other western countries, and the cessation of Jewish immigration led to the decline of the American Jewish working-class and Yiddish culture. Increasingly the Jewish community became middle-class, and a number of Jews attained positions of prominence in politics, the arts, music, science and literature.

The First World War also profoundly altered European Jewry: over 3,000,000 Jews lived in reconstituted Poland; 445,000 in Hungary; 850,000 in expanded Romania; 95,000 in Latvia; 115,000 in Lithuania; 375,000 in Czechoslovakia; 191,000 in Austria; 68,000 in Yugoslavia; 48,000 in Bulgaria and 73,000 in Greece. In these countries the war brought about the destruction of property; in addition large markets were replaced by small economic units, and protective tariffs were introduced. In all these cases governmental authorities were concerned to foster middle-class interests at the expense of minorities.

In this milieu Jews were vulnerable and bereft of political allies. In 1919 Jewish delegates participated in the Paris peace talks in an unsuccessful attempt to ensure that political treaties would protect the rights of minority groups. In Lithuania, Poland, Czechoslovakia, Hungary and Romania the majority of the Jewish population remained loyal to the Jewish faith and were perceived as aliens. In universities and the professions quotas were strictly applied and Jews were excluded from state bureaucracies. Various political parties also advocated anti-Jewish policies. None the less Jewish life flourished and Jewish political parties established Hebrew and Yiddish schools. Eastern European Jewry was also enriched by the creation of such institutions as the Yivo Institute of Jewish Research founded in Vilna and the establishment of yeshivot and Jewish youth movements.

In post-revolutionary Russia most Jewish organizations were dissolved, and poor Jews living in villages were deprived of civil rights. All yeshivot were closed in the 1920s, and the printing of religious books ended. Such anti-Jewish sentiment, however, did not prevent Jews from settling in Russian cities. A considerable number attended institutions of higher education, and in 1921 the New Economic Policy encouraged Jews to establish farming villages. In the 1920s Birobidzhan became a centre for Jewish colonization. However, in 1928 this policy was revoked, and many Jews worked instead as labourers, technicians, scientists and engineers. During this period communists fostered the creation of Yiddish-speaking workers' councils, schools, scholarly institutes, publishing houses and theatres. Although anti-Semitism was officially prohibited, in subsequent years Jewish institutions and cultural programmes ceased to function and Jews were removed from positions of political influence.

Jewry in Palestine, Africa and Asia

In the aftermath of the First World War the Jewish population in Palestine organized a National Assembly and Executive Council. By 1929 the Jewish community (*yishuv*) numbered 160,000; in the next ten years the community increased to 500,000, with 233 agricultural settlements. Nearly a quarter of this population lived in co-operatives, whereas Tel Aviv had 150,000 settlers, Jerusalem 90,000 and Haifa 60,000. Initially the Palestinian Electric Corporation encouraged industrialization, which was later developed by the General Federation of Hebrew Workers (Histradrut). During this early period Palestine was only 160 miles long and 70 miles wide, and contained one million Arabs. The Arab population consisted largely of peasants (*fellahin*)

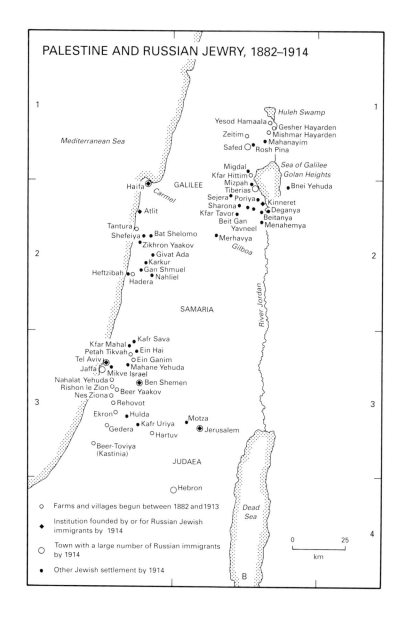

PALESTINE AND RUSSIAN JEWRY, 1882–1914

Mediterranean Sea

Huleh Swamp
Yesod Hamaala ○ ○ Gesher Hayarden
Zeitim ○ ○ Mishmar Hayarden
Mahanayim
Safed ○ • Rosh Pina

Migdal
Kfar Hittim •
Mizpah • Sea of Galilee
Tiberias ○ Golan Heights
Haifa ◉ GALILEE
Carmel
Sejera • Poriya • Bnei Yehuda
Sharona • Kinneret
Kfar Tavor • Deganya
Beit Gan Beitanya
Atlit Yavneel Menahemya
Tantura ○ • Merhavya
Shefeiya • • Bat Shelomo Gilboa
• Zikhron Yaakov
• Givat Ada
• Karkur
Heftzibah ○ ○ • Gan Shmuel
Hadera • Nahliel

SAMARIA

Kfar Mahal • • Kafr Sava
Petah Tikvah ○ • Ein Hai
Tel Aviv ◉ ○ Ein Ganim
Jaffa ○ • • Mahane Yehuda
Mikve Israel
Nahalat Yehuda ○ ◉ Ben Shemen
Rishon le Zion ○ ○ Beer Yaakov
Nes Ziona ○
○ Rehovot
Ekron ○ • Hulda • Motza
○ Gedera • Kafr Uriya ◉ Jerusalem
○ Hartuv

○ Beer-Toviya
(Kastinia)

JUDAEA

○ Hebron

○ Farms and villages begun between 1882 and 1913
◆ Institution founded by or for Russian Jewish immigrants by 1914
○ Town with a large number of Russian immigrants by 1914
• Other Jewish settlement by 1914

River Jordan

Dead Sea

0   25
km

and a number of landowners. Concerned about the increasing influx of Jewish newcomers, Arabs rioted in 1929 following a dispute concerning Jewish access to the Western Wall of the ancient Temple. In response the British curtailed Jewish immigration and the purchase of Arab land.

By the late 1920s Labour Zionism had become a major force in Palestinian Jewish life, and in the next decade various socialist and labour groups joined together in the Israel Labour Party. Within the Zionist movement a right-wing faction criticized Chaim Weizmann, the President of the World Zionist Organization, for co-operating with the British. According to Vladimir Jabotinsky, leader of the Union of Zionist Revisionists, the central aim of the Zionists should be to establish an independent state covering the whole of Palestine. After several Zionist Congresses, the Revisionist movement created its own organization and withdrew from the militia of the *yishuv* (Haganah) and formed its own military force. In 1936 the Arabs, with the support of Syria, Iraq

and Egypt, launched an offensive against Jews, the British and moderate Arabs. In the following year a British Royal Commission proposed that Palestine be partitioned into two separate states with a British zone. Although this proposal was accepted by the Zionists, it was rejected by the Arabs. At the end of the decade the British government produced a White Paper which rejected the concept of partition, limited Jewish immigration to 75,000, and declared that Palestine would become independent in ten years.

As these events took place in Palestine, North African Jewry flourished as a result of French influence. In the 1860s the Alliance Israélite established modern French-language schools for the Jewish population, and such policies continued into the next century. In India the long-established communities continued to exist into the modern period. Under British rule modern Jewry was also active in Alexandria and Cairo, and the Jews of Iraq also played an important role in economic and educational life. At the

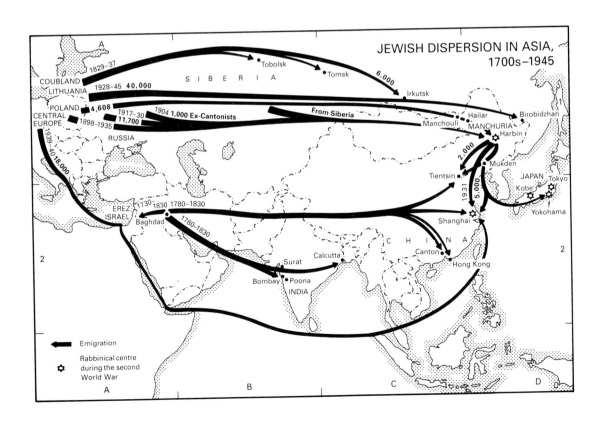

beginning of the nineteenth century Jews in the Caucasus, Georgia and Bukhara were incorporated into the Russian empire and remained loyal to the traditions of their ancestors. In Turkey Sephardic Jews developed cultural traditions based on Ladino, a Jewish Spanish dialect. In Persia Jews lived under oppressive conditions throughout the nineteenth century, but at the end of the century, a revival of Judaeo-Persian literature took place. By the 1920s Persia was modernized and the Jewish community began to create cultural and educational institutions.

Jews in Germany

During the last days of the First World War, the assembly at Weimar drafted a new constitution which transformed Germany into a federal republic. Immediately this new regime faced opposition from the extreme right and left. During 1922–3 there was massive inflation, but during the next five years there was greater stability as well as important intellectual and cultural developments. This period of prosperity was followed by the Great Depression – over six million were unemployed between 1930 and 1933. As a consequence the communists and the Nazis gained considerable support. To cope with this crisis, the government began to rule by presidential decree. After several ineffective conservative coalitions, Field Marshal Paul von Hindenburg appointed Adolf Hitler as Chancellor of Germany on 30 January 1933.

Hitler was born and brought up in Austria. As a frustrated and unsuccessful artist he spent several years in Vienna and subsequently moved to Munich in 1913. Volunteering for the German army, he fought on the Western Front and returned to Munich in 1919, where he joined the national Socialist German Workers' Party, later becoming its leader. Between 1919 and 1924 he combined German nationalism, anti-capitalism and anti-Semitism into a political ideology.

According to Hitler, the Jews were parasites and degenerates. Germany, he believed, lost the war because of treachery by Jewish socialists, liberals and pacifists. Further, he argued that the Bolshevik Revolution was part of a world-wide Jewish plot. Such a fusion of anti-Jewish sentiment and anti-communism provided a justification for the belief that the Germans were entitled to greater living space in eastern Europe: the Jews had taken control over the Slavs and therefore the struggle against communism was synonymous with the attack on Jewry itself. Hitler saw himself as the leader of a heroic battle against a malignant part of Europe – an Aryan victory would provide Germany with control of an empire (*Reich*) which it rightly deserved.

When the Nazis gained power, they dissolved a number of social institutions and absorbed others. In the Spring and Summer of 1933 all political parties were eliminated, strikes were outlawed and trade unions were replaced by a government- and employer-controlled labour front. In May 1933 book burnings took place and scientists, scholars and artists were arrested. In June 1934 a purge of the SA (Stormtroops) eliminated the party's social radicals and made way for the expansion of the SS (Protection Squad). Under Heinrich Himmler, the SS troops took over many of the functions of the police, including the Gestapo (Secret Police), as well as the running of the concentration camps.

After Hindenburg's death in August 1934, Hitler became the party chief and head of state. In September 1935 all sexual liaisons between Jews and non-Jews were described as crimes against the state. In 1938 Jewish communal bodies were put under the control of the Gestapo, and Jews were forced to register their property. Later in the year the Nazi party organized an onslaught against the Jewish population. This event, known as *Kristallnacht* ('night of the broken glass'), was a prelude to the terrors of the death camps.

Jews throughout Germany were victims of this

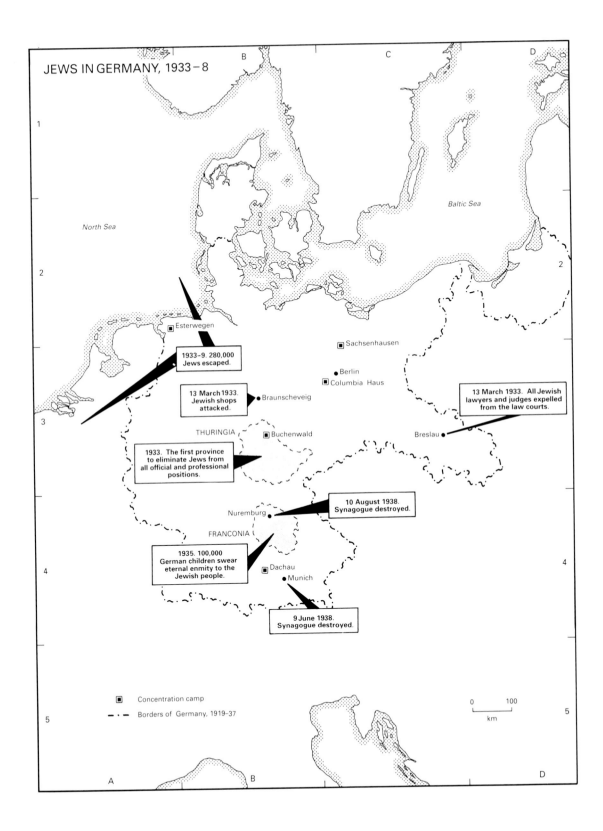

JEWS IN GERMANY, 1933–8

North Sea

Baltic Sea

■ Esterwegen

1933–9. 280,000
Jews escaped.

■ Sachsenhausen

● Berlin
■ Columbia Haus

13 March 1933.
Jewish shops
attacked.

● Braunscheveig

13 March 1933. All Jewish
lawyers and judges expelled
from the law courts.

THURINGIA

■ Buchenwald

Breslau ●

1933. The first province
to eliminate Jews from
all official and professional
positions.

10 August 1938.
Synagogue destroyed.

Nuremburg ●

FRANCONIA

1935. 100,000
German children swear
eternal enmity to the
Jewish people.

■ Dachau
● Munich

9 June 1938.
Synagogue destroyed.

■   Concentration camp
–·–·– Borders of Germany, 1919–37

0   100
km

massacre. In Hoengen, a small village near Aachen, the synagogue was destroyed. According to a witness who observed these events:

> The stormtroops were joined by people who were not in uniform; and suddenly with one loud cry of 'Down with the Jews', the gathering outside produced axes and heavy sledgehammers ... the little synagogue was but a heap of stone, broken glass and smashed up woodwork.... Where the two well-cared-for flowerbeds had flanked both sides of the gravel path leading to the door of the synagogue, the children had lit a bonfire, and the parchment of the Scrolls gave enough food for the flames to eat up the smashed-up benches and doors, and the wood, which only the day before had been the Holy Ark for the Scrolls of the Law of Moses.
>
> (Dan Cohn-Sherbok, *Holocaust Theology* (London: Lamp Press, 1989), pp. 2–3)

14 THE HOLOCAUST

The destruction of Polish and Russian Jewry

The first stage of the Nazis' plan for European Jewry began with the invasion of Poland in September 1939. In every conquered town and village the Germans forced Jews to hand over jewellery, to clear rubble, to carry heavy loads and to scrub floors and lavatories with their prayer shawls. In addition the Germans cut off religious Jews' beards and sidelocks with scissors, or tore them from their faces. When the Jewish population was forced into what Hitler referred to as a huge Polish labour camp, a massive work programme was initiated. The nightmare of these camps was described by numerous eye-witnesses, as in this record of a mass slaughter of Jews at a camp in the village of Stutthof during the Passover of 1940:

> All the Jews were assembled in the courtyard; they were ordered to run, to drop down and to stand up again. Anybody who was slow in obeying the order was beaten to death by the overseer with the butt of his rifle. Afterwards Jews were ordered to jump right into the cesspit of the latrines, which were being built; this was full of urine. The taller Jews got out again since the level reached their chin, but the shorter ones went down. The young ones tried to help the old folk, and as a punishment the overseers ordered the latter to beat the young. When they refused to obey, they were cruelly beaten themselves.
>
> (Cohn-Sherbok, *Holocaust Theology*, p. 3)

The surviving Jews from this camp were subsequently sent to another smaller camp at Gransdorf; only one survivor, a sculptor, was left behind. In the words of a witness to these events:

> The SS men took all his works, put him to a carriage loaded with sand, and forced him to run while flogging him with a lash. When he fell down they turned the carriage over on him; and when he nevertheless succeeded in creeping out of the sand they poured water on him and hanged him; but the rope was too thin and gave way. They then brought a young Jewess, the only one in the camp, and with scornful laughter they hanged both on the rope.
>
> (Cohn-Sherbok, *Holocaust Theology*, pp. 3–4)

The next stage in the plan of extermination began with the invasion of Russia in 1941. This was designed to destroy what was described by the Nazis as the 'Jewish–Bolshevik conspiracy'. At first mobile killing battalions of 500–900 men (the *Einsatzgruppen*), under the supervision of Reinhard Heydrich, began the slaughter of Russian Jewry. Of the 4,500,000 Jews who resided in Soviet territory, more than half fled before the German invasion; those who remained were concentrated in large cities, making it easier for Heydrich's troops to carry out their task. Throughout the country the *Einsatzgruppen* moved into Russian towns, sought out the rabbi

Figure 22 Poland, c. 1939–40 (Yad Vashem Archives, Jerusalem)

or Jewish council and obtained a list of all Jewish inhabitants. The Jews were then rounded up in market places, crowded into trains, buses and trucks and taken to woods where mass graves had been dug. They were then machine-gunned to death. A typical example of such killings was depicted by a civilian works engineer in the 1945 Nuremberg trials:

> People were closely wedged together, lying on top of each other so that only their heads were visible. Nearly all had blood running over their shoulders from their heads. Some of the people shot were still moving. Some lifted their arms and turned their heads to show that they were still alive. The pit was already two-thirds full. I estimated that it held a thousand people.
>
> (Cohn-Sherbok, *Holocaust Theology*, p. 4)

In this slaughter the Jews attempted to escape the onslaught by hiding under floorboards and cellars, but they were buried alive or blasted out with grenades. A few girls offered themselves to stay alive; they were used during the night but killed the next morning. In the initial sweep between October and December 1941, these troops killed over 300,000 Jews; in a second stage that lasted throughout 1942, over 900,000 were murdered.

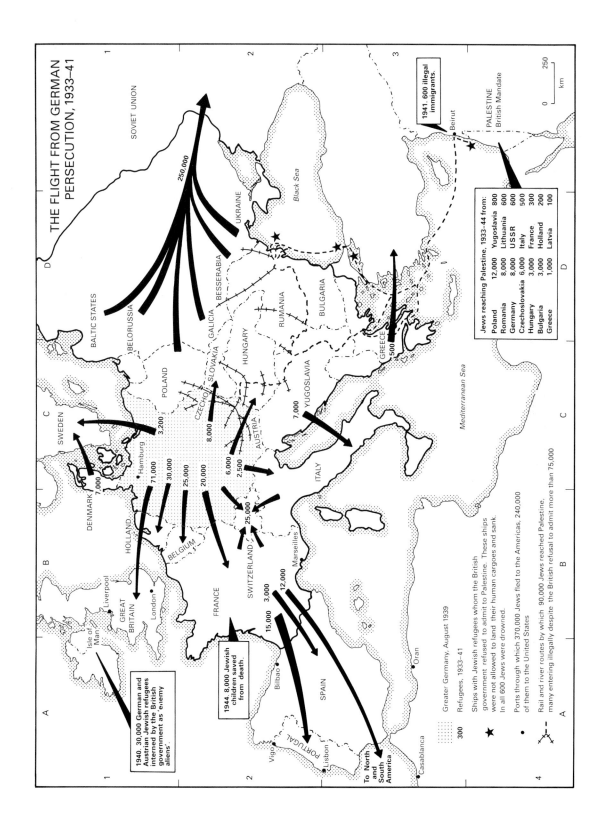

THE FLIGHT FROM GERMAN PERSECUTION, 1933–41

SOVIET UNION

250,000

BALTIC STATES

BELORUSSIA

UKRAINE

Black Sea

GALICIA

BESSERABIA

SWEDEN

3,200

CZECHO.

SLOVAKIA

8,000

RUMANIA

BULGARIA

HUNGARY

Hamburg

DENMARK

7,000

71,000

30,000

25,000

20,000

AUSTRIA

6,000

2,500

YUGOSLAVIA

7,000

HOLLAND

BELGIUM

25,000

SWITZERLAND

ITALY

GREECE

500

Mediterranean Sea

Beirut

1941. 600 illegal immigrants.

PALESTINE
British Mandate

Jews reaching Palestine, 1933–44 from:			
Poland	12,000	Yugoslavia	800
Romania	8,000	Lithuania	600
Germany	8,000	USSR	600
Czechoslovakia	6,000	Italy	500
Hungary	3,000	France	300
Bulgaria	3,000	Holland	200
Greece	1,000	Latvia	100

GREAT
BRITAIN

Liverpool

Isle of
Man

London

1940. 30,000 German and Austrian Jewish refugees interned by the British government as 'enemy aliens'.

FRANCE

1944. 8,000 Jewish children saved from death.

Marseilles

15,000

3,000

12,000

SPAIN

Bilbao

Oran

Vigo

PORTUGAL

Lisbon

Casablanca

To North and South America

- Greater Germany, August 1939

- Refugees, 1933–41

300

★ Ships with Jewish refugees whom the British government refused to admit to Palestine. These ships were not allowed to land their human cargoes and sank. In all 600 Jews were drowned.

• Ports through which 370,000 Jews fled to the Americas, 240,000 of them to the United States

⅄ Rail and river routes by which 90,000 Jews reached Palestine, many entering illegally despite the British refusal to admit more than 75,000

0   250
km

The death camps

Other methods were also employed by the Nazis. Mobile gas vans were sent to each battalion of the *Einsatzgruppen*. Meanwhile the mobile killing operations were being supplemented by the use of fixed centres, the death camps. Six of these were at Chelmno and Auschwitz in the Polish territories, and at Treblinka, Sobibor, Majdanek and Belzec in the Polish 'General Government'. Construction of this mass murder industry began in 1941. Two civilians from Hamburg went to Auschwitz to teach the staff how to use Zyklon-B gas. In September 1941 the first gassing took place in Auschwitz Block II; then work began at Birkenau, the central killing centre in Auschwitz. The first death camp to be completed was Chelmno near Lodz, which started functioning in December 1941. Subsequently Belzec became operational, and the building of Sobibor began in March 1942. At the same time Majdanek and Treblinka were transformed into death centres.

One of the survivors of a convoy of Jews who travelled from Paris to Auschwitz later recounted the terrors of this journey:

> Piled up in freight cars, unable to bend or to budge, sticking one to another, breathless, crushed by one's neighbour's every move, this was already hell. During the day, a torrid heat, with a pestilential smell. After several days and several nights, the doors were opened. We arrived worn out, dehydrated, with many ills. A newborn baby, snatched from its mother's arms, was thrown against a column. The mother, crazed from pain, began to scream. The SS man struck her violently with the butt end of his weapon over the head. Her eyes haggard, with fearful screams, her beautiful hair became tinted with her own blood. She was struck down by a bullet in her head.

> (Cohn-Sherbok, *Holocaust Theology*, p. 6)

On arrival at the camps, Jews were ordered out of the train and separated into groups. According to a survivor of Treblinka, women and children were sent to the left, men to the right:

The women all went into the barracks on the left, and as we later learned, they were told at once to strip naked and were driven out of the barracks through another door. From there, they entered a narrow path lined on either side by barbed wire. This path led through a small grove to the building that housed the gas-chamber. Only a few minutes later we could hear their terrible screams, but we could not see anything, because the trees of the grove blocked our view.

> (Cohn-Sherbok, *Holocaust Theology*, pp. 6–7)

At Treblinka the women on arrival were shaved to the skin; their hair was later packed up for despatch to Germany. At the Nuremberg Tribunal one of those who survived gave an account of this procedure:

> Because little children at their mothers' breasts were a great nuisance during the shaving procedure, later the system was modified and babies were taken from their mothers as soon as they got off the train. The children were taken to an enormous ditch; when a large number of them were gathered together they were killed by firearms and thrown into the fire.

> (Cohn-Sherbok, *Holocaust Theology*, p. 7)

Here, too, no one bothered to see whether all the children were really dead. Sometimes one could hear infants wailing in the fire. When mothers succeeded in keeping their babies with them and this interfered with the shaving, a German guard took the baby by its legs and smashed it against the wall of the barracks until only a bloody mass remained in his hands. The unfortunate mother had to take this mass with her to the 'bath'.

The most horrible of all horrors were the gas chambers. An eye-witness to the killings at Belzec later recounted a typical occurrence:

> A little before seven, there was an announcement: 'The first train will arrive in ten minutes!' A few minutes later a train arrived from Lemberg: forty-five carriages with more

CONCENTRATION CAMPS

Chelmno Death camp

■ Concentration camp

North Sea

Baltic Sea

USSR

ESTONIA

Vaivara ■
Klooga ■

LATVIA

LITHUANIA

■ Stutthof

■ Neuengamme

■ Ravensbrück

■ Bergen-Belsen ■ Sachsenhausen

■ Treblinka

■ Chelmno

POLAND

Mittelbau
■ Dora

Gross
Rosen

■ Buchenwald ■

■ Sobibor

■ Majdanek

■ Belzec

■ Auschwitz

GERMANY

Flossenberg ■

■ Plaszow

Natzweiler ■

CZECHOSLOVAKIA

■ Dachau

■ Mauthausen

FRANCE

AUSTRIA

HUNGARY

ROMANIA

■ Jasenovac

■ Gospič

■ Sajmište

YUGOSLAVIA

ITALY

ALBANIA

BULGARIA

0   250
km

than six thousand people; two hundred Ukrainians assigned to this work flung open the doors and drove the Jews out of the cars with leather whips. A loudspeaker gave instructions: 'Strip, even artificial limbs and glasses. Hand all money and valuables in at the "valuables" window. Women and girls are to have their hair cut in the "barber's" hut.' Then the march began. Barbed wire on both sides, in the rear two dozen Ukrainians with rifles.

Stark naked men, women, children and cripples passed by.... SS men pushed the men into the chambers.... Seven to eight hundred people in ninety-three square metres. The doors closed.... Twenty-five minutes passed. You could see through the window that many were already dead, for an electric light illumin-ated the interior of the room. All were dead after thirty-two minutes.... Jewish workers on the other side opened the wooden doors. They had been promised their lives in return for doing this horrible work, plus a small percentage of the money and valuables collected.

The people were still standing like columns of stone, with no room to fall or lean. Even in death you could tell the families, all holding hands. It was difficult to separate them while emptying the room for the next batch. The bodies were tossed out, blue, wet with sweat and urine, the legs smeared with excrement and menstrual blood. Two dozen workers were busy checking mouths they opened with iron hooks.... Dentists knocked out gold teeth, bridges and crowns with hammers.

(Cohn-Sherbok, *Holocaust Theology*, pp. 7–8)

Jewish resistance

By September 1942 German troops had conquered most of Europe. Yet as the murder of Jews continued, resistance spread. On 24 September the Jews of the Belorussian town of Korzec set the ghetto on fire, and a number of Jews established a partisan band. On 25 September, in Kaluszyn near Warsaw, the chairman of the Jewish Council in Lukow near Lublin collected money from Jews assembled in the main square in the expectation that he could use the funds to ransom the Jewish community. When he discovered the deportation would take place, he shouted: 'Here is your payment for our trip, you bloody tyrant!' Tearing the money into shreds, he slapped the German supervisor in the face and was shot on the spot by the Ukrainian guards. In the same month a former Jewish soldier in the Polish army, who was being held with several hundred other prisoners in a prison camp in Lublin, escaped with seventeen Jews, forming a small partisan group.

In the Warsaw ghetto, the Jewish Fighting Organization prepared itself for action. On 29 October a member of the Organization killed the commander of the Jewish police in the ghetto. In the Bialystok ghetto resistance was also taking place with the assistance of German soldiers from whom they obtained weapons. Near Cracow six members of the Jewish Fighting Organization set off for the forests armed with pistols and a knife, but were betrayed by local peasants. The next month the Jewish Fighting Organization in Cracow sabotaged railway lines, raided a German clothing store and killed several Germans. In Marcinkance the chairman of the Jewish Council called out to the Jews who had been brought to the railway station. 'Fellow Jews, everybody run for his life. Everything is lost!' As the Jews ran toward the ghetto fence, attacking the guards with their fists, over a hundred were shot. Yet despite the insurmountable odds, some Jews in other situations did manage to escape from the Nazis. As one survivor recounted:

The moans of the elderly, the screams of the children ... were being drowned by the clatter of the death train as it moved through the French countryside of contrasting bucolic

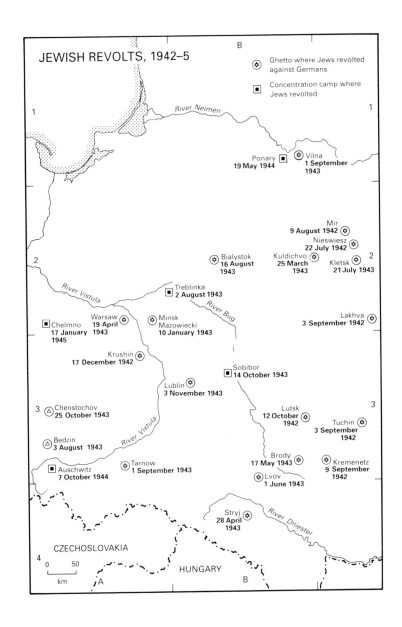

JEWISH REVOLTS, 1942–5

⊛ Ghetto where Jews revolted against Germans

■ Concentration camp where Jews revolted

River Neimen

Ponary ■
19 May 1944

Vilna ⊛
1 September 1943

Mir ⊛
9 August 1942

Nieswiesz ⊛
22 July 1942

Bialystok ⊛
16 August 1943

Kuldichvo ⊛
25 March 1943

Kletsk ⊛
21 July 1943

River Vistula

Treblinka ■
2 August 1943

River Bug

Lakhva ⊛
3 September 1942

Chelmno ■
17 January 1945

Warsaw ⊛
19 April 1943

Minsk ⊛
Mazowiecki
10 January 1943

Krushin ⊛
17 December 1942

Sobibor ■
14 October 1943

Lublin ⊛
3 November 1943

Chenstochov ⊛
25 October 1943

Lutsk ⊛
12 October 1942

Tuchin ⊛
3 September 1942

Bedzin ⊛
3 August 1943

River Vistula

Brody ⊛
17 May 1943

Kremenetz ⊛
9 September 1942

Auschwitz ■
7 October 1944

Tarnow ⊛
1 September 1943

Lvov ⊛
1 June 1943

Stryj ⊛
28 April 1943

River Dniester

CZECHOSLOVAKIA

0   50
km

HUNGARY

---

beauty and serenity.... We chose the moment of escape very carefully. It had to come at a time when the train would slow down for a curve. It also had to avoid the floodlights which the guards were aiming over the entire length of the concave curvature of the train during the period of reduced speed.... At this split second, we had to take our chances and

leap before the beams of the floodlights would fall on us. We jumped.

(Cohn-Sherbok, *The Crucified Jew*, p. 203)

In November Polish Jews who had escaped the deportation to Treblinka organized a small group to protect those Jews who were in hiding. The news of executions in the labour camps in

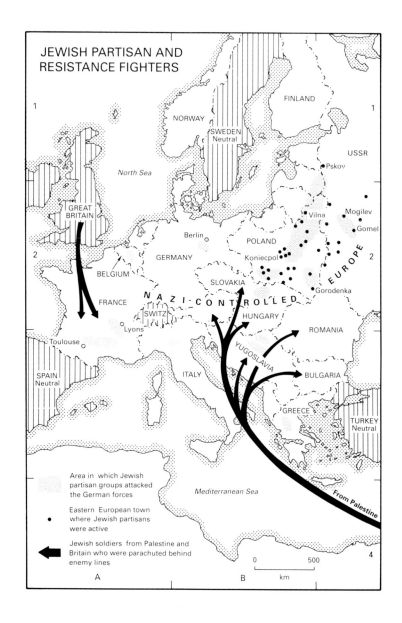

JEWISH PARTISAN AND
RESISTANCE FIGHTERS

Area in which Jewish
partisan groups attacked
the German forces

• Eastern European town
where Jewish partisans
were active

◀ Jewish soldiers from Palestine and
Britain who were parachuted behind
enemy lines

December stimulated plans for resistance in Warsaw. An eye-witness wrote: 'Aryeh Wilner was the first to cry out: "Come, let us destroy ourselves. Let's not fall into their hands alive." The suicides began.... Then someone discovered a hidden exit, but only a few succeeded in getting out this way. The others slowly suffocated in the gas.'

Street by street the ghetto had been eliminated. In the fighting 7,000 Jews lost their lives, and 30,000 were deported to Treblinka.

Figure 23   Round-up of Jews in Warsaw during the Second World War (Yivo Institute for Jewish Research, New York)

The final stage of terror

Despite the Jewish Resistance in Warsaw and elsewhere, the slaughter of the Jews continued. The advance of the Red Army on the Eastern Front since early 1943 led to the decision to dig up the corpses of Jews and burn them. On 15 June at the Janowska death pits in Lvov hundreds of Jewish labourers were forced to dig up those who had been murdered and extract gold teeth and remove rings from the fingers of the dead.

The pace of the killing was unchanging. On 4 October Himmler addressed his SS officers. The Jewish race was being eliminated, he explained:

> Most of you know what it means when one hundred corpses are lying side by side, or five hundred, or one thousand. To have stuck it out and at the same time – apart from

exceptional cases of human weakness – to have remained decent fellows, that is what has made us hard. This is a page of glory in our history which has never to be written.... we had the moral right, we had the duty to world peace, to destroy this people which wished to destroy us.

(Cohn-Sherbok, *The Crucified Jew*, p. 206)

During the Winter of 1943 the murder of Jews continued without pause. At Birkenau on Christmas Day Jewish women who had been starved were brought from the barracks. Trucks drove up to the block where they were assembled, and women were piled into them. The victims knew they were going to the gas chamber and tried to escape and were massacred. According to an account of this incident, when the lorry motors started, a terrible noise arose – the death cry of thousands of young women. As they tried to break out, a rabbi's son cried out: 'God, show them your power – this is against you.' When nothing happened, the boy cried out: 'There is no God.'

As the months passed Jews continued to be subjected to equally terrible events. In Kovno several thousand children were rounded up, driven off in trucks and murdered. As an observer of this action related:

I saw shattered scenes. It was near the hospital. I saw automobiles which from time to time would approach mothers with children, or children who were on their own. In the back of them, two Germans with rifles would be going as if they were escorting criminals. They would toss the children in the automobile. I saw mothers screaming. A mother whose three

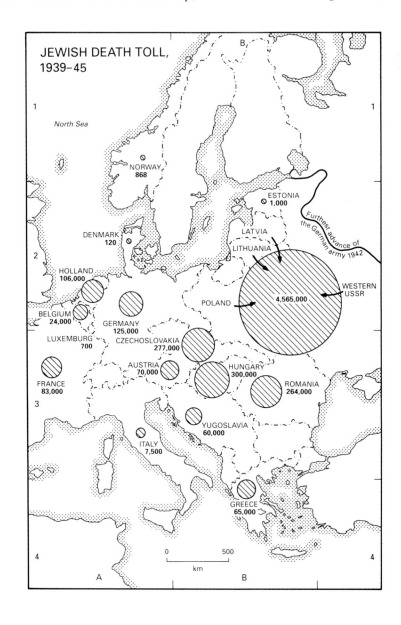

JEWISH DEATH TOLL, 1939–45

North Sea

NORWAY 868

ESTONIA 1,000

DENMARK 120

LATVIA

LITHUANIA

Furthest advance of the German army 1942

HOLLAND 106,000

POLAND

4,565,000

WESTERN USSR

BELGIUM 24,000

GERMANY 125,000

LUXEMBURG 700

CZECHOSLOVAKIA 277,000

AUSTRIA 70,000

HUNGARY 300,000

ROMANIA 264,000

FRANCE 83,000

YUGOSLAVIA 60,000

ITALY 7,500

GREECE 65,000

0 500 km

children had been taken away – she went up to this automobile and shouted at the German, 'Give me the children', and he said, 'You may have one.' And she went up into that automobile, and all three children looked at her and stretched out their hands. Of course, all of them wanted to go with their mother, and the mother didn't know which child to select and she went down alone, and she left the car.

(Cohn-Sherbok, *The Crucified Jew*, p. 207)

By the Summer of 1944 the last deportations took place. More than 67,000 were deported from the Lodz ghetto to Birkenau. Most were selected for the gas chamber, but some were chosen for medical experimentation. According to an account:

When the convoys arrived, Dr Mengele espied, among those lined up for selection, a hunch-backed man about fifty years old. He was not alone; standing beside him was a tall hand-some boy of fifteen or sixteen. The latter, however, had a deformed right foot.... Father and son – their faces wan from their miserable years in the Lodz ghetto.... I first examined the father in detail, omitting nothing.... Before proceeding to the examination of the boy I conversed with him at some length. He had a pleasant face, an intelligent look, but his

morale was badly shaken.... Scarcely half an hour later SS Quartermaster Sergeant Muss-feld appeared with four Sonderkommando men. They took the two prisoners into the furnace room and had them undress. Then the Ober's revolver cracked twice.

(Cohn-Sherbok, *The Crucified Jew*, p. 207)

At Birkenau the Day of Atonement was celebrated on 1 October with a note of religious exaltation despite the horror of the camp:

The moon shone through the window. Its light was dazzling that night and gave the pale wasted faces of the prisoners a ghostly appear-ance. It was as if all the life had ebbed out of them. I shuddered with dread, for it suddenly occurred to me that I was the only living man among corpses. All at once the oppressive silence was broken by a mournful tune. It was the plaintive tones of the ancient '*Kol Nidre*' prayer.... When at last he was silent, there was exaltation among us, an exaltation which men can experience only when they have fallen as low as we had fallen and then, through the mystic power of a deathless prayer, have awakened once more to the world of the spirit.

(Cohn-Sherbok, *The Crucified Jew*, p. 208)

Jewry after the Holocaust

During the Holocaust six million Jews died at the hands of the Nazis, yet by the 1980s the Jewish community had significantly grown in size. Out of a total of 13,500,000 Jews, about 3,500,000 live in Israel. However, the largest Jewish community is in America: 5,700,000 reside in the United States, 310,000 in Canada, 250,000 in Argentina, 130,000 in Brazil and 40,000 in Mexico (as well as smaller populations in other South American countries). The next largest community is in Russia, consisting of about 1,750,000. In addition some eastern European countries also have a large number of Jews, such as Hungary with 75,000 and Romania with 30,000. In western

Europe there are approximately 1,250,000 Jews: 670,000 in France, 360,000 in Britain, 42,000 in West Germany, 41,000 in Belgium, 35,000 in Italy, 28,000 in the Netherlands and 21,000 in Switzerland. In Africa 105,000 live in South Africa, and 17,000 in Morocco. In Asia there are 35,000 Jews in Iran, and 21,000 in Turkey. In Australia and New Zealand the Jewish community consists of about 75,000.

These Jewish populations have had a complex history since the war. In some cases the Jewish population was reduced to a fraction of its size prior to the Nazi onslaught. The Jewish community of Salonica, for instance, was 60,000

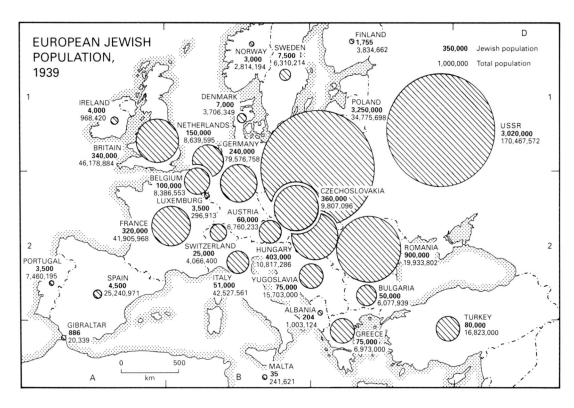

EUROPEAN JEWISH POPULATION, 1939

FINLAND
1,755
3,834,662

NORWAY
3,000
2,814,194

SWEDEN
7,500
6,310,214

350,000 Jewish population
1,000,000 Total population

D

1

IRELAND
4,000
968,420

DENMARK
7,000
3,706,349

POLAND
3,250,000
34,775,698

USSR
3,020,000
170,467,572

NETHERLANDS
150,000
8,639,595

BRITAIN
340,000
46,178,884

GERMANY
240,000
79,576,758

BELGIUM
100,000
8,386,553

LUXEMBURG
3,500
296,913

CZECHOSLOVAKIA
360,000
9,807,096

FRANCE
320,000
41,905,968

AUSTRIA
60,000
6,760,233

SWITZERLAND
25,000
4,066,400

HUNGARY
403,000
10,817,286

ROMANIA
900,000
19,933,802

2

PORTUGAL
3,500
7,460,195

SPAIN
4,500
25,240,971

ITALY
51,000
42,527,561

YUGOSLAVIA
75,000
15,703,000

BULGARIA
50,000
6,077,939

TURKEY
80,000
16,823,000

ALBANIA
204
1,003,124

GIBRALTAR
886
20,339

GREECE
75,000
6,973,000

0   500
km

A

B

MALTA
35
241,621

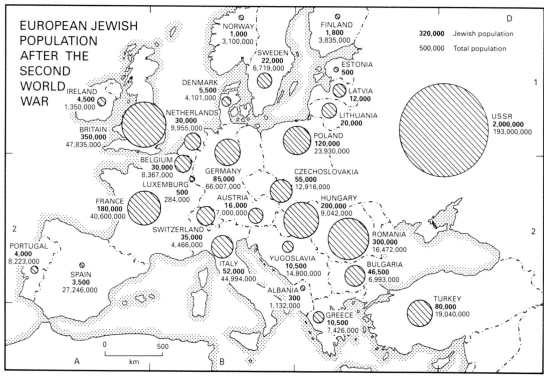

EUROPEAN JEWISH POPULATION AFTER THE SECOND WORLD WAR

NORWAY
1,000
3,100,000

FINLAND
1,800
3,835,000

320,000 Jewish population
500,000 Total population

D

SWEDEN
22,000
6,719,000

ESTONIA
500

1

DENMARK
5,500
4,101,000

LATVIA
12,000

IRELAND
4,500
1,350,000

LITHUANIA
20,000

NETHERLANDS
30,000
9,955,000

POLAND
120,000
23,930,000

USSR
2,000,000
193,000,000

BRITAIN
350,000
47,835,000

BELGIUM
30,000
8,367,000

GERMANY
85,000
66,007,000

CZECHOSLOVAKIA
55,000
12,916,000

LUXEMBURG
500
284,000

FRANCE
180,000
40,600,000

AUSTRIA
16,000
7,000,000

HUNGARY
200,000
9,042,000

2

SWITZERLAND
35,000
4,466,000

ROMANIA
300,000
16,472,000

PORTUGAL
4,000
8,223,000

ITALY
52,000
44,994,000

YUGOSLAVIA
10,500
14,800,000

BULGARIA
46,500
6,993,000

SPAIN
3,500
27,246,000

ALBANIA
300
1,132,000

TURKEY
80,000
19,040,000

GREECE
10,500
7,426,000

0   500
km

A

B

in 1939 but only 1,500 in the 1980s; Vienna shrank from 200,000 to fewer than 8,000; Berlin Jewry was reduced from approximately 175,000 to about 6,000; and the Jews of Poland dwindled from 3,300,000 to about 5,000. However, in other countries Jewish numbers increased as a result of immigration. In France, for example, Sephardic immigrants from the Muslim world swelled the Jewish population; in Britain a large number of newcomers increased the community and added to its cultural development.

In the United States Jewish refugees had a profound effect on American Jewry. These immigrants included adherents of European liberalism as well as Hasidim. As numbers of Jews increased, earlier religious groups gained strength and influence. On the left of the religious spectrum the Reform movement increasingly adopted a more favourable attitude to Zionism, and in matters of ritual observance moved toward a more traditional stance; none the less in the 1970s reformers took the radical step of ordaining women to the rabbinate and redefined Jewish identity to include children of Jewish fathers and non-Jewish mothers. In both the Conservative and Orthodox movements, tension between liberals and traditionalists frequently occurred, reflecting differing attitudes to Americanization and co-operation with other Jews.

In contrast with Jewish life in the New World, Jewish activities in the Soviet Union were officially restricted after the war. Israel was frequently denounced as a bourgeois tool of American capitalism, Yiddish schools were closed and an attack was waged against Jewish writers, painters, musicians and intellectuals.

This campaign extended to Czechoslovakia: in the 1950s a number of Jews were accused of Trotskyite–Titoist–Zionist conspiracy and executed. During this period a cadre of Russian Jews were accused of plotting to poison Joseph Stalin in conjunction with British, American and Zionist agents. Their trial was to have been a prelude to the deportation of Jews to Siberia, but Stalin died before it could take place. Stalin's successor Nikita Khruschev altered the orientation of anti-Jewish propaganda from spying to economic criminality; during his reign the number of synagogues was reduced from 450 to 60. After Khrushchev's fall there was a brief respite, but following the Six Day War in 1967 a new campaign was launched against Jewry. In 1971 Leonid Brezhnev allowed a sizeable number of Jews to leave the Soviet Union, but in the 1980s fewer visas were granted as the Soviet campaign against Zionism intensified. With the policy of *glasnost* and the collapse of the Soviet Union, Jewish immigration greatly increased, yet such a policy has been accompanied by the growth of Jew-hatred. Parallel with such a rise of anti-Jewish sentiment the Arab world has disseminated propaganda against the Jews. Such polemics were based in part on the *Protocols of the Elders of Zion*, which circulated widely in Arab countries. Extracts and summaries from this anti-Semitic forgery were used in Arab textbooks and training manuals for the Arab military forces. In addition, in 1962 blood-libel material appeared as a government publication of the United Arab Republic. Such attitudes have been fostered throughout the Arab world and serve as a major obstacle to peace in the Middle East.

15 ISRAEL

The early struggle

The quest for a Jewish state was set in motion by the events of the nineteenth century. Following the inspiration of early Zionist leaders, the First Zionist Congress met on 29 August 1897 in the Great Hall of the Basle Municipal Casino under the leadership of Theodor Herzl. Subsequently Herzl cultivated important figures in Turkey, Austria, Germany and Russia to further his plans. In 1902 Herzl appeared before the Commission, declaring that further Jewish immigration to Britain should be accepted but that the ultimate solution to the refugee problem was the recognition of the Jews as a people and the finding by them of a legally recognized home.

This appearance brought Herzl into contact with the Colonial Secretary, Joseph Chamberlain, who subsequently suggested to Herzl that a Jewish homeland could be established in Uganda. Fearful of the plight of Russian Jewry, Herzl was prepared to accept the proposal. As a result Lord Lansdowne, the Foreign Secretary, wrote in a letter:

> If a site can be found which the [Jewish Colonial] Trust and His Majesty's Commission consider suitable and which commends itself to HM Government, Lord Lansdowne will be prepared to entertain favourable proposals for the establishment of a Jewish colony of settlement, on conditions which will enable the members to observe their national customs.
>
> (Dan Cohn-Sherbok, *Israel: The History of an Idea* (London: SPCK, 1992), p. 150)

After Herzl read Lansdowne's letter to the Zionist Congress, a number of Russian delegates who viewed the Uganda Plan as a betrayal of Zionism walked out. At the next congress, Uganda was formally rejected as a place for a national homeland.

After Herzl's death, David Wolffsohn became the leader of the Zionists and continued to agitate for the creation of a Jewish national home. In Britain Chaim Weizmann pressed for the acceptance of this plan with the support of the liberal MP Herbert Samuel. In a meeting with the Foreign Secretary, Sir Edward Grey, on 9 November 1914, Samuel asked about a homeland for the Jewish people. In reply Grey said that the idea had always had a strong sentimental appeal to him, and he would be prepared to work for it if the opportunity arose. Later in the day Samuel attempted to enlist the support of Lloyd George, the Chancellor of the Exchequer. When Samuel later put his plan to the Cabinet, it was resisted by his cousin Edwin Montague. Later in the year, when Lloyd George became Prime Minister and Arthur Balfour was appointed Foreign Secretary, the Zionist cause was given a more sympathetic hearing. In January 1917 British troops began the assault on Palestine; at the same time the Tsar was overthrown and the provisional Prime Minister Kerensky ended Russia's anti-Semitic code.

At the end of the month Germany engaged in U-boat warfare, thereby drawing America on to the Allied side. In the light of these events, the US government became a supporter of a Jewish

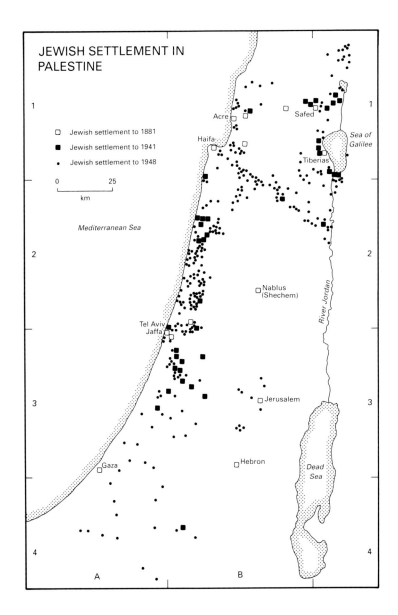

JEWISH SETTLEMENT IN
PALESTINE

□ Jewish settlement to 1881

■ Jewish settlement to 1941

• Jewish settlement to 1948

0   25
km

Mediterranean Sea

Acre

Safed

Haifa

*Sea of
Galilee*

Tiberias

Nablus
(Shechem)

River Jordan

Tel Aviv
Jaffa

Jerusalem

Hebron

*Dead
Sea*

Gaza

home in Palestine. In the same year Balfour as Foreign Secretary wrote to Lord Rothschild, the head of the English Jewish community, promising British commitment to a Jewish homeland in Palestine. The original draft of this letter (the text of which was agreed on by both sides beforehand) stated that Palestine should be reconstituted as a whole as a Jewish national home with internal autonomy, and that there should be an unrestricted right of Jewish immigration. This document was not approved by the Cabinet until 31 October 1917, but substantial changes were made. Palestine was not equated with the national home, nor was there any reference to unrestricted Jewish immigration. Further the rights of the Arabs were safeguarded. The central passage of the letter, subsequently known as the Balfour Declaration, read:

His Majesty's Government view with favour the establishment in Palestine of a national home for the Jewish people, and will use their

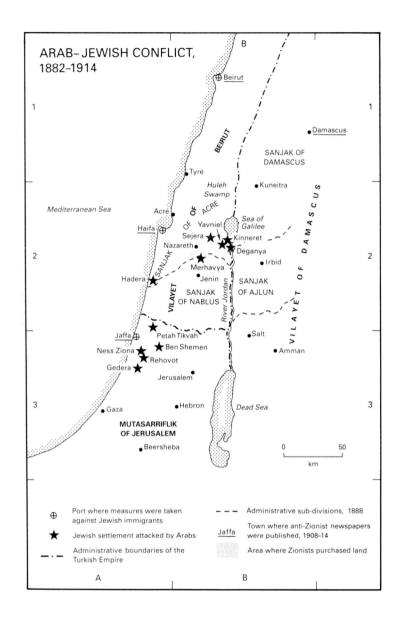

ARAB–JEWISH CONFLICT, 1882–1914

Beirut

Damascus

SANJAK OF
DAMASCUS

BEIRUT

Tyre

Huleh Swamp

Kuneitra

Mediterranean Sea

Acre

SANJAK   OF   ACRE

Haifa

Yavniel

Sea of Galilee

Sejera ★

★ Kinneret

Nazareth

★ Deganya

Irbid

★ Merhavya

Jenin

SANJAK
OF AJLUN

Hadera ★

VILAYET

SANJAK
OF NABLUS

River Jordan

Jaffa

Petah Tikvah

★ Ben Shemen

Salt

Ness Ziona ★

Rehovot

Amman

Gedera ★

Jerusalem

VILAYET   OF   DAMASCUS

Gaza

Hebron

Dead Sea

**MUTASARRIFLIK
OF JERUSALEM**

Beersheba

0   50
km

⊕   Port where measures were taken
     against Jewish immigrants

★   Jewish settlement attacked by Arabs

– · –   Administrative boundaries of the
        Turkish Empire

– – –   Administrative sub-divisions, 1888

Jaffa   Town where anti-Zionist newspapers
        were published, 1908–14

        Area where Zionists purchased land

best endeavours to facilitate the achievement of this object, it being clearly understood that nothing shall be done which may prejudice the civil and religious rights and political status enjoyed by Jews in any other country.

A month after the Balfour Declaration was published, General Allenby captured Jerusalem. When Weizmann went to meet him in 1918, Allenby was overwhelmed by military and administrative difficulties. Weizmann was told the time was not propitious to implement the British plan: 'Nothing can be done at present', he stated. 'We have to be extremely careful not to hurt the susceptibilities of the population.' Yet despite such obstacles as well as opposition from various quarters Britain secured the Palestine mandate at the peace negotiations and steps were undertaken to create a national Jewish homeland.

Aftermath of the First World War

At the end of the nineteenth century a number of agricultural settlements, funded by such philanthropists as Moses Montefiore and Edmund de Rothschild, were established in Palestine by Jewish settlers (the first Aliyah). At the beginning of the twentieth century in the wake of Russian pogroms, a second wave of Jewish immigrants (the second Aliyah) emigrated to the Holy Land. These pioneers set up the new garden suburb of Jaffa (later Tel Aviv) and founded kibbutzim as well as agricultural settlements. In 1909 the young men of the second Aliyah, who had previously participated in Jewish defence groups in Russia, established the Society of Shomerim (Watchmen) to protect these new settlements. Under the leadership of the Russian-born writer Vladimir Jabotinsky and the Russian war hero Joseph Trumpeldor, a Jewish regiment (the Zion Mule Corps) was founded, and participated in the First World War. After the war neither the Zionist authorities nor the British showed any desire to keep the Jewish Legion in existence. Jabotinsky, however, believed its continuation was necessary for Jewish survival and formed a self-defence organization (which later became the Haganah).

With the rise of Arab nationalism, the Jewish settlement in Palestine came increasingly under threat. In March 1920 the Arabs attacked Jewish settlements in Galilee when Trumpeldor was killed; this was followed by Arab riots in Jerusalem. In response, Jabotinsky's self-defence force went into action and Jabotinsky and others were arrested, tried by a military court, and given fifteen years' hard labour. Arab rioters were also convicted and imprisoned. Following these events, Lloyd George sent out Herbert Samuel as High Commissioner, to the fury of the Arab population. Intent on implementing the Balfour Declaration — which aimed to safeguard the civil and religious rights of non-Jewish communities — Samuel criticized the Zionists for failing to recognize the importance of Arab nationalist aspirations.

The Zionists had few resources for appeasing the Arab population in the early 1920s and were therefore not anxious to heed Samuel's words. None the less Samuel pursued a policy of even-handedness, pardoning the Arab extremists who had started the riots of 1920. Following this act, he confirmed Sheikh Hisam, who was elected Grand Mufti of Jerusalem by the electoral college of pious Arab Muslims, in preference to the extremist Haj Amin Al-Husseini. Subsequently the Al-Husseini family and the nationalist extreme wing who had led the 1920 riots embarked on a campaign against the electoral college.

Within the British staff an anti-Zionist, Ernst T. Richmond (who acted as an adviser to the High Commissioner on Muslim affairs), persuaded Sheikh Hisam to step down and urged Samuel to allow Haj Amin to take his place. On 11 July 1921 Samuel saw Haj Amin, who gave assurances that he and his family would be dedicated to peace. Three weeks later riots occurred in Jaffa and elsewhere in which forty-five Jews were killed. This error of judgement was compounded when Samuel fostered the creation of a supreme Muslim Council which was transformed by the Mufti and his followers into a means of terrorizing the Jewish population. Further, Samuel encouraged Palestinian Arabs to contact their neighbours to promote Pan-Arabism. As a result the Mufti was able to generate anti-Zionist feeling within the Pan-Arab movement.

Although the British government initially agreed that all Jews should be free to emigrate to Palestine, immigration eventually became a pressing issue. After the Arab riots, Samuel suspended Jewish immigration, and three boat-loads of Jews fleeing from Poland and the Ukraine were sent back from Israel. According to Samuel, mass migration could not be allowed; not surprisingly this policy led to vehement Jewish protests. Under Samuel's successor Lord Plumer the country prospered, yet Jewish resentment continued. Although Weizmann adopted a moderate stance toward Palestinian development,

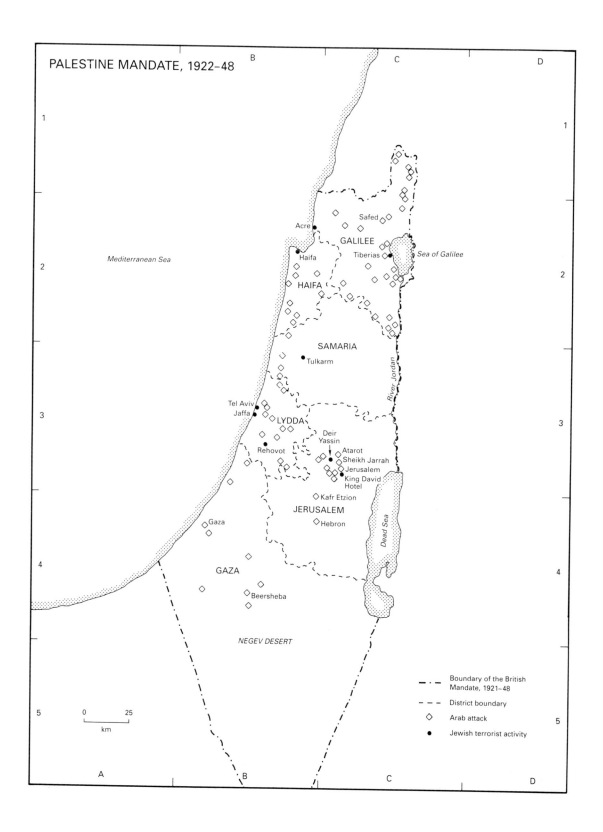

PALESTINE MANDATE, 1922–48

Mediterranean Sea

Acre

Safed

GALILEE

Haifa

Tiberias

Sea of Galilee

HAIFA

SAMARIA

Tulkarm

River Jordan

Tel Aviv
Jaffa

LYDDA

Deir
Yassin

Rehovot

Atarot
Sheikh Jarrah
Jerusalem
King David
Hotel

Kafr Etzion

JERUSALEM

Dead Sea

Gaza

Hebron

GAZA

Beersheba

NEGEV DESERT

Boundary of the British
Mandate, 1921–48

District boundary

◇ Arab attack

● Jewish terrorist activity

0   25
km

A   B   C   D

187

other leaders such as Jabotinsky were more impatient. In 1922 Churchill ended the ban on immigration, but his White Paper none the less insisted that immigration must reflect the economic capacity of the country. Unwilling to accept British policy, Jabotinsky believed that immigration should be the sole concern of Jewish authorities. On this basis, he left the Zionist executive in 1923, and in 1925 founded the Union of Zionist-Revisionists which sought to attract the largest number of Jews in the shortest possible time. This movement was hailed in eastern Europe, where its youth wing Betar wore uniforms and received military training.

The establishment of a Jewish state

Despite such efforts to encourage Jewish immigration, the Jewish population in Palestine grew gradually. But from 1929, as the economic and political situation grew worse throughout Europe, a large number of Jews sought to enter the country. In 1929 a massacre took place in Palestine in which 150 Jews were killed; this led to a further limit on immigration despite the fact that hundreds of thousands of Jews sought entry into Palestine. As more and more Jews were allowed to settle, Arab resentment intensified. Each year there were more than 30,000 arrivals, and in 1935 the number grew to 62,000. In response, in April 1936 a major Arab uprising took place. On 7 July 1937 a commission headed by Lord Peel recommended that Jewish immigration be reduced to 12,000 a year, and restrictions were placed on land purchases. In addition a three-way partition was suggested: the coastal strip, Galilee and the Jezreel valley should be formed into a Jewish state, whereas the Judaean hills, the Negev and Ephraim should be the Arab state. This plan was rejected by the Arabs, and another revolt took place in 1937. In the following year, the Pan-Arab conference in Cairo adopted a policy whereby all Arab communities pledged that they would take action to prevent further Zionist expansion.

After the failure of the tripartite plan in London in 1939 the British abandoned the policy of partition. In May 1939 a new White Paper was published stating that only 75,000 more Jews could be admitted over five years, and thereafter none except with Arab agreement. At the same time Palestine should proceed with plans to become independent.

Although the Jews supported the allies, Jewry was committed to overturning British policy as enshrined in the 1939 White Paper. During this period the British attempted to prevent illegal immigrants from landing in Palestine: if their ships got through they were captured and deported. In November 1940 the *Patria*, which was about to set sail for Mauritius carrying 1,700 deportees, was sabotaged by the Haganah; it sank in Haifa Bay with the loss of 250 refugees. Two years later the *Struma*, a refugee ship from Romania, was refused landing permission, turned back by the Turks, and sank in the Black Sea with the loss of 770 passengers. Such events, however, did not alter Britain's determination to prevent the entry of illegal immigrants.

In 1943 Menahem Begin, formerly chairman of Betar, took over control of the Revisionist military arm, the Irgun. With 600 agents under his control, he blew up various British buildings. On 6 November 1944 the ultra-extreme group, the Stern Gang (which had broken away from the Irgun), murdered Lord Moyne, the British Minister for Middle Eastern Affairs. Outraged by this act, the Haganah launched a campaign against both the Sternists and the Irgun. While he was fighting the British and other Jews, Begin organized a powerful underground force in the belief that the Haganah would eventually join him in attacking the British. In 1945 a united Jewish resistance movement was created which embraced the various Jewish military forces, and on 31 October it began blowing up railways. In retaliation the British made a raid on the Jewish Agency on 29 June 1946, arresting 2,718 Jews. Begin, however, persuaded the Haganah to blow up the King David Hotel, where a segment of the British administration was located. When Weizmann heard of this plan he was incensed, and the Haganah was ordered to desist. Begin refused, and on 22 July 1946 the explosion took place, killing 27 British, 41 Arabs, 17 Jews and 5 others. In consequence the Haganah commander Moshe Sneh resigned, and the resistance movement divided. The British then proposed a tripartite plan of partition which was rejected by both Jews and Arabs. Exasperated by this conflict, the British Foreign Secretary, Ernest Bevin, declared he was handing over this dispute to the United Nations.

Despite this decision, Begin continued with his campaign of terror, insisting on the right of the Irgun to retaliate against the British. In April 1947, after three members of the Irgun were convicted and hanged for destroying the Acre prison fortress, Begin ordered that two British sergeants be hanged. Such an act of revenge provoked world-wide condemnation, and anti-

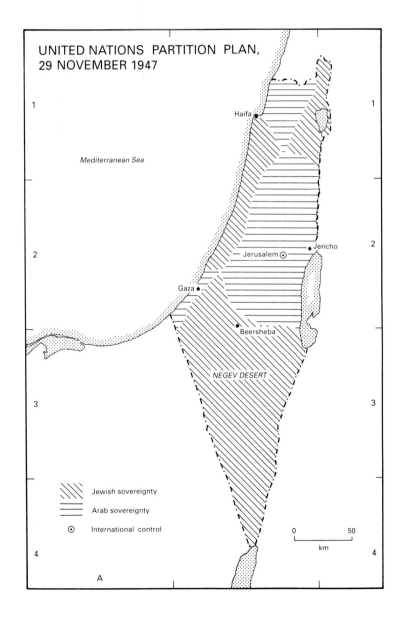

UNITED NATIONS PARTITION PLAN, 29 NOVEMBER 1947

Jewish riots took place throughout Britain. These incidents encouraged the British to leave Palestine as soon as possible, and also coincided with the succession of Harry S. Truman as President of the United States. Sympathetic to the Jewish cause and anxious for the support of American Jewry in the 1948 election, Truman pressed for the creation of a Jewish state. In May 1947 the Palestinian question came before the United Nations, and a special committee was authorized to formulate a plan for the future of the country. The majority recommended a binational state, but the majority suggested that there be both an Arab and a Jewish state as well as an international zone in Jerusalem. On 29 November this recommendation was endorsed by the General Assembly.

After this decision was taken, the Arabs began to attack Jewish settlements. Although the Jewish commanders were determined to repel this assault, their resources were not considerable compared with the Arab side. The Haganah had 17,600 rifles, 2,700 sten-guns, about 1,000 machine guns and approximately 20,000–43,000 men in various stages of training. The Arabs, on the other hand, had a sizeable liberation army as well as the regular forces of the Arab states including 10,000 Egyptians, 7,000 Syrians, 3,000 Iraqis, 3,000 Lebanese as well as 4,500 soldiers from the Arab Legion of Transjordan. By March 1948 over 1,200 Jews were killed; in April Ben Gurion ordered the Haganah to link the Jewish enclaves and consolidate as much territory as possible under the United Nations plan. Jewish forces then occupied Haifa, opened up the route to Tiberias and eastern Galilee and captured Safed, Jaffa and Acre. On 14 May Ben Gurion read out the Scroll of Independence in the Tel Aviv Museum:

> By virtue of our national and intrinsic right and on the strength of the resolution of the United Nations General Assembly, we hereby declare the establishment of a Jewish state in Palestine, which shall be known as the State of Israel.

War between Jews and Arabs

On 11 June a truce was concluded, but in the next month conflict broke out and the Israelis seized Lydda, Ramallah and Nazareth as well as large areas beyond the partition frontiers. Within ten days the Arabs agreed to another truce, but outbreaks of hostility continued. In mid-October the Israelis attempted to open the road to the Negev settlements and took Beersheba. On 12 January 1949 armistice talks took place in Rhodes and an armistice was later signed by Egypt, Lebanon, Transjordan and Syria. These events created the continuing Arab–Palestinian problem: 656,000 Arab inhabitants fled from Israeli-held territories: 280,000 to the West Bank; 70,000 to Transjordan; 100,000 to Lebanon; 4,000 to Iraq; 75,000 to Syria; 7,000 to Egypt; and 190,000 to the Gaza Strip.

On the basis of the 1949 armistice, the Israelis sought agreement on the boundaries of the Jewish state. The Arabs, however, refused to consider this proposal – instead they insisted that Israel return to the 1947 partition lines without giving any formal recognition of the new state. Further, despite the concluding of the armistice, *fedayeen* bands continued to attack Israeli citizens, and boycotts and blockades sought to injure Israel's economy. After King Abdullah was assassinated on 20 June 1951, a military junta ousted the Egyptian monarch; on 25 February 1954 President Gemal Abdul Nasser gained control of the country. From September 1955 the Soviet bloc supplied weapons to the Arabs, and this encouraged Nasser to take steps against the Jewish state. From 1956 he denied Israeli ships access to the Gulf of Aqaba. In April 1956 he signed a pact with Saudi Arabia and Yemen, and in July he seized the Suez Canal. Fearing Arab intentions, Israel launched a pre-emptive strike

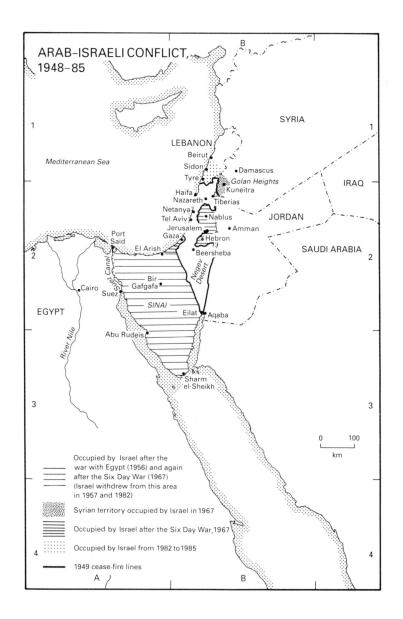

ARAB-ISRAELI CONFLICT, 1948–85

SYRIA

Mediterranean Sea

LEBANON

Beirut
Sidon
Tyre
Haifa
Nazareth
Netanya
Tel Aviv
Jerusalem
Gaza

Damascus
Golan Heights
Kuneitra
Tiberias
Nablus
Amman
Hebron

IRAQ

JORDAN

SAUDI ARABIA

Port Said
El Arish
Beersheba

Suez Canal

Negev Desert

Cairo

Bir Gafgafa

Suez

EGYPT

SINAI

Eilat
Aqaba

Abu Rudeis

River Nile

Sharm el-Sheikh

0   100
km

Occupied by Israel after the war with Egypt (1956) and again after the Six Day War (1967) (Israel withdrew from this area in 1957 and 1982)

Syrian territory occupied by Israel in 1967

Occupied by Israel after the Six Day War, 1967

Occupied by Israel from 1982 to 1985

1949 cease-fire lines

on 29 October, and in the war that followed Israel captured all the Sinai as well as Gaza, and opened a sea route to Aqaba.

At the end of the Sinai War Israel undertook to withdraw from Sinai as long as Egypt did not remilitarize it and UN forces formed a protective *cordon sanitaire.* This arrangement endured for ten years, but attacks still continued during this period. In 1967 Nasser launched another offensive, and on 15 May he moved 100,000 men and armour into Sinai and expelled the UN army. On

22 May he blockaded Aqaba; several days later King Hussein of Jordan signed a military agreement in Cairo. On the same day Iraqi forces took up positions in Jordan. In the face of this Arab threat, Israel launched a strike on 5 June, destroying the Egyptian air force on the ground. On 7 June the Israeli army took the Old City, thereby making Jerusalem its capital. On the next day the Israeli forces occupied the entire Left Bank, and during the next few days captured the Golan Heights and reoccupied Sinai.

191

Figure 24   Jerusalem during Israel's War for Independence, 1948 (Central Zionist Archives, Jerusalem)

Despite such a crushing defeat, the Six Day War did not bring security to the Jewish state. Nasser's successor President Anwar Sadat expelled Egypt's Soviet military advisers in July 1972, cancelled the country's political and military alliance with other Arab states, and together with Syria attacked Israel on Yom Kippur, 6 October 1973. At the outbreak of war the Egyptians and the Syrians broke through Israeli defences, but by 9 October the Syrian advance had been repelled. On 10 October the American President Richard Nixon began an airlift of advanced weapons to Israel; two days later the Israelis engaged in a counter-attack on Egypt and moved toward victory. On 24 October a cease-fire came into operation.

Later after the Labour coalition lost the May 1977 election and handed over power to the Likud headed by Menahem Begin, Sadat offered to negotiate peace terms with Israel. On 5 September 1978 at the American presidential home Camp David, the process of reaching such an agreement began and was completed thirteen days later (although another six months were required before a detailed treaty was formulated). The treaty specified that Egypt would recognize Israel's right to exist and provide secure guarantees for her southern border. In return Israel would hand over Sinai. In addition she would undertake to negotiate away much of the West Bank and make concessions over Jerusalem as long as a complementary treaty was agreed with the Palestinians and other Arab countries. This latter step, however, was never taken – the proposal was rejected by the Palestinian Arabs.

In the years that followed, Arab influence grew immeasurably, because of the Arabs' control of oil in the Middle East. As the price of oil

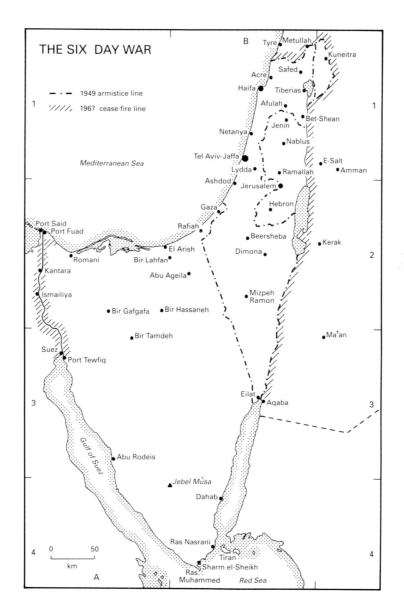

THE SIX DAY WAR

- – · – 1949 armistice line
- ///// 1967 cease-fire line

Mediterranean Sea

B Tyre Metullah
Kuneitra
Acre Safed
Haifa Tiberias
Afulah
Jenin Bet-Shean
Netanya
Nablus
Tel Aviv-Jaffa
E-Salt
Lydda Ramallah Amman
Ashdod Jerusalem
Gaza Hebron
Rafiah
Port Said Beersheba
Port Fuad Kerak
El Arish
Romani Dimona
Bir Lahfan
Kantara Abu Ageila
Ismailiya Mizpeh Ramon
Bir Gafgafa Bir Hassaneh
Bir Tamdeh Ma'an
Suez
Port Tewfiq
Eilat Aqaba
Gulf of Suez
Abu Rodeis
▲ *Jebel Mûsa*
Dahab
Ras Nasrani
0   50
Tiran
km
Ras Sharm el-Sheikh
A Muhammed *Red Sea*

increased, Arab revenue provided huge sums for the purchase of armaments. At the UN the Arab world exerted its power, and in 1975 the General Assembly passed a resolution equating Zionism with racism. Further, Yasser Arafat, the leader of the Palestine Liberation Organization, was accorded head of government status by the UN. Fearing the growing threat of Palestinian influence and terrorism, Israel launched an advance into southern Lebanon in June 1982, destroying PLO bases. This Israeli onslaught and subse-

quent occupation served as the background to the killing of Muslim refugees by Christian Falangist Arabs in the Sabra and Shatilla camps on 16 September 1982. Throughout the world this atrocity was portrayed as Israel's fault. In response to this criticism, the Israeli government ordered an independent judicial inquiry which placed some blame on the Israeli Minister of Defence, Ariel Sharon, for not having prevented this massacre.

Figure 25 The Western Wall of the ancient Temple mount, Jerusalem (Richard Stoneman)

The *intifada*

After the Israeli conquest during the Yom Kippur War, the State of Israel took control of the Occupied Territories. In the following years the Palestinians staged demonstrations, strikes and riots against Israeli rule. By 1987 the Palestinians in the West Bank and Gaza were largely young people who had benefited from formal education. Yet despite such educational advances, they suffered from limited job expectations and this situation led to political radicalism. Such frustration came to a head on 9 December 1987 in Jabaliya, the most militant of the Gaza refugee camps. An Israeli patrol was trapped there during a protest about the death of four Jabaliya residents who were killed in a road accident the previous day. The soldiers shot their way out,

killing one youth and wounding ten others. This event provoked riots throughout the Occupied Territories. By January 1989, the Israel Defence Forces declared that 352 Palestinians had died, more than 4,300 were wounded, and 25,600 arrested. In addition, 200 Arab homes had been sealed or demolished. As hostilities increased, the *intifada* (resistance) demonstrated that occupying the West Bank and the Gaza Strip would be a perpetual problem.

The Jewish state was unprepared for such a situation, and the army was forced to improvise. As time passed, the *intifada* became more resilient and its tactics changed to ambushes, small-scale conflicts and selective strikes. In addition the technology of modern communications was used to apply pressure against the Israelis. In the view of many observers, this uprising had transformed the Palestinian people.

Despite having such an impact, the *intifada* created tensions with the Palestinian community. As the resistance developed, Islamic revivalism spread from the Gaza Strip to the West Bank and Jerusalem and posed a serious threat to secular Palestinian nationalism. Such a division was aggravated when the PLO endorsed a two-stage solution to the Palestinian problem. Such a policy was bitterly condemned by fundamentalists. Hamas, the Islamic Resistance Movement, insisted on a Muslim Palestine from the Mediterranean to the Jordan. Clause 11 of its Manifesto declared:

The Islamic Resistance Movement believes that all the land of Palestine is sacred to Islam, through all the generations and forever, and it

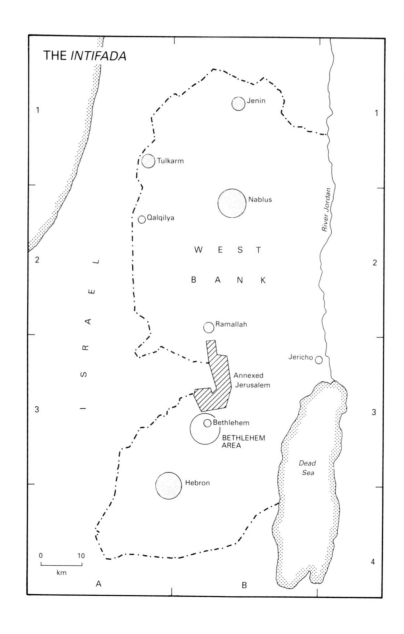

THE *INTIFADA*

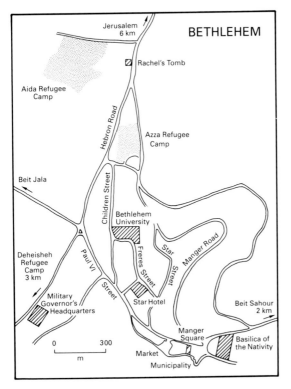

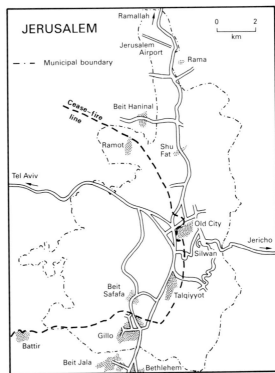

is forbidden to abandon it or part of it, or to yield it or part of it. No Arab state individually has the right, nor do all of the Arab states collectively, nor does any king or president individually, nor do all the kings and presidents collectively. No organization individually has the right, nor do all the organizations collectively, whether they are Palestinian or Arab.

Yasser Arafat, however, adopted a more pragmatic approach and abandoned such maximalist formulations of the Palestinian position in favour of a policy which took into account the reality of Israel's existence.

The *intifada* was generally regarded as more than a local skirmish, and throughout the world Israelis were viewed as guilty of brutality. As a result, there was a growing feeling that Israel should abandon the Occupied Territories. Thus a poll conducted by Professor Elihu Katz, Director of the Hebrew University's Israel Institute of Applied Social Research, in January 1989

revealed considerable sympathy toward the idea of a Palestinian state. Concluding his findings, Professor Katz wrote:

> Some 30 per cent of Israeli Jews (half of the left and 10 to 20 per cent of the right) are willing to grant the essential prerequisites for a Palestinian state: negotiations, substantial territorial concessions and recognition. If questions are worded to make evident that security and peace might be obtained in exchange for these concessions, the favourable proportion increases substantially to 50 per cent or more.
>
> (Cohn-Sherbok, *Israel: The History of an Idea*, pp. 162–3)

Thus after several years of Palestinian revolt in the Occupied Territories, the Israeli population appears more prepared to settle its dispute with its Arab inhabitants, as has been evidenced by recent peace talks between Israel and the Palestinians.

FURTHER READING

General

Baron, Salo Wittmayer, *A Social and Religious History of the Jews*, New York: Columbia University Press, 1952–76.

Ben-Sasson, H. H. (ed.), *A History of the Jewish People*, Cambridge, Mass.: Harvard University Press, 1976.

Cohn-Sherbok, Dan, *The Jewish Heritage*, Oxford: Basil Blackwell, 1988.

de Lange, Nicholas, *Judaism*, Oxford: Oxford University Press, 1986.

Dubnow, Simon, *History of the Jews*, vols 1–5, New Jersey: Thomas Yoseloff, 1969.

Encyclopaedia Judaica, vols 1–16, Jerusalem: Keter Publishing House, 1972.

Finkelstein, Louis (ed.), *The Jews: Their History, Culture and Religion*, New York: Harper & Row, 1960.

Graetz, Heinrich, *History of the Jews*, vols 1–6, Philadelphia: Jewish Publication Society of America, 1949.

Jewish Encyclopedia, vols 1–12, New York: Funk & Wagnalls, 1901–5

Johnson, Paul, *A History of the Jews*, London: Weidenfeld & Nicolson, 1987.

Margolis, Max and Marx, Alexander, *A History of the Jewish People*, Philadelphia: Jewish Publication Society, 1927.

Rayner, John and Goldberg, David, *The Jewish People*, Middlesex: Viking, 1987.

Seltzer, Robert M., *Jewish People, Jewish Thought*, New York: Macmillan, 1980.

Trepp, Leo, *A History of the Jewish Experience*, New York: Behrman House, 1973.

The Ancient Near East and the Israelites

Albright, William Foxwell, *From the Stone Age to Christianity*, Garden City, N.Y.: Doubleday & Co., 1959.

Anderson, G. W., *The History and Religion of Israel*, London: Oxford University Press, 1966.

Bright, John, *A History of Israel*, Philadelphia: Westminster Press, 1972.

De Vaux, Roland, *Ancient Israel*, vols 1–2, New York: McGraw-Hill, 1961.

Frankfort, H., Frankfort, H. A., Wilson, John A. and Jacobsen, Thorkild, *Before Philosophy*, Baltimore: Penguin, 1951.

Noth, Martin, *The History of Israel*, New York: Harper & Row, 1960.

Pritchard, James, *Archeology and the Old Testament*, Princeton, N.J.: Princeton University Press, 1958.

Pritchard, James (ed.), *The Ancient Near East: An Anthology of Texts and Pictures*, Princeton, NJ: Princeton University Press, 1958.

—— *The Ancient Near East*, vol. 2, *A New Anthology of Texts and Pictures*, Princeton, N.J.: Princeton University Press, 1975.

Wright, G. Ernest (ed.), *The Bible and the Ancient Near East: Essays in Honour of William Foxwell Albright*, Garden City, N.Y.: Doubleday, 1965.

Captivity and return

Bickerman, Elias, *From Ezra to the Last of the Maccabees: Foundations of Postbiblical Judaism*, New York: Schocken Books, 1972.

Blenkinsopp, Joseph, *Prophecy and Canon: A Contribution to the Study of Jewish Origins*, Notre Dame, Ind.: Notre Dame Press, 1977.

Hengel, Martin, *Judaism and Hellenism: Studies in their Encounter in Palestine During the Early Hellenistic Period*, Philadelphia: Fortress Press, 1977.

Kaufmann, Yehezkel, *History of the Religion of Israel: From the Babylonian Captivity to the End of Prophecy*, New York: Ktav, 1978.

Nicklesburg, George W. E., *Jewish Literature Between the Bible and the Mishnah*, London: SCM Press, 1981.

Schalit, Abraham (ed.), *The Hellenistic Age: Political History of Jewish Palestine from 332 BCE–67 CE*, New Brunswick, N.J.: Rutgers University Press, 1972.

Schürer, Emil, *The History of the Jewish People in the Age of Christ*, vols 1–2, Edinburgh: T. & T. Clark, 1973, 1979.

Smith, Morton, *Palestinian Parties and Politics that Shaped the Old Testament*, New York: Columbia University Press, 1971.

Tcherikover, Victor, *Hellenistic Civilization and the Jews*, Philadelphia: Fortress Press, 1974.

Zeitlin, Solomon, *The Rise and Fall of the Jewish State*, vols 1–3, Philadelphia: Jewish Publication Society, 1962–78.

From Herod to rebellion

Avi-Yonah, Michael (ed.), *The Herodian Period*, New Brunswick, N.J.: Rutgers University Press, 1975.

Leon, Harry J., *The Jews of Ancient Rome*, Philadelphia: Jewish Publication Society, 1960.

Neusner, Jacob, *Early Rabbinic Judaism: Historical Studies in Religion, Literature and Art*, Leiden: E. J. Brill, 1975.

—— *From Politics to Piety: The Emergence of Pharisaic Judaism*, Englewood Cliffs, N.J.: Prentice-Hall, 1973.

Rivkin, Ellis, *A Hidden Revolution: The Pharisees' Search for the Kingdom Within*, Nashville, Tenn.: Abingdon, 1978.

Safrai, S. and Stern, M., *The Jewish People in the First Century: Historical Geography, Political History, Social, Cultural, and Religious Life and Institutions*, vols 1–2, Philadelphia: Fortress Press, 1974–6.

Sanders, E. P., *Paul and Palestinian Judaism*, Philadelphia: Fortress Press, 1977.

Sandmel, Samuel, *Judaism and Christian Beginnings*, New York: Oxford University Press, 1978.

Yadin, Yigael, *Masada: Herod's Fortress of the Zealots' Last Stand*, New York: Random House, 1966.

Vermes, Geza, *Jesus the Jew: A Historian's Reading of the Gospels*, London: Collins, 1973.

Jewry in Palestine and Babylonia

Avi-Yonah, M., *The Jews of Palestine: A Political History from the Bar Kokhba Wave to the Arab Conquest*, New York: Schocken, 1976.

Lieberman, Saul, *Greek in Jewish Palestine*, New York: Feldheim, 1965.

Montefiore, C. G. and Loewe, H. (eds), *A Rabbinic Anthology*, New York: Schocken, 1974.

Moore, George Foot, *Judaism in the First Centuries of the Christian Era: The Age of the Tannaim*, vols 1–3, Cambridge, Mass.: Harvard University Press, 1927–30.

Neusner, Jacob, *A History of the Jews in Babylonia*, vols 1–4, Leiden: E. J. Brill, 1965–70.

—— *Talmudic Judaism in Sasanian Babylonia: Essays and Studies*, Leiden: E. J. Brill, 1976.

—— *There We Sat Down: Talmudic Judaism in the Making*, Nashville, Tenn.: Abingdon, 1972.

Parkes, James, *The Conflict of the Church and the Synagogue: A Study in the Origin of Anti-Semitism*, New York: Meridian Books, 1961.

Strack, Hermann L., *Introduction to the Talmud and Midrash*, Philadelphia: Jewish Publication Society, 1931.

Urbach, Ephraim E., *The Sages: Their Concepts of Beliefs*, vols 1–2, Jerusalem: Magnes Press, 1975.

Judaism under Islam in the Middle Ages

Ashtor, Eliyahu, *The Jews of Moslem Spain*, vols 1–2, Philadelphia: Jewish Publication Society, 1973–9.

Fischel, W., *Jews in the Economic and Political Life of Medieval Islam*, New York, 1937.

Goitein, S. D., *A Mediterranean Society: The Jewish Communities of the Arab World as Portrayed in the Documents of the Cairo Geniza*, vols 1–3, Berkeley and Los Angeles: University of California Press, 1967–78.

—— *Jews and Arabs: Their Contacts Through the Ages*, New York: Schocken, 1964.

Goiten, S. D. (ed.), *Religion in a Religious Age*, Cambridge, Mass.: Association for Jewish Studies, 1974.

Lewis, Bernard, *The Jews of Islam*, London, 1984.

Mann, J., *The Jews in Egypt Under the Fatmid Caliphs*, vols 1–2, London, 1920–2.

Nemoy, Leon (ed.), *Karaite Anthology: Excerpts from the Early Literature*, New Haven: Yale University Press, 1952.

Stillman, Norman A. (ed.), *The Jewish Arab Lands: A History and Source Book*, Philadelphia, 1979.

Ye'or, Bar, *The Dhimmi: Jews and Christians Under Islam*, London, 1985.

Jews in Medieval Christian Europe

Abrahams, Israel, *Jewish Life in the Middle Ages*, New York: Athenaeum, 1964.

Baer, Yitzhak, *A History of the Jews of Christian Spain*, vols 1–2, Philadelphia: Jewish Publication Society, 1961.

Finkelstein, Louis, *Jewish Self-government in the Middle Ages*, New York: Feldheim, 1964.

Grayzel, Solomon, *The Church and the Jews in the Thirteenth Century*, New York: Herman Press, 1966.

Kamen, Henry, *The Spanish Inquisition*, New York: Hippocrene Books, 1974.

Katz, *Exclusiveness and Tolerance: Studies in Jewish–Gentile Relations in Medieval and Modern Times*, New York: Schocken, 1962.

Lowenthal, Marvin, *The Jews of Germany: A Story of Sixteen Centuries*, Philadelphia: Jewish Publication Society, 1938.

Newman, Abraham A., *The Jews in Spain: Their Social, Political and Cultural Life*, vol. 1–2, Philadelphia: Jewish Publication Society, 1942.

Roth, Cecil, *A History of the Jews in England*, London: Oxford University Press, 1949.

Synan, E. M., *The Popes and the Jews in the Middle Ages*, New York: Macmillan, 1965.

Medieval Jewish thought

Agus, Jacob Bernard, *The Evolution of Jewish Thought from Biblical Times to the Opening of the Modern Era*, London and New York: Abelard-Schuman, 1959.

Blau, Joseph L., *The Story of Jewish Philosophy*, New York: Random House, 1962.

Husik, Isaac, *A History of Jewish Philosophy*, Philadelphia: Jewish Publication Society, 1958.

Jacobs, Louis, *A Jewish Theology*, London: Darton, Longman & Todd, 1973.

Jacobs, Louis (ed.), *Jewish Mystical Testimonies*, New York: Schocken, 1977.

Katz, Steven (ed.), *Jewish Philosophers*, New York: Bloch Publishing Co., 1975.

Maimonides, Moses, *The Guide for the Perplexed*, Chicago University Press, 1963.

Scholem, Gershom, *Kabbalah*, New York: Quadrangle/The New York Times Book Co., 1974.

—— *Major Trends in Jewish Mysticism*, New York: Schocken, 1954.

The Zohar, vols 1–5, London: Soncino Press, 1933–4.

Western European Jewry in the early modern period

Barzilay, Isaac E., *Between Reason and Faith: Anti-Rationalism in Italian Jewish Thought, 1250–1650*, The Hague: Mouton, 1967.

Katz, Jacob, *Tradition and Crisis: Jewish Society at the End of the Middle Ages*, New York: The Free Press, 1961.

Roth, Cecil, *History of the Jews of Venice*, New York: Schocken, 1975.

—— *The House of Nasi: Dona Gracia*, Philadelphia: Jewish Publication Society, 1947.

—— *The House of Nasi: The Duke of Naxos*, Philadelphia: Jewish Publication Society, 1948.

—— *The Jews in the Renaissance*, Philadelphia:

Jewish Publication Society, 1950.

Ruderman, David B., *Kabbalah, Magic and Science, The Cultural Universe of a Sixteenth Century Physician*, Cambridge, Mass.: Harvard University Press, 1988.

Scholem, Gershom, *Sabbatai Sevi: The Mystical Messiah, 1626–1676*, Princeton, N.J.: Princeton University Press, 1973.

Stern, Selma, *The Court Jew: A Contribution to the History of the Period of Absolutism in Central Europe*, Philadelphia: Jewish Publication Society, 1950.

Yerushalmi, Yosef Hayim, *From Spanish Court Jew to Italian Ghetto: Isaac Cardoso*, New York: Columbia University Press, 1971.

Eastern European Jewry in the early modern period

Band, Arnold (ed.), *Nahman of Bratslav: The Tales*, New York, Paulist Press, 1978.

Ben-Amos, Dan and Mintz, Jerome R. (eds), *In Praise of the Baal Shem Tov: The Earliest Catalogue of Legends about the Founder of Hasidism*, Bloomington, Ind.: Indiana University Press, 1970.

Dawidowicz, Lucy S. (ed.), *The Golden Tradition: Jewish Life and Thought in Eastern Europe*, New York: Holt, Rinehart & Winston, 1966.

Dresner, Samuel H., *The Zaddik: The Doctrine of the Zaddik according to the Writings of Rabbi Yaakov Yosef of Polnoy*, New York: Schocken, 1974.

Dubnov, Simon, *History of the Jews in Russia and Poland*, New York: Ktav, 1973.

Greenberg, Louis, *The Jews in Russia*, New York: Schocken, 1976.

Levitas, Isaac, *The Jewish Community in Russia, 1772–1884*, New York: Octagon Press, 1970.

Poliakov, Leon, *The History of Anti-Semitism*, vols 1–3, New York: Vanguard Press, 1965–76.

Rabinowitsch, W. Z., *Lithuanian Hasidism from its Beginnings to the Present Day*, London: Vallentine, Mitchell, 1970.

Zborowski, Mark and Herzog, Elizabeth, *Life is with People: The Culture of the Shtetl*, New York: Schocken, 1962.

Jews in Europe in the eighteenth and nineteenth centuries

Albert, Phyllis Cohen, *The Modernization of French Jewry: Consistory and Community in the Nineteenth Century*, Hanover, N.H.: University Press of New England, 1977.

Altmann, Alexander, *Moses Mendelssohn: A Biographical Study*, Philadelphia: Jewish Publication Society, 1973.

Chazan, Robert and Raphael, Marc Lee (eds), *Modern Jewish History: A Source Reader*, New York: Schocken, 1974.

Elbogen, Ismar, *A Century of Jewish Life*, Philadelphia: Jewish Publication Society, 1960.

Hertzberg, Arthur, *The French Enlightenment and the Jews*, New York: Columbia University Press, 1968.

Jospe, Eva (ed.), *Moses Mendelssohn: Selections from his Writings*, New York: Viking Press, 1975.

Katz, Jacob, *Out of the Ghetto: The Social Background of Jewish Emancipation 1770–1870*, Cambridge, Mass.: Harvard University Press, 1973.

Kobler, Franz, *Napoleon and the Jews*, New York: Schocken, 1975.

Mendelssohn, Moses, *Jerusalem and Other Writings*, New York: Schocken, 1969.

Sachar, Howard Morley, *The Course of Modern Jewish History*, New York: Dell, 1977.

The development of reform Judaism

Davis, Moshe, *The Emergence of Conservative Judaism: The Historical School in Nineteenth Century America*, Philadelphia: Jewish Publication Society of America, 1965.

Geiger, Abraham, *Judaism and its History*, New York: Bloch Publishing Co., 1911.

Marcus, Jacob R., *Israel Jacobson: The Founder of the Reform Movement in Judaism*, Cincinnati, Ohio: Hebrew Union College, 1972.

Meyer, Michael, *A Response to Modernity: A History of the Reform Movement*, Oxford: Oxford University Press, 1988.

Petuchowski, Jakob J., *Prayerbook Reform in*

Europe: The Liturgy of European Liberal and Reform Judaism, New York: World Union for Progressive Judaism, 1968.

Petuchowski, Jacob J. (ed.), *New Perspectives on Abraham Geiger*, New York: Hebrew Union College Press, 1975.

Philipson, David, *The Reform Movement in Israel*, New York: Ktav, 1967.

Plaut, Gunther W. (ed.) *The Growth of Reform Judaism: American and European Sources until 1948*, New York: World Union for Progressive Judaism, 1965.

—— *The Rise of Reform Judaism: A Sourcebook of its European Origins*, New York: World Union for Progressive Judaism, 1963.

Weiner, Max (ed.), *Abraham Geiger and Liberal Judaism: The Challenge of the Nineteenth Century*, Philadelphia: Jewish Publication Society, 1962.

Jewry in the nineteenth and early twentieth centuries

Glazer, N., *American Judaism*, Chicago: University of Chicago Press, 1972.

Laqueur, W., *A History of Zionism*, New York: Schocken, 1976.

Poliakov, L., *The History of Anti-Semitism*, 3 vols, Vanguard Press, 1965–76.

Reinharz, J., *Fatherland or Promised Land: The Dilemma of the German Jew 1893–1914*, University of Michigan Press, 1975.

Sachar, *The Course of Modern Jewish History*, Delta, 1958.

The Holocaust

Cohn-Sherbok, D., *Holocaust Theology*, London: Lamp Press, 1989.

Dawidowicz, L. S., *The War Against the Jews 1937–1945*, New York: Holt, Rinehart & Winston, 1975.

Dawidowicz, L. S. (ed.), *A Holocaust Reader*, New York: Behrman House, 1976.

Gilbert, Martin, *The Holocaust*, London: Macmillan, 1984.

Levin, N., *The Holocaust: The Destruction of European Jewry 1933–1945*, New York: Schocken, 1973.

Israel

Cohn-Sherbok, Dan, *Israel: The History of an Idea*, London: SPCK, 1992.

Hurewitz, Jacob Coleman, *The Struggle for Palestine*, New York: Norton, 1950.

Laqueur, Walter, *A History of Zionism*, London: Weidenfeld & Nicolson, 1972.

Lewis, Bernard, *The Middle East and the West*, London: Weidenfeld & Nicolson, 1968.

Lucas, Noah, *The Modern History of Israel*, London: Weidenfeld & Nicolson, 1974.

Moore, John Norton (ed.), *The Arab–Israeli Conflict: Readings and Documents*, Princeton, N.J.: Princeton University Press, 1977.

O'Brien, Conor Cruise, *The Siege*, London: Weidenfeld & Nicholson, 1986.

Sachar, Howard M., *A History of Israel from the Rise of Zionism to Our Time*, Oxford: Basil Blackwell, 1977.

Vital, David, *The Formative Years*, New York: Oxford University Press, 1982.

—— *The Origins of Zionism*, Oxford: Clarendon Press, 1975.

GAZETTEER

This gazetteer indicates places shown on maps. Each reference uses co-ordinates based on the letters and numbers on the edges of the maps. Major geographical features (e.g. Dead Sea, Mediterranean Sea, Dniester River) are only included where they are significant. Where there are two maps on a page they are lettered a and b. Some references extend over more than one square. A4–3 indicates that the name starts in square A4 and ends in square A3. If you cannot locate a name within the designated square, check the key for a numbered location.

Aargau 102 B3
Abana, River 23 D1
Abbasid Caliphate 75 C2–D2; 85 C2; 100 C2
Abel 33 B2
Abel-beth-maachah 20 B1; 23 C1
Abel-meholah 20 B3
Abila 41 C2; 43 C2; 61 D2
Abilene 41 C1; 48 C1
Abu Ageila 193 B2
Abu Rodeis/Abu Rudeis 191 A3; 193 A3
Abu Salabikh 2b B2
Abu Shahrein see Eridu
Abu Sukhair 2b B1
Abydos 9 C4; 81 C2
Abyssinia 69 D4; 75 C4; 85 C3; 100 C3; 106 C4; 133 E3
Accaron 41 A3; 61 B3
Acco 20 A2; 26 B2; 28 B2; 33 A2; 83 D3; 95 B2
Achaea 54a A1–B1; 54b A1–B1; 63 C2
Achshaph 14 B1
Achzib 28 B2 & B4; 51 B1
Acrabatha 41 B3
Acrabbein 51 B2
Acrabeta 61 C3
Acre see Ptolemais
Acre, Sanjak of 185 A2–B2
Acre, Wilayat of 111 B1
Adab 2b B2
Adam 14 C3; 20 B3
Adana 69 D2
Aden 73a B3; 85 C3; 100 C3; 133 E3
Adesa 41 B3
Adhruh 73a B1
Adiabene 58 C2; 62 B1
Adida 41 B3; 43 B3; 61 B3
Adora 41 B4; 43 B4; 61 B4
Adoraim 23 B5
Adrarnyttium 63 C2; 67 D2

Adrianople (Edirne) 77 B3; 81 C2; 91 C2; 106 C2; 109 C3; 118 D2
Adullam 14 B4; 17b A3; 23 B4; 38 B3; 41 B4
Aegean Sea 54a B1; 54b B1
Aegina 67 C2
Africa 116 C2–3
Afulah 193 B1
Agade 2b B1
Agde 69 B1
Aghlabid Emirate 75 A2–B2
Agreda 97 D2
Agrigento 69 B2; 113 A5
Aguilar 104 C3
Ahlab 28 B1
Ahwas/Ahwaz 62 C3; 73b C2
Ai 5 A3; 14 B4
Aiath 38 C2
Aijalon 14 B4; 17B A3; 20 A3; 23 B4
'Ain Qudeirat see Kadesh-barnea
'Ajlūn 110 B1; 185 B2
Akkad 2b A1–B1
Akshak 2b B1
Al 'Ubad 2b 2B
Alagón 97 D2
Alalah 5 B1
Albania 181a C2; 181b C2
Albany 153 D1
Alcalá de Henares 97 C2
Alcoutim 104 B3
Aleksander see Alexandrów
Alema 41 C2
Aleppo 69 D2; 73b C1; 75 C2; 83 D3; 85 C2; 87 B2; 100 C2; 106 C2; 109 D4; 116 C2; 118 E3; 133 E2
Aleppo, Sultanate of 87 B2
Alexandria 9 B1; 58 C2; 63 D3; 67 D3; 69 C3; 73b B2; 81 D4; 85 B2; 88 E4; 91 D3; 95 B2; 100 B2; 106 C2
Alexandrium 43 C3; 46 B3; 61 C3

Alexandrów (Aleksander) 130a A2; 130b A2
Algeciras 97 B4
Algiers 91 B2; 116 C2; 132 D2
Alhambra 104 C3
Al-Hiba 2b C2
Alik see Olyka
Aljezur 104 B3
Almah 111 B1
Almería 97 C4
Almohad Empire 85 A2; 100 A2
Alpes-Maritimes 136 C3
Alsace 102 A3–B3; 135; 138 B2–C2
Altkirch 135 B3
Altona 154 C1
Alusa 41 A5
Amadia 85 C2; 100 C2
Amalekites 17b A4; 19 A4
Amastris 67 D2
Amathus/Ammathus 41 B3; 43 C3; 61 C3
Amboina 116 E3
Amdur see Indura
Amida 69 D2
Amisus 58 C2
Amman (Philadelphia) 41 C3; 43 C3; 46 C3; 48 C4; 61 D3; 65 A2; 87 B3; 185 B3; 191 B2; 193 C1
Ammon (Ammanitis) 17a C3; 17b B3–C2; 20 B3–C3; 23 D3; 26 C3–D3; 32 A2–B2; 33 C3; 41 B3–C3
Amorion 81 D2
Amsterdam 91 B1; 92 B1; 102 A1; 109 A1; 116 C1; 118 B1; 132 D1; 145 A2; 150 A2; 154 B2
Ananiah 38 C2
Anat 62 A2
Anathoth 28 B4
Ancyra 58 C2
Andalusia 93 B3–2; 97 B3–C3; 104 B3–C3
Ankara 67 D2

Brazil 116 A3–B3

Breslau 85 B1; 88 C1; 89 C1; 92 B1; 100 B1; 102 D2; 109 B2; 145 B2; 150 C3; 155 D2; 168 C3

Brest-Litovsk 91 C1; 109 C1; 122a B2; 122b B1; 126 B2; 128 B3; 130b B2; 140 A2; 142 D2; 148 B2; 161 B3

Brindisi 81 B2; 113 D2

Brisk 122a A2; 145 C2

Britain/British Isles 83 A1–B1; 132 D1; 138 B1–2; 154 A1–2; 159 B2; 163 C2–D2; 172 B1; 177 A1–2; 181a A1; 182b A1

Brittany 75 A1

Brixia 67 C1

Brody 116 C1; 122a B2; 122b C2; 124 C3; 128 B4; 145 C2; 150 D3; 155 F2; 161 B3; 176 B3

Brook of Egypt (Nahal-musur) 2a A2

Brumath 135 B2

Brunswick 115 B1; 138 C2; 154 C2

Brussels 89 B1

al-Bu´ayna 110 B1

Bubastis (Pibeseth) 9 B1

Buchach see Buczazc

Bucharest 109 C3; 155 G4

Buchenwald 168 B3; 174 B3

Buczazc (Buchach) 128 B4; 130a B2; 130b B3

Buda 106 B1; 150 C4

Budapest 88 C2; 102 D3

Bug, River 124 B2; 176 B2–3

Bukhara 73b D1; 107 E2; 133 F2

Bukovina 128 B5–C5; 130a B3; 130b B3

Bulgaria 75 B2–C2; 85 B1; 88 D2; 100 B1; 138 D3–E3; 172 D2–3; 177 B3–C3; 181a C2; 181b C2

Burgos 93 B1; 97 C1; 104 C2

Burgundy 75 A1–B1

Bursa 106 C2

Buschwiller 135 B3

Busk 124 B3

Byblos/Byblos Gebal (Jebeil) 5 B2; 19 B1; 81 E3

Byelaya Tzerkov 124 D3

Byeltzy 124 C4

Byzantine Empire 75 B2–C2

Cabra 97 C4

Caceres 104 B3

Cadiz 58 A2; 73b A1; 104 B4

Caesarea (Asia Minor) 58 C2; 63 D2; 67 D2

Caesarea (Israel) 46 B2; 48 A3; 50

A2; 51 B2; 65 A2; 67 D2; 69 D2; 67 D2; 111 B1

Caesarea Philippi 48 C1; 53 B1

Cairo (Fostat) 36 C3; 73b B2; 75 C2; 77 B4; 79; 81 D4; 83 D4; 85 B2; 87 A4; 91 D3; 100 C2; 106 C3; 109 D5; 118 E4; 133 E2; 191 A2

Calah (Kalhu) 2a B1; 32 B1; 34 D2

Calatayud 93 C1; 104 C2

Calcutta 133 G2; 166 C2

California 153 A1–2

Callinicum 67 D2; 81 E2

Cana 53 B2

Canaan 3 A3–B2; 6a A2

Canada 132 B1; 152 A1–B1; 163 A2–B2

Canton 166 C2

Cape Town 116 C3

Capercotnei 51 B1; 61 C2

Capernaum 48 C2; 51 C1; 53 B2

Caphor Salama 41 B3

Cappadocia 54a D1; 54b D1; 63 D2

Capua 58 B2; 67 C2; 113 B2

Caralis 69 B2

Carcassone 83 B2

Carchemish 2 B1; 3 B1; 5 B1; 6a B1; 32 B1; 34 B2

Carmel (North Judah) and Mount Carmel 14 B2; 17a B2; 23 B2; 33 A2; 165 A2

Carmel (South Judah) 17b B3

Carmona 97 B3

Carnaim 41 C2

Carthage 58 B2; 67 B2; 69 B2

Casablanca 172 A3

Casphor 41 C2

Caspian Sea 75 D1

Castejon 104 C2

Castellón 104 D2

Castile 93 B2–1; 97 B1–C3; 104 B2–C3

Castrillo 97 C1

Castrojeriz 97 C1

Catalayud 75 A1; 97 D2

Catalonia 93 C1–D1; 97 D2–E2

Catana/Catania 67 C2; 113 B5

Catanzaro 113 C4

Cattaro 91 C2

Ceara 116 B3

Cedron 41 A3

Cenchreae 54a B2

Central America 132 A3

Central Asia 36 D1

Ceylon 85 E3; 100 E3; 107 F4; 116 D2

Chalcedon 67 D2

Chalcis 41 C1; 81 C3

Charleston 132 B2; 152 B3

Château-Salins 135 A1

Chechiny 122b B2

Chelm 122a B2; 122b B2; 126 B2

Chelmno 122b A1–B1; 174 C3; 176 A2

Cheminik 126 C3

Chenstochow 176 A3

Chephirah 38 C2

Cherkassy 148 C3

Chernigov 91 C1; 124 D3; 140 A3; 148 C2

Chernobyl 126 D2; 128 D3; 130a C2; 130b C2

Cherson 75 C1

Chicago 152 A2; 153 C2

Chigirin 124 D3

China 107 G2–3; 133 G2; 166 C2–D2

Chinnereth 14 C2; 23 C2

Chinnereth, Sea of 28 C2 see also Galilee, Sea of

Chinon 88 B2

Chios 81 C3

Chorazin 53 B2

Chortkow see Czortków

Chryslers Farm 152 B2

Chudnov 124 C3

Chufut-Kale (Bakhchisarai) 77 B2

Ciechanow 88 C1

Ciechanowiec 122a B2; 122b B1; 126 B2

Cilicia 32 A1; 54a D2; 54b D2

Cincinnati 152 A2; 153 C2

Circesion 62 A1

Cleveland 152 B2; 153 C2

Cnidus 54a B2

Cochaba 51 C1

Cochin 116 D2

Coimbra 93 A2; 97 A2; 104 B2

Colmar 135 B2

Cologne 58 B1; 69 B1; 75 B1; 83 B2; 85 A1; 88 B1; 100 A1; 102 B2; 109 A2; 154 B2

Colombo 116 D2

Colonia (Cologne) 58 B1 see also Cologne

Colorado 153 B2

Columbia Haus 168 C3

Concordia 67 C1

Congress Poland 150 C2–D2

Constance 88 B2; 89 C2

Constantinople 36 C2; 69 C2; 75 C2; 77 B3; 81 C2; 83 C3; 85 B1; 91 C2; 100 B1; 106 C2; 116 C2; 118 D2 see also Istanbul

Kerman 36 E2; 73b C2; 75 D2
Kerson 148 C3
Kfar Azia 51 B3
Kfar Hittim 165 B1
Kfar Tavor 165 B2
Khafaje 2b B1
Khaibar 73b C2
al-Khalīl (Hebron) 110 B2 *see also*
    Hebron
Kharkov 91 D1; 148 C3–D3; 161
    C3
Khaybar 67 E3; 69 D3; 73a B1
Khazar/Khazaria 75 C1–D1; 92
    C1–2
Kheibar 58 D3
Kherson 140 C4; 148 C4
Khiva 36 E1; 73b C1
Khotan 85 E2; 100 E2; 107 E2
Khust 142 E3
Khwarizm 75 D1–E1; 85 D2; 100
    D2
Kidnov 122a B1
Kielce 140 A3; 148 A2; 161 A3
Kiev 75 C1; 85 B1; 88 D1; 91 C1;
    92 C1; 100 B1; 109 C2; 122a C2;
    122b C2; 124 D3; 128 D3; 130a
    C2; 130b C2; 140 B3; 148
    B3–C3; 150 E3; 161 C3
Kinda 73a C3
King David Hotel 187 C3
King's Highway 11 D2
Kinneret 165 B2; 185 B2
Kir-hareseth 23 C5; 33 B4
Kiriath-arba (Hebron) 14 B4 *see also*
    Hebron
Kiriath-jearim 14 B4; 17b A3; 23
    B4; 38 C2
Kiriath-sepher (Debir) 14 B4; 17a
    A4
Kis 73b C2
Kish 2b B1
Kishinev 91 C1; 140 B4; 145 D3;
    148 B3; 150 E4; 161 B4
Kishon, River 14 B2
Kletsk 122a B2; 176 C2
Klevan 124 C3
Klooga 174 C2
Kobe 166 D2
Kobrin 124 C2; 128 B2; 130a B2;
    130b B2
Kock (Kotsk) 128 A3; 130a B2;
    130b B2
Kojdanów *see* Dzerzhinsk
Kolin 142 C3
Kolki 124 C3
Komarno 128 B4; 130a B2; 130b
    B2

Koniecpol 177 B2
Königsberg 88 C1; 145 C1; 150 C2;
    155 E2
Konitz 88 C1
Konotop 124 D3
Konstantynow 122b C2
Konya, Sultanate of 87 A1–B1
Kopys 124 D2
Korets (Korzec) 128 C3; 130a B2;
    130b C2
Koretz 124 C3
Korneuburg 89 C2
Korsun 124 D3
Kosów 128 B5; 130a B3; 130b B3
Kotsk *see* Kock
Kovel 122a B2; 122b B2; 124 C3;
    126 B2
Kovno 124 C1; 142 D1; 148 B1; 150
    D2; 161 B2
Kozienice (Kuznitz) 128 A3; 130a
    A2; 130b B2
Krasnik 124 B3
Krasny 124 D2
Krasny Ostrow *see* Kukizow
Kremenchug 140 C3; 148 C3; 161
    C4
Kremenets 122a B2; 122b C2; 128
    C4; 145 C2; 150 D3
Krementez 176 C3
Krichev 124 D2
Krotoszyn 122a A2; 122b A2
Krushin 176 A3
Kudisos *see* Kedesh/Kudisos
Kufa 73b C2
Kukizow (Krasny Ostrow) 77 A2
Kuldichvo 176 B2
Kuneitra 185 B2; 191 B2; 193 C1
Kurland 148 B1
Kursk 148 C2
Kutais 88 E2
Kutów *see* Kuty
Kuty (Kutów) 128 B5; 130a B3;
    130b B3
Kuzhmir *see* Kazimierz
Kuznitz *see* Kozienice

Laa 89 C2
Lachish 14 B4; 17a A3; 23 B5; 28
    B4; 38 B3
Lachowiec 122a B2; 128 C2
Ladder of Tyre 41 B1
Ladyzhin 124 C2
Lagash (Telloh) 2b C2
Laguardia 88 A2
Laish/Dan 17a B1 *see also* Dan
al-Lajjūn 110 B1
Lakhovich *see* Lyakhovichi

Lakhva 176 C2
Lampsacus 63 C2
Lancaster 152 B2
Lanciano 113 B1
Lańcut 128 A4; 130a B2; 130b B2
Landau 135 C1
Landes 136 A2
Laodicea 54b C2; 63 D2; 67 D2
Lapethus 67 D2
Larissa 58 B2; 67 C2
Larsa 2a C2; 2b B2; 6a C2
Latvia 161 B1–2; 174 C2; 179 B2;
    182a C1
Lauterbourg 135 C1
Lavello 113 C2
Lebanon 65 A2; 191 B1
Lebanon Mountains 19 B2
Leczna 122b B2
Leczyca 122b A1
Lehi 17a B3
Leipnik 142 C3
Leipzig 102 C2; 116 C1; 154 D2
Lemba 61 C4
Lemberg *see* Lvov
Léon 75 A1; 93 B1; 97 B1; 104
    B2–C3
Leontini 67 C2
Leontopolis 9 B2; 63 D3
Lérida 97 E2; 104 D2
Lesczow 122b B2
Leshnev (Leszinów) 128 B4
Lesko (Lisko) 130a B2; 130b B2
Leszinów (Leshnev) 128 B4
Leszn/Leszno 122a A2; 122b A2;
    133 D1
Letichev 124 C3
Lezajsk (Lyzhansk) 128 A4; 130b
    B2
Libava 161 A2
Libnah 14 B4; 23 B4; 28 B4
Lida 142 E1
'Limes Palestinae' 51 A4–B4
Lincoln 88 B1
Linz 88 C2
Liozno 128 D1
Lisbon 116 B2
Lisbon 83 A2; 93 A2; 97 A3; 104
    A3; 172 A3
Lithuania 36 B1–C1; 91 C1; 102
    D1; 106 B1–C1; 109 C1; 122a;
    122b; 126 B1–C1; 128 B1–C1;
    130a B1; 130b B1; 142 E1; 145
    C1; 148 B1; 150 D2; 161 B2; 166
    A1; 174 C2; 179 B2; 182a C1
Little Bitter Lake 11 A2
Little Poland 122b A2–B2
Liverpool 172 B1

Nicomedia (Izmit) 67 D2; 69 C2; 77 B3
Nicopolis 91 C2
Nicosia 58 C2
Niebla 97 B4
Niederbronn 135 B1; 135 C1
Nieswiesz 176 C2
Nihawend 73b C2
Nikolaev 140 C4; 148 C3
Nikolsburg 109 B2; 142 C3; 150 B3
Nikopol 75 B1
Nile, River 9 B1–C5; 75 C3; 100 B2–C2; 106 C3
Nineveh 2a B1; 6a C1; 32 B1; 34 D2; 67 E2
Ningbo 107 G4
Nippur 2a C2; 2b B2; 6a C2; 34 D3; 62 B2; 63 E2; 67 E2
Nishapur 73b C1; 75 D2
Nisibis 58 C2; 62 A1; 63 D2; 67 E2
Nitra 142 C3
No (Thebes) 9 C4; 58 C3
Nob 17b B3; 28 B4; 38 C2
Noph see Memphis
Nord 136 B1
Nordhausen 83 B1; 102 C2
North Africa 36 B3–C3; 67 A2–D3; 73b A2–B2; 116 C2; 132–3 D2
North America 116 A1–2; 132 A1–2 & B1; 152; 163 A2–B3
North Dakota 153 B1
Norway 138 C1; 159 C1; 179 A1; 181a B1; 182b B1
Norwich 88 B1
Novogrudok 122a B2; 142 E1
Nowe Miasto 77 A1
Nowy Sacz (Zanz) 128 A4; 130a A2; 130b A2
Nubia 67 D3
Numidia 63 B2; 69 B2
Nuremburg 83 B2; 85 B1; 89 C2; 102 C2; 154 C3; 168 B4
Nuzi 6a C1

Obernai 135 B2
Odessa 77 B2; 140 C4; 145 D3; 148 C4; 150 E4; 155 H3; 161 B4
Oea 69 B2
Oescus 67 C1
Ofakim 77 B4
Okbara 85 C2; 100 C2
Okop 128 C5
Olbia 67 D1
Oldenburg 154 C1
Olkusz 122b A2
Olyka (Alik) 124 C3; 130a B2; 130b B2

On (Heliopolis) 9 B2
Ono 38 B1
Opatów (Apta) 122a A2; 122b B2; 126 A3; 128 A3; 130a A2; 130b B2
Ophrah 14 C2
Opole 130a B2; 130b B2
Oporto 83 A2; 93 A1
Oppeln 122b B2
Oran 91 A2
Orda 61 B4
Orël 148 C2
Orgeon 153 A1
Oria 75 B2; 81 B2; 83 C3; 113 D2
Orivellas 89 A2
Orkuta 88 C2
Oronaim 61 C5
Orontes, River 5 B1–2
Orsha 124 D2
Oster 124 D3
Ostia 58 B2
Ostrava/Ostróg 83 C2; 109 C2; 122a B2; 122b C2; 124 C3; 126 C3; 128 C4; 130b C2; 140 B3
Otranto 75 B2; 81 B2; 85 B1; 100 B1; 113 D2
Ottoman Empire 91 C2–D2 and C3–D3; 102 E4; 106 B2–C2; 109 C3; 128 C5; 133 E2; 138 D3–E4
Ovruch 130a C2; 130b C2
Oxford 83 B1
Oxyrhynchus 9 B3; 58 C3; 67 D3; 69 C3

Padua (Padova) 88 C2; 109 A2; 145 B3; 150 A4
Palencia 104 C2
Palermo 69 B2; 85 B2; 100 B2; 113 A4
Palestine 165; 172 E4
Palma 93 D2; 104 E2
Palmyra 63 D2; 67 D2
Pamphylia 54a C2; 54b C2
Pamplona 93 C1; 104 C1
Paneas 41 C1
Pannonia 58 B1; 67 C1
Panticapaeum 63 D1; 67 D1; 69 D1
Papa 155 E3
Paphos 54a C2
Papumnia 62 B2
Paralia 41 A3–B3; 61 B4–3
Parathon 41 B3
Paremyshlany see Przemyślany
Paris 69 B1; 83 B2; 85 A1; 88 B1; 89 B1; 91 B1; 100 A1; 116 C1; 132 D1; 150 A3; 154 A3
Parthian Empire 63 E2

Passau 75 B1; 89 C2; 102 C3
Patara 54b C2; 67 D2
Patrae/Patras 63 C2; 67 C2; 81 B3; 106 B2
Pavia 109 A2
Pechina 97 C4
Pegae 61 B3
Peki'in/Pekiin 63 A2; 111 B1
Pella 41 B2; 43 C3; 46 C2; 51 C2; 61 C2
Pelusium see Sin
Penuel 5 B3; 23 C3
Peraea 46 C3; 61 C3
Peran, Wilderness of 11 C3
Pereyaslav 124 D3
Pergamum 58 C2; 63 C2; 67 D2; 69 C2
Perge 63 D2
Pernambuco 116 B3
Perpignan 83 B2; 93 D1; 104 D1
Persia 36 E2; 67 E2; 92 D2; 95 C2–D2; 116 D2
Pessinus 58 C2; 67 D2
Pest 150 C4; 155 E3
Petah Tikvah 165 A3; 185 A2
Petrovo Selo 88 C2
Pfastatt 135 B3
Pforzheim 88 B2
Pharpar, River 23 D1
Phaselis/Phasaelis 46 B3; 63 D2; 67 D2
Philadelphia (Amman) see Amman
Philadelphia (USA) 152 B2; 153 D2
Philippi 54a B1; 54b B1; 58 B2; 63 C2
Philippines 133 G3–H3
Philistines and Philistia 17a A3; 17b A3–2; 19 A4; 20 A4–3; 23 A5–B4; 26 B4–3; 29
Philoteria 41 B2; 43 C2; 61 C2
Phoenicia and Phoenicians 17a B1; 23 B2–C1; 28 B2–C1; 32 A2–1; 43 C2–1; 61 C1
Pibeseth (Bubastis) 9 B1
Piedmont 138 C3
Pilica 122b C2
Pinczów 122a A2; 122b B2; 124 B3; 130a A2; 130b A2
Pinsk 91 C1; 109 C1; 122a B2; 122b C1; 124 C2; 126 C2; 128 C3; 130a B2; 130b C2; 133 E1; 140 B2; 148 B2; 161 B3
Piotrkow 140 A3; 148 A2
Piryatin 124 D3
Pisidian Antioch 54a B1; 54b B1
Pithom 11 A2
Plaszow 174 C3

Sierentz 135 B3
Sighet 128 B5; 130a B3; 130b B3
Sigüenza 97 C2
Sikhnin/Siknin 51 B1; 65 A2
Silesia 91 C1; 102 D2
Silhi 62 B2
Simferopol 140 C4
Simmari 113 C4
Sin (Pelusium) 9 C1
Sin, Wilderness of 11 B3–C3
Sinai 11 B3–C3; 191 A2–B2
Singara 69 D2
Sinope 58 C2; 63 D2; 67 D2
Sippar 2a C2
Siraf 75 D2; 95 D2
Sirbonis, Lake 1 B1
Skole 130a B2; 130b B3
Skurz 88 C1
Skvira (Skver) 128 D4; 130a C2;
    130b C2
Slavuta 130a B2; 130b C2
Slonim 122a B2; 128 B2; 130a B1;
    130b B1; 148 B2; 150 D2
Slovakia 177 B2
Slutsk/Slutzk 109 C1; 122a B2;
    122b C1; 128 C2; 140 B2; 148
    B2
Smolensk 122a C1; 148 C1; 161 C2
Smorgon 161 B2
Smyrna (Izmir) 36 C2; 81 C3; 91
    C2; 109 C3; 116 C2; 118 D3
Sobibor 174 C3; 176 B3
Sochaczew 89 D1; 128 A2; 130a
    A2; 130b A2
Socoh 17b A3; 20 A3; 23 B3 & B4
Sodom 3 A3; 6a A2
Sofia 106 B2; 109 C3
Solkhat (Stary-Krym) 77 B2
Solothurn 102 B3
Songhai Empire 106 A3
Sorek 17a A3
Soria 97 C2; 104 C2
Soultz 135 B3
Soultzmatt 135 B3
South America 116 A3–4; 132 B3
South China Sea 107 G4–H4
South Dakota 153 B1
Soutz-sous-Forêts 135 C1
Soviet Union 172 E1; 177 C1; 179
    B2–C2; 181a C1–D1; 181b
    C1–D1
Spain 58 A1–2; 69 A1–2; 73b A1;
    83 A2–3; 88 A2–3; 89 A2–3; 91
    A2; 92 A2; 93; 97; 100 A1; 106
    A2; 132 D2; 138 A3–B3; 159
    A3; 172 A2–3; 177 A3; 181a A2;
    182a A2

Spalato 91 B2
Sparta 58 B2; 63 C2
Speyer 83 B2; 85 A1; 100 A1; 102
    B2
Spoleto, Duchy of 69 B1–2
Squillace 113 C4
Starodub 124 D2
Starokonstantinov 124 C3; 161 B3
Starosielce 130a B1; 130b B1
Stary Bykhov 124 D2
Stary-Krym (Solkhat) 77 B2
Stefanesti (Shtelunesht) 130a C3;
    130b C3
Stelisk (Strzeliska) 130a B2; 130b
    B2
Sternberg 89 C1
Stobi 58 B2
Stolin 128 C3; 130a B2; 130b C2
Strasburg 109 A2; 135 C2; 150 A3
Strato's Tower 41 A2; 43 B3; 61 B2
Strelisk 128 B4
Stretin 130a B2; 130b B2
Stribro 88 C1
Stryi 176 B4
Strzeliska (Stelisk) 130a B2; 130b
    B2
Stura 136 C2
Stutthof 174 C3
Al-Subayba 110 B1
Succoth 5 B3; 11 A2; 14 C3; 17a
    B2; 23 C3
Sudylikow/Sudlykow 128 C4; 130a
    C2; 130b C2
Suez 191 A2; 193 A3
Sūfin 111 B2
Suljuk Sultanate of Iconium 100 C1
Sumatra 116 E3
Sumer 2b B1–C2
Sura 58 C2; 62 B2; 63 E2; 65 C2;
    67 E2; 69 D2; 73b C2; 83 E3; 95
    C2
Surat 166 B2
Susa 2a C2; 32 C2; 58 C2; 62 C2;
    63 E2; 67 E2
Suwalki 148 B2–1
Svestopol 161 C5
Sweden 138 C1; 159 C1; 172 C1;
    177 B1; 181a B1; 182b B1
Switzerland 88 B2; 89 B2–C2; 132
    D1; 138 C2–3; 150 A3; 159 B3;
    172 B2; 177 A2; 181a B2; 182b
    B2
Sychar 53 B3
Syene 9 C5
Syracuse (Sicily) 67 C2; 113 B5
Syria 20 B1–C1; 32 A2–B2; 46 B1;
    48 B1–C1; 54a D2; 54b D2; 62

D2; 116 C2; 118 E3; 191 B1
Szalacs 88 D2
Szatmar see Satu Mare
Szczebrzeszyn 122b B2
Szeged 150 C4
Szydlów/Szydlowiec 88 C1; 122b
    B2; 130a A2; 130b B2

Taanach 14 B2; 17a B2; 20 B3; 23
    B3; 26 C2
Tabor, Mount 17a B2; 17b B2; 61
    C2
Tabriz 73b C1; 75 D2; 85 C2; 95
    C1; 100 C2; 106 D2
Tadmor 2a B1; 3 B2; 5 C2; 6a B1;
    32 B2
Taenarum 67 C2
al-Tafila 111 B3
Tahpanhes 9 C1
al-Tāʾif 73a B2
Taima 58 C3
Talavera 104 C2
Talbotton 152 B3
Talnoye (Talna) 130a C2; 130b
    C3
Talvera de la Reina 97 C2
Tanais 36 C2; 69 D1
Tangier 69 A2; 116 B2
Tanis (Zoan) 9 B1
Tantura 165 A2
Tappuah 14 B3; 20 B3; 23 B4
Taranto 83 C3; 113 C3
Tarazona 97 D2
Tarentum 63 C2; 69 B2
Tarichaea 61 C2
Tarnograd/Tarnogrod 122b B2;
    130a B2; 130b B2
Tarnopol 91 C1; 128 C4; 150 D3
Tarnow 150 C3; 176 A3
Tarracina 63 B2
Tarraco 63 A2; 67 B2
Tarragona 69 A2; 75 A1; 93 C1; 97
    E2; 104 D2
Tarsus 2a A1; 6A A1; 32 A1; 54a
    D2; 54b D2; 58 C2; 63 D2; 67
    D2
Tashkent 36 E1
Tasnad 88 D2
Taurida 148 C4
Taymā 67 E3; 73a B1; 73b C2
Tehran 106 D2
Tekoa 23 B4; 38 C3; 41 B4; 51 B3
Tekoa, Wilderness of 41 B4–3
Tel Aviv 65 A2; 165 A3; 184 B2;
    187 B3; 191 B2; 193 B1
Telemessus 67 D2
Tell Agrab 2b B1